Internal Displacement

The crisis of internally displaced persons (IDPs) was first confronted in the 1980s, and the problems of those suffering from this type of forced migration have grown continually since then. This volume traces the normative, legal, institutional, and political responses to the challenges of assisting and protecting IDPs.

Drawing on official and confidential documents as well as interviews with leading personalities, *Internal Displacement* provides an unparalleled analysis of this important issue and includes:

- an exploration of the phenomenon of internal displacement and of policy research about it
- a review of efforts to increase awareness about the plight of IDPs and the development of a legal framework to protect them
- a "behind the scenes" look at the creation and evolution of the mandate of the representative of the secretary-general on IDPs
- a variety of case studies illustrating the difficulties in overcoming the operational shortcomings within the UN system
- a foreword by former UN high commissioner for refugees Sadako Ogata

Internal Displacement is written by two lucid analysts and will appeal to students, scholars, and practitioners with interests in war and peace, forced migration, human rights, and global governance.

Thomas G. Weiss is Presidential Professor of political science at The CUNY Graduate Center and Director of the Ralph Bunche Institute for International Studies, where he is co-director of the United Nations Intellectual History Project.

David A. Korn is a retired U.S. foreign service officer and former ambassador who served in overseas postings in Europe, the Middle East, North Africa, South Asia, and sub-Saharan Africa.

About the series

The "Global Institutions Series" is edited by Thomas G. Weiss (The CUNY Graduate Center, New York, USA) and Rorden Wilkinson (University of Manchester, UK) and designed to provide readers with comprehensive, accessible, and informative guides to the history, structure, and activities of key international organizations. Every volume stands on its own as a thorough and insightful treatment of a particular topic, but the series as a whole contributes to a coherent and complementary portrait of the phenomenon of global institutions at the dawn of the millennium.

Books are written by recognized experts, conform to a similar structure, and cover a range of themes and debates common to the series. These areas of shared concern include the general purpose and rationale for organizations, developments over time, membership, structure, decision-making procedures, and key functions. Moreover, current debates are placed in historical perspective alongside informed analysis and critique. Each book also contains an annotated bibliography and guide to electronic information as well as any annexes appropriate to the subject matter at hand.

The volumes currently under contract include:

The United Nations and Human Rights (2005)
by Julie Mertus (American University)

The UN Secretary-General and Secretariat (2005)
by Leon Gordenker (Princeton University)

UN Global Conferences (2005)
by Michael Schechter (Michigan State University)

The UN General Assembly (2005)
by M.J. Peterson (University of Massachusetts, Amherst)

Internal Displacement
Conceptualization and Its Consequences (2006)
by Thomas G. Weiss (The CUNY Graduate Center) and David A. Korn

The World Intellectual Property Organization
Resurgence and the Development Agenda
by Chris May (University of the West of England)

The Life and Times of the UN Security Council
by Edward C. Luck (Columbia University)

Global Environmental Institutions
by Beth DeSombre (Wellesley College)

Group of 7/8
by Hugo Dobson (University of Sheffield)

World Economic Forum
by Geoffrey Pigman (University of Kent)

The World Trade Organization
by *Bernard Hoekman (World Bank) and Petros Mavroidis (Columbia University)*

The International Organization for Standardization and the Global Economy
Setting Standards
by *Craig Murphy (Wellesley College) and JoAnne Yates (Massachusetts Institute of Technology)*

For further information regarding the series, please contact:

Craig Fowlie, Publisher, Politics & International Studies
Taylor & Francis
2 Park Square, Milton Park, Abingdon
Oxford OX14 4RN, UK

+44 (0)207 842 2057 Tel.
+44 (0)207 842 2302 Fax

Craig.Fowlie@tandf.co.uk
www.routledge.com

Internal Displacement
Conceptualization and its consequences

Thomas G. Weiss and David A. Korn

Routledge
Taylor & Francis Group

LONDON AND NEW YORK

First published 2006
by Routledge
2 Park Square, Milton Park, Abingdon, Oxon OX14 4RN

Simultaneously published in the USA and Canada
by Routledge
270 Madison Ave., New York, NY 10016

Routledge is an imprint of the Taylor & Francis Group, an informa business

© 2006 Thomas G. Weiss and David A. Korn

Typeset in Times New Roman by Taylor & Francis Books
Printed and bound in Great Britain
by TJ International Ltd, Padstow, Cornwall

British Library Cataloguing in Publication Data
A catalogue record for this book is available from the British Library

Library of Congress Cataloging in Publication Data
A catalog record for this book has been requested

ISBN10: 0-415-77080-7   ISBN13: 978-0-415-77080-4 (hbk)
ISBN10: 0-415-77079-3   ISBN13: 978-0-415-77079-8 (pbk)

Never doubt that a small group of thoughtful, committed citizens can change the world. Indeed, it is the only thing that ever has.

Margaret Mead[1]

Contents

List of illustrations

About the authors

Thomas G. Weiss is Presidential Professor of political science at The Graduate Center of The City University of New York and director of the Ralph Bunche Institute for International Studies, where he is also co-director of the United Nations Intellectual History Project and editor of Global Governance and served as research director of the International Commission on Intervention and State Sovereignty. He has written extensively about international organization, peace and security, humanitarian action, and development. His recent authored books include Ahead of the Curve? UN Ideas and Global Challenges (Indiana University Press, 2001, named "outstanding academic title of 2003" by Choices); The Responsibility to Protect: Research, Bibliography, and Background (International Research Development Center, 2001); The United Nations and Changing World Politics, 4th edition (Westview, 2004); Military-Civilian Interactions: Humanitarian Crises and the Responsibility to Protect, 2nd edition (Rowman & Littlefield, 2005); UN Voices: The Struggle for Development and Social Justice (Indiana University Press, 2005); and Sword & Salve: Confronting New Wars and Humanitarian Crises (Rowman & Littlefield, 2006). Two recent edited volumes are Terrorism and the UN: Before and After September 11 (Indiana University Press, 2004); and Wars on Terrorism and Iraq: Human Rights, Unilateralism, and U.S. Foreign Policy (Routledge, 2004). He is currently at work authoring The UN and Global Governance: An Idea and its Prospects and editing the Oxford Handbook on the United Nations.

David A. Korn is a retired U.S. foreign service officer and former ambassador who served in overseas postings in Europe, the Middle East, North Africa, South Asia, and sub-Saharan Africa. He was a member of the State Department team in negotiations that led to the 1978 Camp David agreements, the 1979 Egyptian–Israeli peace treaty, and the establishment of the international force to monitor demilita-

rization of the Sinai peninsula. He received the presidential merito-
rious service award in 1985 for his leadership of the American embassy
in Addis Ababa during a period of crisis in U.S.–Ethiopian relations.
He is the author of the 1990 Middle East Watch book Human Rights
in Iraq, and of four other books: Ethiopia: The United States and the
Soviet Union; Stalemate: The War of Attrition and Great Power
Diplomacy in the Middle East, 1967–1970; Assassination in Khartoum;
and Exodus Within Borders.

Foreword

Sadako Ogata

Former United Nations High Commissioner for Refugees

Internal Displacement: Conceptualization and Its Consequences explores "sovereignty as responsibility" as the most powerful idea that has emerged in the international arena in the last decade. Evolving rapidly from a humanitarian issue, the question of internally displaced persons (IDPs) came to challenge state sovereignty as the founding principle of international relations.

In the years when international relations were defined as relations between sovereign states, the distinction between refugees and IDPs also had to be consigned within the framework of the interstate order. The need to protect refugees far outweighed the urgency to protect internally displaced persons, in terms of the confines of both legal as well as institutional structures. In the aftermath of the Second World War, a humanitarian agency, United Nations High Commissioner for Refugees (UNHCR), was created to protect and assist refugees, who were defined as the main victims of state persecution and interstate war. State sovereignty was considered supreme and inviolable. Those left in refugee-like situations within state boundaries were to be treated and settled within the sovereign responsibility of the state.

The 12 years between 1992 and 2004 mark a period of growing numbers of IDPs, mainly due to the increase in internal conflicts. IDPs became prominent victims of both persecution and conflict. Francis Deng was appointed as the first representative of the UN secretary-general on internally displaced persons, subsequently joined by Roberta Cohen as co-director of the Project on Internal Displacement that provided support for the mandate. Their outstanding analytical and normative contribution culminated in the adoption of the "Guiding Principles on Internal Displacement," which in turn provided the basis for mobilizing action.

During the same period, UNHCR, the agency that protected and assisted the largest number of refugees and IDPs, followed a more eclectic approach. It decided to engage in the protection of IDPs when they fled their homes for reasons similar to what forced refugees to cross international borders. To UNHCR, which has the mandate to protect refugees, these IDPs comprised "would-be refugees" equally deserving of humanitarian attention. UNHCR thus extended major efforts on assisting IDPs, frequently resorting to setting up camps and settlements within their country, or undertaking cross-border assistance operations.

The prevalence of internal conflicts challenges the foundation of contemporary international relations, premised on the principle of state sovereignty. The causes of most conflicts derive from internal power struggles over who controls sovereign power, which may coincide with ethnic or sectarian cleavages within society. The state apparatus often has been party to the internal feud, if not the cause, and proved incapable if not unwilling to protect its people. Worse still, displacement of certain groups at times has become the very objective of the state. In such contexts, state sovereignty can be recovered only during the post-conflict peace-building process, as the state gradually is expected to develop its capacity to protect its people. In short, sovereignty can only be recognized in relation to the degree to which states exercise responsibility over their people.

Internal Displacement is "must" reading for both scholars and practitioners. No team is better placed than Thomas G. Weiss and David A. Korn to tell this story. Few scholars have written as much or as knowledgeably as Tom Weiss about the problems of assisting and protecting people caught in the throes of war. Weiss and Korn have accomplished a formidable task in this book—to intellectually challenge the customary principle of state authority by examining the evolution in ideas related to IDPs. It comprises two components. First, by studying the changing "ideas" toward assisting and protecting IDPs, it traces the impact on the evolving notion of sovereignty in contemporary international relations. Second, it analyzes the dynamics of how "ideas" can change law, norms, and even institutional frameworks. As the authors remind us, people and ideas matter. This book opens intellectual doors to possibilities of affecting necessary changes for protecting people in our times.

Editor's foreword

The current volume is the fifth in a new and dynamic series on "global institutions." The series strives (and, we believe, succeeds) to provide readers with definitive guides to the most visible international and intergovernmental aspects of what we know as global governance. Remarkable as it may seem, there are relatively few books that offer in-depth treatments of prominent global bodies and processes, much less an entire series of concise and complementary volumes. Those that do exist are either out of date, inaccessible to the non-specialist reader, or seek to develop a specialized understanding of particular aspects of an institution or a process rather than offer an overall account of its functioning. Similarly, existing books have often been written in highly technical language or have been crafted "in-house" and are notoriously self-serving and narrow in focus.

The advent of electronic media has helped by making public information and resolutions more widely available, but it has also complicated matters further. The growing reliance on the internet and other electronic methods of finding information about key international organizations and processes has served, ironically, to limit the educational materials to which most readers have ready access—namely, books. Public relations documents, raw data, and loosely refereed websites do not offer intelligent analysis. Official publications compete with a vast amount of electronically available information, much of which is suspect because of its ideological or self-promoting slant. Paradoxically, the growing range of purportedly independent websites offering analyses of the activities of particular organizations have emerged, but one inadvertent consequence has been to frustrate access to basic, authoritative, critical, and well-researched texts. The market for such has actually been reduced by the ready availability of myriad electronic materials of varying quality.

For those of us that teach, research, and practice in the area, this access to information has been at best frustrating. Tom Weiss and I were delighted, then, when Routledge saw the value of our idea to put together a series that bucks this trend and provides key reference points to the most significant global institutions. They are betting that serious students and professionals will want serious analyses. We have assembled a first-rate line-up of authors to address that market. Our intention is to provide one-stop shopping for readers—students (both undergraduate and graduate), interested negotiators, diplomats, practitioners from nongovernmental and intergovernmental organizations, and interested parties alike—seeking information about most prominent institutional aspects of global governance.

Internal Displacement: Conceptualization and Its Consequences

In the post-Cold War era, the number of internally displaced persons (IDPs)—people exiled within the borders of their countries of origin— has far outstripped the number of refugees (people similarly exiled but who *cross* international boundaries in the pursuit of safe haven). Yet, unlike refugees, who are able to call upon the resources and expertise of the United Nations High Commissioner for Refugees, no international institution exists for dealing with IDPs. Instead, they often have to rely on ad hoc arrangements and those nonstate actors that are willing and are able to assist and, on occasion, protect them.

Attempts to address the problem of IDPs are afoot within the UN system, though they are at present frustratingly inadequate. A 1992 UN resolution opened up the way for an examination of internal displacement, though it fell far short of setting out the foundations for a United Nations commissioner for internally displaced persons or other institutional machinery. Had it not been for the foresight and enthusiasm of a small group of people—led by Francis M. Deng, the representative of the secretary-general on IDPs—UN involvement in the area would have come to naught. However, against the odds, this group of people has begun to make a difference. This book is concerned with the process of making a difference—normatively, legally, and operationally.

Ironically, it is this very absence of any organization and the desperate need for one that tempted us to place a book on the phenomenon of displacement in our series on global institutions. This clearly is not the only arena of global governance where there is a vast disparity between international needs and capacities. As the authors point out, "people and ideas matter," and there are lessons here for handling other challenges facing the planet.

No two people are better placed or qualified to explore the emergence and development of UN involvement in IDPs than Tom Weiss and David Korn. Weiss has more than three decades of experience of working in and writing about the UN system and is *the* leading authority in the field. Korn's diplomatic career has spanned precisely those parts of the world wherein internal displacement is most acute, and he has written widely on the subject. Moreover, their networks and unrivalled access to primary sources, both archival and interviews, have given them unique insights. Their collective expertise is much in evidence throughout.

Weiss and Korn offer one of those rare academic works that captures events and developments in an accessible, engaging, and provocative fashion. It is important not only for its insight into the development of a response to the problematic of internal displacement, the incisiveness of its account, and for documentation of processes hidden from view, but also for its examination of a process that has the *capacity* to develop into a more formal and adequate institutional response to the plight of these vulnerable people. As one of those who read the manuscript prior to production put it, this book really is "a page turner." It deserves to be read by all who are interested in the problems of forced migration and the international responses thereto as well as in international institutionalization, global governance, and the impact of norms and ideas. As always, comments and suggestions from readers are welcome.

Rorden Wilkinson
University of Manchester, UK
May 2006

Acknowledgments

We are delighted that Routledge agreed to place this book in a series about "global institutions," although a most critical problem with the international handling of internally displaced persons (IDPs) is actually the absence of an institution with a mandate to protect and succor them. As its title suggests, this study offers a guide to the history, structure, and concrete activities of efforts in the post-Cold War era to address the phenomenon of internal displacement. Our writing of this book has been collaborative from the outset. We have struggled to cede any pride of authorship to getting the story right. While readers who know one of us well undoubtedly will find passages that reflect a particular approach to an issue, this book is a joint undertaking.

We are grateful to the Brookings-University of Bern Project on Internal Displacement for not attaching conditions to our work and for giving us full access to all project files. In particular, Francis Deng and Roberta Cohen generously gave of their time to clarify issues and respond to question upon question. This kind of openness of spirit should characterize more of the institutions that deal with internal displacement and refugees. The rigid rules blocking access to and use of archives and files of such institutions as the UN High Commissioner for Refugees (UNHCR) and the International Committee of the Red Cross (ICRC) are regrettable—not only for researchers but also for these institutions themselves that purportedly wish to learn lessons from the past so as better to assist future victims of armed conflicts.

We are also grateful to those who shared their knowledge through interviews, some of them multiple times. These are reflected in the text whether a person is quoted directly or anonymously or not at all. We would like to single out the following for their help and insights: Kenneth Bacon, Simon Bagshaw, Paula Banerjee, Mark Bowden, Joel Charny, Jeff Crisp, Jan Egeland, Elizabeth Ferris, Bill Frelick, Elissa Golberg, Robert Goldman, Richard Haass, Walter Kälin, Iain Levine, Martin

Macpherson, Sarah Maguire, Carolyn Makinson, Ian Martin, Susan Martin, Georg Mautner-Markoff, Dennis McNamara, Erin Mooney, Bertram Ramcharan, Elisabeth Rasmusson, Ranabir Samaddar, Gimena Sanchez-Garzoli, Ed Schenkenberg, Meera Sethi, Hugo Slim, Donald Steinberg, John Steinbruner, Christian Strohal, Wegger Strommen, Jeevan Thiagarajah, Manisha Thomas, Roger Winter, and I. William Zartman.

We also gratefully acknowledge detailed comments from several readers who took the time to read earlier drafts carefully, suggest additions, and correct errors or interpretations or lack of subtlety. Jeff Crisp, Leon Gordenker, and Gil Loescher provided critical looks from outside for the final draft, whereas Roberta Cohen, Francis M. Deng, and Erin Mooney were kind enough to scrutinize two full drafts of our presentation from inside. The final judgment on what appears here, however, is ours.

We wish to record our profound gratitude to Ausama Abdelhadi, an advanced graduate student in political science at The CUNY Graduate Center. Sammy's help in chasing down sources and his critical eye for the logic of the argument were essential in improving the text that is before readers. Zeynep Turan tidied up early drafts. Danielle Zach's careful attention to editing details improved substantially the quality of the presentation. Balkees Jarrah and Joy Miller of the Brookings Institution painstakingly prepared the appendices.

Notwithstanding the many individuals who helped make this book possible or improved the final text, none bears responsibility for any remaining lapses in fact or interpretation. They helped develop the stories and improve them, but we alone are responsible for the text.

T.G.W. and D.A.K.
New York and Washington, D.C.
May 2006

List of abbreviations

ASIL	American Society of International Law
AU	African Union
CAP	consolidated appeals process
CHA	Consortium of Humanitarian Agencies [Sri Lanka]
CHR	Commission on Human Rights
CIS	Commonwealth of Independent States
CUNY	City University of New York
DfID	Department for International Development [UK]
DHA	Department of Humanitarian Affairs [replaced by OCHA]
DPA	Department of Political Affairs
DPKO	Department of Peacekeeping Operations
DRC	Democratic Republic of the Congo
ECDFC	Ecumenical Commission for Displaced Families and Communities [Philippines]
ECHA	Executive Committee on Humanitarian Affairs
ECOSOC	Economic and Social Council
ECOWAS	Economic Community of West African States
ERC	emergency relief coordinator
HC	humanitarian coordinator
HIWG	Humanitarian Issues Working Group
FGM	female genital mutilation
GAD	Grupo de Apoyo y Organizaciones de Desplazados [Colombia]
GCIM	Global Commission on International Migration
IASC	Inter-Agency Standing Committee
ICC	International Criminal Court
ICISS	International Commission on Intervention and State Sovereignty
ICJ	International Court of Justice
ICRC	International Committee of the Red Cross

ICVA	International Council of Voluntary Agencies
IDD	Internal Displacement Division [within OCHA]
IDP	internally displaced person
IDU	Internal Displacement Unit [within OCHA, replaced by IDD]
IFRC	International Federation of the Red Cross and Red Crescent Societies
IGAD	Inter-Governmental Authority on Development
IGO	intergovernmental organization
IMF	International Monetary Fund
InterAction	American Council for Voluntary International Action
IOM	International Organization for Migration
MOU	memorandum of understanding
MSF	Médecins sans Frontières [Doctors without Borders]
NATO	North Atlantic Treaty Organization
NGO	nongovernmental organization
NRC	Norwegian Refugee Council
OAS	Organization of American States
OAU	Organization of African Unity
OCHA	Office for the Coordination of Humanitarian Affairs
ODA	overseas development assistance
OHCHR	Office of the High Commissioner for Human Rights
OLS	Operation Lifeline Sudan
OSCE	Organization for Security and Co-operation in Europe
PID	Project on Internal Displacement
RC	resident coordinator
RPG	Refugee Policy Group
RSG	representative of the secretary-general [on internally displaced persons]
SAIS	School of Advanced International Studies [Johns Hopkins University]
SCHR	Steering Committee for Humanitarian Response
SPLM/A	Southern People's Liberation Movement/Army [Sudan]
UNDP	UN Development Programme
UNHCR	UN High Commissioner for Refugees
UNICEF	UN Children's Fund
USAID	U.S. Agency for International Development
USCR	U.S. Committee for Refugees
WCC	World Council of Churches
WFP	World Food Program
WHO	World Health Organization

Introduction

The most reliable indicator of suffering in war zones is usually the number of "refugees"—that is, in the vernacular or according to the text of the 1951 UN Convention on Refugees, exiles who flee across the borders of their country of origin. Physical displacement is *prima facie* evidence of vulnerability because people who are deprived of their homes and communities and means of livelihood are unable to resort to traditional coping capacities. When such people are forced migrants *within* their own countries, especially as a result of war, they often are even more vulnerable. Whereas international law entitles refugees to physical security and human rights protection in addition to assistance to offset their other vulnerabilities, no such legal guarantees exist for those who participate in an "exodus within borders."[1] Thus, agencies seeking to help persons who have not crossed a border require permission from the very political authorities who may be responsible for the displacement.

Over the past two decades, the ratio of refugees to internally displaced persons (IDPs)—that is, forced migrants who physically remain within their own countries—has seen a dramatic reversal. The number of refugees at the beginning of the twenty-first century is fewer than 10 million and the number of IDPs is considerably higher—depending on who is counting, as many as 25 million people have been displaced by wars in some 40 countries (12 to 13 million in Africa, 5 to 6 million in Asia, 3 million in Europe, and 2 to 3 million in the Americas) and a similar or even greater number were displaced by natural disasters and development projects.[2] When IDP data were first gathered in 1982, there was one IDP for every ten refugees;[3] at present the ratio is approximately 2.5:1.

At the outset of the 1990s, the massive number of IDPs and the changing nature of warfare suggested to watchful observers that what formerly had seemed a modest blemish on the international humanitarian system was an ugly structural scar. The fastest growing category of war-affected populations had, and still has, no institutional sponsor or formal international legal framework, leading one analyst to describe them as "orphans of conflict."[4] At the same time, diminishing refugee populations continue to benefit from well-developed institutional and legal efforts by the United Nations High Commissioner for Refugees (UNHCR). Moreover, the anodyne lingo of "internal displacement" fails to convey immense human suffering. IDPs lack food, shelter, and physical and legal security, and according to a Centers for Disease Control study, they could have death rates 60 times higher than non-displaced populations in their home countries.[5]

In 1992, UN secretary-general Boutros Boutros-Ghali submitted the first analytical report on IDPs to the UN Commission on Human Rights (CHR) in Geneva.[6] The commission in turn, but not without controversy, approved resolution 1992/73 authorizing him to appoint a representative to explore "views and information from all Governments on the human rights issues related to internally displaced persons, including an examination of existing international human rights, humanitarian and refugee law and standards and their applicability to the protection of and relief assistance to internally displaced persons." But the commission limited the scope for reporting to existing laws and mechanisms, possible additional measures to strengthen the application of such laws, and new ways to address the protection needs that are not covered by existing instruments.[7] Nonetheless, many states were still uneasy with this potential intrusion into domestic jurisdiction while many humanitarian agencies were leery about the likely bureaucratic fall-out.

Shortly thereafter Boutros-Ghali designated Francis M. Deng, a former Sudanese diplomat and a senior fellow at the Brookings Institution, to serve as the representative of the secretary-general (RSG) on internally displaced persons. The CHR consistently extended his mandate for two- and three-year terms until July 2004, when Deng's extension ran into UN time limits for such mandates; he was replaced by Walter Kälin, a Swiss jurist whose title became representative of the secretary-general on the human rights of internally displaced persons.

This book recounts the history and politics of the period from 1992 to 2004. To the extent that some critical decisions and literature appeared earlier as well as through December 2005 that shed light on the story, we also examine them. Readers should be aware that we are analyzing the impact of idea-mongering, research, advocacy, and bureaucratic politics on the headquarters of governments, intergovernmental organizations (IGOs), and nongovernmental organizations

(NGOs). Our own experience teaches us that such influences also make a significant difference on the ground in operational activities, but our perspective here is on the center not the periphery. Determining the extent to which new discourse, legal standards, and organizational mandates translate themselves into better assistance and protection in the field would be another book.

It may be early to offer a measured judgment, but there are advantages in trying to capture a story while it is still fresh, especially because the central idea behind the effort to assist and protect IDPs— "sovereignty as responsibility"—has so rapidly made its way into the everyday vocabulary of international affairs as well as into the policy- and decision-making of aid and protection agencies.[8] This idea has two essential parts: governments are responsible for the human rights of their citizens as part of the essence of statehood; when they are unwilling or unable to provide for the security and well-being of their citizens, an international responsibility arises to protect vulnerable individuals.

Retirements are an artificial moment to celebrate or cry. But even in this post-modern era, they provide a logical point at which to review the past before continuing. We are presented with such a moment when 12 years after the establishment of his mandate, Francis Deng departs and the new representative begins his tenure.

In the interest of truth in packaging, we specify our association as consultants with work on IDPs over the years. We trust that our reputations for integrity will withstand attempts to portray this history as celebratory. This text is not a hagiography, and warts appear. But at a moment when cynicism is so widespread about the ability of any individual to make a difference in the international arena, this story should be told. It shows how individuals and groups working outside the diplomatic circuit can affect the norms that to a considerable extent shape international action. The effect of these actors on developing a hitherto unacceptable set of policy guidelines and far-reaching conceptual alterations in legal standards also affects the fates of our forgotten brethren in vile IDP camps.

We should be straightforward about our own normative agenda from the outset. We seek a better understanding of the origins, history, problems, and positive contributions toward addressing the protection and assistance needs of IDPs. On the one hand, this could result in improved strategies and tactics in the first decades of the twenty-first century. On the other hand, a better comprehension of the deficiencies of the current generation of international organizations could lead to the swift identification of appropriate remedies as well.

Why is it worthwhile analyzing these efforts? As students of international organizations and norms, our answer is: "People matter. Ideas Matter."[9] There are two organizing themes that frame this volume: the institutional "model" of how this issue was pursued; and the power of conceptualizing sovereignty as responsibility, including the need for international protection, and its concrete manifestation in special efforts for IDPs.

Regarding the first, Deng was asked to pursue his mandate on a voluntary, part-time basis—a dubious yet common practice for the cash-pressed world organization in the human rights arena. He and his collaborators actively and successfully solicited cooperation from a wide range of experts and autonomous research institutions along with financial resources from public and private sources. The development of a comprehensive global approach for effective assistance and protection of IDPs has been independently formulated and financed since that time under the guidance of the Project on Internal Displacement (PID), set up specifically to support the mandate of the representative. Indeed, much of the work set out in specific UN resolutions or directives from the secretary-general for the RSG was only possible because the PID took the lead. The project was born of necessity—given the miserably inadequate resources to deal with such problems—and the intertwining between the ·mandate and the PID makes it impossible to consider one in isolation from the other.

Since the outset of the effort, the Brookings Institution has been its main organizational location, but the project has collaborated with a series of other partners: initially with the Refugee Policy Group (RPG) and the U.S. Committee for Refugees (USCR), and then with the Ralph Bunche Institute for International Studies at The Graduate Center of The City University of New York, and the Paul H. Nitze School of Advanced International Studies (SAIS) at Johns Hopkins University. Deng and Roberta Cohen—a human rights specialist and former U.S. deputy assistant secretary of state for human rights—served as co-directors, with Cohen doubling as senior adviser to Deng as representative until his mandate expired in mid-2004. At that point, Walter Kälin, the new representative, joined Cohen as co-director in what is now the Brookings-University of Bern project.

Starting from scratch and without an official and assessed UN budget, the PID's productivity and output have been impressive. As mentioned, since 1993 the CHR has regularly extended the mandate of the RSG. In the period covered by this volume, Deng reported annually to the CHR and at least biannually to the General Assembly, and he undertook 28 country missions, with many more field visits.[10] The

PID conducted 16 regional and country workshops and seminars, many of which were made to dovetail with the country missions.[11] Independent research and analysis put this issue squarely on the public policy map.[12]

The main reason for discussing the nuts-and-bolts of this experiment is that a controversial idea, namely, the succor and protection of IDPs through the realization of sovereignty as responsibility, clashed directly with the customary prerogatives of state authorities who often believe that sovereignty means that they can do as they wish with their citizens. The idea moved quickly in the intergovernmental arena largely as a result of research and pressure from outside of the United Nations. There are other illustrations—for example, NGOs and the signing of the Universal Declaration of Human Rights in 1948 and both women's and environmental groups and the host of conferences in the 1970s and 1990s on gender and sustainable development.

However, the Project on Internal Displacement is a far more circumscribed and identifiable entity that provides a window into the world of normative and policy change at the nexus of ideas, institutions, and individuals. Perhaps "model" is too grand a word, but this history is an attempt to better understand the dynamics of international normative and institutional change, and the PID provides an unusual case study of people who have made a difference. In an anarchical world[13]—that is, in absence of a central overarching international authority—one central challenge of what is now commonly called "global governance" is to seek out and rely upon a range of nonstate actors who can help solve problems that go beyond the capacity of individual states.[14] In many ways, the PID is a nonstate actor *par excellence* that has punched above its weight in filling gaps not addressed either by states or by their creations, intergovernmental organizations. This achievement was recognized in 2004 when Francis Deng and Roberta Cohen received the prestigious Grawemeyer Award for "ideas changing the world order."

The second framing theme for readers, conceptualizing sovereignty as responsibility, illustrates how ideas matter in international relations. The actual consequences are less than esoteric because the efforts under the mandate and conducted by the PID amount to finding a straightforward way to navigate around the shoals, or contradictions, of state sovereignty. This dominant organizing principle of the international system since the Peace of Westphalia in 1648 has never been as sacrosanct as many of its most die-hard defenders claim—Stephen Krasner went so far as to call it "organized hypocrisy."[15] At the dawn of the twenty-first century, sovereignty remains enshrined as the essential lens through which we understand the way that the world operates. This, for example, in spite of the fact that globalization erodes the power of the state to guarantee outcomes and act independently,[16] or that human rights norms and conventions circumscribe the autonomy of state authorities to do what they please to their populations or sometimes suffer opprobrium and sanctions.

In examining the trajectory and utility of the notion of sovereignty as responsibility, it is useful to refer briefly to *The Structure of Scientific Revolutions*, Thomas S. Kuhn's classic that outlined the process by which a dominant paradigm in science is replaced by a new one. The process starts with a theory that directs research by defining a problem, explaining it, and predicting solutions. The normal procedure is to solve puzzles arising from the paradigm. In the course of pursuing research, however, anomalies are uncovered. A crisis results if the old paradigm proves unable to accommodate the anomalies. In Kuhn's terms, "the anomalous has become the expected."[17]

As human rights abuses grew, in spite of the host of international conventions and treaties and declarations, how were we to deal with the Westphalian paradigm of sovereignty and its guarantee of nonintervention in domestic jurisdiction? How can we maintain this worldview while human rights abuses grow to the point that there is nothing anomalous about them? Sovereignty as responsibility does not qualify as a new paradigm, or world view, but it is a way to square the sovereignty circle for those caught in the throes of war or under the thumbs of murderous leaders. The efforts by the RSG and the PID represent an alternative, which helps the paradigm of sovereignty adapt to the anomalies that it has uncovered—in this case, the clash between respect for human rights and noninterference in the internal affairs of states. Rather than seeing the paradigm as an all-or-nothing proposition that must collapse under the weight of accumulated deficits, concepts interact with evidence. They evolve and transform. This is a view of science more in debt to Karl Popper: by peeling away the layers through open debate of what is demonstrably falsifiable, we come closer to the truth of the concepts at the core of a model.[18]

The motivation in writing this volume and a central proposition behind it is captured in the subtitle, *Conceptualization and its Consequences*. International organizations and especially the United Nations have played a central role in bringing ideas and issues into the limelight on the world stage, and helping in the concrete realization of new policies and programs.[19] The phenomenon of internal displacement and the conceptualization of sovereignty as responsibility—including the various dimensions of international protection—have had substantial normative, legal, and operational consequences during what, by historical standards, represents a remarkably brief period of time (1992–2005). They are: the recognition of the category itself; the acceptance of the Guiding Principles on Internal Displacement; the promotion of national and international protection for IDPs; and the integration of internal displacement into the machinery of donors, IGOs, regional organizations, and NGOs. The mandate of the representative provided the platform, and the PID provided the intellectual firepower and institutional base.

But before examining the consequences, what precisely do we mean by "ideas"? We define them as normative or causal beliefs held by individuals that influence their attitudes and actions, in this case, toward the protection and succor of human beings. The two types, *normative* and *causal*, are worth distinguishing. Normative ideas are broad, general beliefs about what the world should look like. That there should be a more equitable allocation of world resources is an example. Causal ideas are more operational notions about what strategy will have a desired result or what tactics will achieve a particular strategy. At the UN, causal ideas often take an operational form—for instance, the target of 0.7 percent of national income as overseas development assistance. Causal ideas are more specific, but they usually are much less than fullblown theories.[20] As ideas, both sovereignty as responsibility and specific measures to benefit IDPs have normative and causal dimensions.

The recent research about the role of ideas can be grouped into three broad categories. The first, institutionalism—such as Judith Goldstein and Robert O. Keohane's analyses of foreign policy[21] and Kathryn Sikkink's on developmentalism in Latin America[22]—is concerned with how organizations shape the policy preferences of their members. Ideas can be particularly important to the policymaking process during periods of upheaval. In thinking about the end of the Second World War, of the Cold War, or of post-9/11 challenges, for instance, ideas provide a conceptual road map that can be used to understand changing preferences and definitions of vital interests of state and nonstate actors alike. This approach helps us to situate the dynamics at work among ideas, multilateral institutions, and national policies. It also enables us to begin thinking about how the UN influences elite and popular images, as well as how opinion-makers affect the world organization. Again, sovereignty as responsibility and efforts to assist and protect IDPs have helped shape the way that individuals, institutions, and countries define the world in which they operate as well as the language used to talk about the human consequences of war and horrendous human rights abuses.

The second category consists of expert-group approaches, which include Peter Haas's epistemic communities,[23] Peter Hall's work on analyzing the impact of Keynesian economists,[24] and Ernst B. Haas's analysis of knowledge and power[25] as well as more recent work by Kathryn Sikkink on transnational networks of activists.[26] These approaches examine the role of intellectuals in creating ideas, of technical experts in diffusing them and making them more concrete and scientifically grounded, and of all sorts of people in influencing the positions adopted by a wide range of actors, including and especially governments. Networks of knowledgeable experts influence a broad spectrum of international politics through their ability to interact with policy-makers irrespective of location and national boundaries.[27] Researchers working on HIV/AIDS or climate change can have an impact on policy by clarifying an issue from which decision-makers may deduce what is in the interests of their administrations. Researchers also can help to frame the debate on a particular issue, thus narrowing the acceptable range of bargaining in international negotiations. They can introduce standards for action. These networks can help provide justifications for alternatives, and often build national or international coalitions to support chosen policies and to advocate for change. In many ways, the idea of sovereignty as responsibility and the existence of the category of IDPs have been the work of a small group of experts and activists who have doggedly developed the notion and kept it before governments.

The third category consists of so-called constructivists such as Alexander Wendt[28] and John G. Ruggie.[29] They seek to determine the potential for individuals, their governments, and international institutions to be active agents for change rather than mere robots whose behavior reflects the status quo. The critical approaches of those more influenced by the Italian school of Marxism, such as Robert Cox and his followers,[30] are also pertinent because they view the work of all organizations and their ideologies, including the United Nations, as heavily determined by material conditions. The UN system has spawned or nurtured a large number of ideas that have called into question conventional wisdom as well as reinforced it. Indeed, influencing the definition of who counts as a victim of armed conflicts and expanding the benefits whether or not borders have been crossed or sovereign authorities agree can usefully be seen as reflecting such constructivist, or ideational, concerns.

And what then are the consequences of ideas? We begin with an apt quote from *The Economist*: "You can record the 20th century as a story of astonishing technical progress. You can tell it as a rise and fall of powers, or as a painful recovery from modern society's relapses into barbarism. But if you leave out ideas, you leave out what people were ready to live and die for."[31]

This history of internally displaced persons and the conceptualization of sovereignty as responsibility help substantiate four propositions that figure in recent academic literature about the role of ideas in international relations. Readers should keep them in mind as our story unfolds. The first is that ideas can change the nature of international public policy discourse. It is hard to imagine an idea that is better than IDPs to illustrate the importance of crucial changes in discourse and reframing of possible solutions to international challenges. It is now impossible to have a conversation about armed conflict and humanitarian action without thinking about the challenges posed by those victims who have not crossed an international border. It is no longer feasible for donors, UN organizations, or private relief agencies to ignore this particular type of war victim as they articulate the rationale for programs before oversight committees or boards of directors.

The second proposition is that ideas can help governments as well as individuals to define and redefine their identities and interests. One special concern is to gauge the impact of ideas over time on the willingness of governmental and international bureaucracies to embrace, or at least consider, the perspective of common interests rather than narrower self-interests. This kind of impact includes the ability of new ideas to provide a tactical guide to policy and action when older and existing norms conflict, or when sequencing or priorities are disputed. The recognition of the need to override state sovereignty with military force in cases of genocide, mass murder, and forced displacement is a powerful example of how states have redefined, on occasion, their interests to include the basic human rights protection of war victims, including IDPs.[32]

The third proposition is that ideas can alter prospects for forming new coalitions of political or institutional forces. For example, such issue-areas as AIDS, gender, sustainability, or land-mines illustrate the way that many private groups across the North and the South were able to form coalitions to challenge orthodoxy. As we demonstrate, IDPs were a way for NGOs and some sympathetic governments to move the plight of these victims of forced displacement from the shadows and into the limelight on the international public policy stage. These new partners worked to provide not only enhanced visibility and improved aid and protection but also the development of soft international law in the form of the Guiding Principles on Internal Displacement.[33]

The fourth possible influence is that ideas become embedded in institutions and challenge not only the founding principles of those organizations; once an entity exists, an idea may take on a life of its own and also help set future agendas. Again, we see that the acceptance of IDPs as a category and as a priority for donors led to the creation of new units not just within governments but also within established intergovernmental and nongovernmental organizations. This fourth manifestation of ideas can readily be observed and charted over time.

For most of his mandate, Deng routinely explained and justified his work to donors and to the public—and the Brookings project gave concrete form to the approach—in terms of "pillars" that provide the basic structure for this book: improving the knowledge base; raising international awareness and advocacy; promulgating international law; and promoting an international institutional framework. The dynamic and evolving activities of the mandate and the close interaction with the PID can be gleaned from the evolution in the pillars. To begin with, the pillars consisted of the normative framework, the institutional framework, and the country focus. Then other ongoing activities, basically underway as well since the outset, were also conceptualized as pillars: raising awareness and the research agenda. Later, another pillar was added, civil society and capacity-building. The international protection of IDPs—that is, the responsibility of outsiders for the security and assistance of those whose governments were unable or unwilling to respect their human rights—was present throughout.

Chapters 1 and 2, "Putting the Issue on the Map" and "Shaping the Mandate in the Early Years, 1992–1993," provide the historical backdrop for what follows. The following three chapters focus on the critical next half-decade, until 1998—the year that marked the publication of two major books and of international legal guidelines for IDPs. Chapter 3, "Creating the Project on Internal Displacement and Improving the Knowledge Base and Awareness, 1993–1998," focuses on progress in constructing Deng's first two pillars. Chapter 4, "Giving Birth to the Guiding Principles, 1993–1998," concerns the work to identify the international legal underpinnings for IDPs. Chapter 5, "Laying Institutional Foundations, 1993–1998," examines the early attempts to address the UN's institutional shortcomings, Deng's fourth pillar. Chapter 6, "Evolution of the Concept and Project, 1999–2005," and Chapter 7, "Evolution of the Law and Institutions, 1999–2005," together provide an overview of the last half-decade of Deng's tenure and the adaptation of the PID to new needs and demands. Chapter 8, "Whither and Whether, Inside-Outsiders or Outside-Insiders?," concludes the volume with a summary of Deng's legacy as Walter Kälin takes the baton.

1   Putting the issue on the map

Resolution 1992/73, which the 53-member United Nations Commission on Human Rights approved on 5 March 1992 near the close of its annual session in Geneva's stately Palais des Nations, did not seem like a ground-breaking initiative. It called for the secretary-general to:

> Designate a representative to seek again views and information from all Governments on the human rights issues related to internally displaced persons, including an examination of existing international human rights, humanitarian and refugee law and standards and their applicability to the protection of and relief assistance to internally displaced persons.

One year earlier the commission had asked the previous secretary-general to prepare "an analytical report" on IDPs. That report, issued in the name of newly appointed Boutros Boutros-Ghali in February 1992, concluded with a call for the establishment of a "focal point" (in UN jargon, a person or an institution with responsibility for an issue) within the human rights system for internally displaced persons.[1]

The phenomenon of internal displacement was real enough. Around the globe millions of people were being forced from their homes by a spreading rash of state breakdowns, civil wars, and other violent disorders, with no assured access to international humanitarian relief and even less prospect of international protection from the worst sorts of abuses. Was a study all that the UN's main human rights body could think of? A look to the history of the UN's handling of refugees provides insights for an answer.

At its close, the Second World War left tens of millions uprooted in Europe and Asia. The vast majority had fled across borders for sanctuary while others who could not or did not wish to escape remained within the boundaries of their home countries. The Cold War followed and had a different effect. Refugees continued to play a prominent role as political pawns, fleeing from the East to the West where they were granted asylum, in part to make a political statement. Meanwhile, geopolitical competition between the two superpowers, the Soviet Union and the United States, led to the channeling of massive economic and arms assistance to client Third World regimes, which assured a fragile artificial stability in many parts of the globe for much of the Cold War.

Victims of persecution who crossed frontiers fell under the 1951 Convention on Refugees. The Office of the UN High Commissioner for Refugees was specifically charged to assist and protect them. Those who remained within their home state, however, were far harder to help. Given the international system's prevailing norms, outsider access to victims required permission from the very authorities who were abusing them. Human rights groups, both intergovernmental and nongovernmental, confronted the traditional bulwark, state sovereignty and its corollary principle, nonintervention in domestic affairs.

The Soviet invasion of Afghanistan in 1979 and the accompanying civil war was soon followed by the eruption of internal armed conflicts in southern Africa (in Mozambique and Angola) and in Central America (in El Salvador, Nicaragua, and Guatemala). Beginning in the early 1980s, these wars prompted a dramatic rise in the numbers of displaced. But this time, the proxy wars in the East–West conflict meant that most of those forcefully uprooted were IDPs rather than refugees.

As the grip of the Cold War loosened, and particularly after its end, fewer political points could be scored by accepting refugees, especially when so many came from the poorest of countries instead of Eastern Europe. Asylum regimes tightened as "the end of the Cold War swept away any remaining ideological motive for accepting refugees."[2] Hence, both the nature of the wars and the politics of asylum changed. Refugee numbers diminished while IDPs shot up still further. As the superpowers abandoned Africa in the 1990s and were no longer jockeying in an ideological war, stability crumbled; refugee numbers continued to fall, but IDP numbers continued to increase.

There are a number of explanations for the dramatic rise of internally displaced persons. The nature of warfare changed, as belligerents directly targeted civilians, and brutal ethnic cleansing left returning refugees without secure homes. Moreover, not only was the phenomenon of internal displacement better understood than a decade earlier, but better data also were available. If we fast forward to the present, statistics indicate that the ratio of IDPs to refugees is 2.5:1, as depicted in Figure 1.1. Some recent research also suggests that refugee

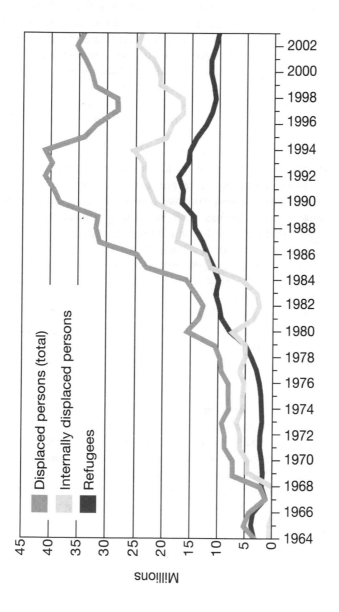

Figure 1.1 IDPs and refugees, 1964–2003.
Source: Andrew Mack, ed., *Human Security Report 2005* (Vancouver: Human Security Centre, 2005), 103.

flows may be greater in the face of state-sponsored genocide than civil wars; and that refugee numbers (relative to IDPs) will be greater if armed conflict occurs in a country whose neighbors are relatively wealthy and democratic rather than poor and authoritarian.[3]

Statistics are one thing, but what was the actual meaning for a war victim who fell into this category? If someone fled across an international border seeking safety from persecution, she or he could qualify for refugee status and for international assistance and protection under the 1951 Refugee Convention, the implementing arm of which is the UN High Commissioner for Refugees, headquartered in Geneva, with 5,000 strong and an annual budget of $1 billion. But if that same individual stopped short of crossing an international border, the hope for succor and protection would be non-existent from the home government, which in most cases either was the oppressor or had no means to help. If that person were lucky, UNHCR might have an extra tent and food if the IDP happened to mingle with a refugee population from another armed conflict, or if it was one of those special situations in which the secretary-general, Security Council, or General Assembly specifically asked UNHCR to help the internally displaced. If it happened to be on the scene, the International Committee of the Red Cross (ICRC) might also offer help.

But there was and still is no internationally accredited agency with a mandate to reach inside state borders—overriding state sovereignty in the process—to assist and protect internally displaced persons in any and all circumstances. What in 1982 had been a minor institutional lacuna, at least in terms of numbers, had become within less than a few years a glaring hole in the international safety net for victims of armed conflicts.

Journalists hate the term and the acronym. "Internally displaced persons" is an awkward mouthful, and "IDP" lacks pizzazz and offers no immediate clarity of meaning for those seeking sound-bites rather than writing legal treatises. For years reporters and editors were reluctant to use it. An outspoken Richard Holbrooke called it "odious terminology."[4] He and others preferred anything, even a circumlocution, or calling the internally displaced "internal refugees," or, inaccurately, simply "refugees." Even those in humanitarian and human rights organizations as well as other professionals working on uprooted people do not much like it. For instance, a special issue on Africa in *National Geographic* in September 2005 contained the following: "Number of refugees: 15 million—3.3 million who have fled their native countries because of conflict, some 12 million who are internally displaced."[5]

"Refugees" immediately evokes the image of people fleeing persecution. "Internally displaced persons" is too many words, too clinical, too antiseptic. It does not automatically conjure up any identifiable image of distress. It does not convey the fact that in many instances these people are the most destitute of the destitute, those most exposed to hunger and disease and abuse by governments and rebel movements, the populations with the highest death rates recorded among all those whom humanitarians seek to assist. Or that they are, in their overwhelming majority, women and children, the most vulnerable of the vulnerable.

Try as they might, neither journalists nor others could come up with anything more concise or evocative that did not blur the line between people uprooted inside their own country and those who had crossed a border. "Internally displaced persons," soon shorthanded to "IDPs," became the term of art. Interestingly, in the wake of the devastation of Hurricane Katrina in New Orleans in August and September 2005, the term "displacees" became commonplace after African-Americans reacted negatively to being labeled "refugees" and the implication that somehow they were the "other." The acronym "IDP" suddenly was not something relegated to the documents of UN organizations or private charities working in Africa but quite pertinent for the American South. Perhaps there would be room to adopt "displacees" as the alternative—it has the same number of syllables and rhymes with "refugees."

The first substantial institution to make a public issue of how the numbers of internally displaced persons had burgeoned was the United States Committee for Refugees, a Washington-based private voluntary organization that issues an annual worldwide refugee survey. In its 1982 accounting, USCR estimated a total of 1.2 million persons in "refugee-like situations" within their own countries.[6] By 1985 USCR was recording such a surge in the number of internally displaced—to over 9 million—that it decided to establish a distinct reporting category for them. By 1987 the 15 million mark had been crossed, about the same as refugees; and by 1992 the number of internally displaced persons from wars was edging toward 25 million, surpassing the figure for refugees. The report of the Independent Commission on International Humanitarian Issues, chaired by two princes—former UN high commissioner for refugees Sadruddin Aga Khan and Jordan's then crown prince Hassan Bin Talal—also contained a significant treatment of the phenomenon in its examination of the "uprooted."[7]

Well before that, however, the sheer numbers of the internally displaced had brought to light the fact that neither the UN's elaborate humanitarian assistance machinery nor its more limited human rights apparatus had institutional arrangements for their assistance or protection. A UN-sponsored Conference on the Plight of Refugees, Returnees and Displaced Persons in Southern Africa, held in Oslo in August 1988, was the first to draw attention officially to this gap in the UN system.[8] The conference proceedings prompted a resolution in the General Assembly in the fall of that year, calling on Secretary-General Javier Pérez de Cuéllar to study the need for an international mechanism to coordinate relief programs for the internally displaced. He did not welcome the initiative. In a report issued in 1989, Pérez de Cuéllar replied that he did "not believe it necessary or appropriate to establish a new mechanism or arrangement to ensure the implementation or overall coordination of relief programs to internally displaced persons."[9] He nevertheless designated United Nations Development Programme (UNDP) resident representatives, in their capacities as UN resident coordinators, to be "focal points" for coordinating relief for internally displaced populations in the countries to which they were assigned.

The step was important symbolically as an acknowledgment of the need for the UN to gear up to deal with the challenge of internal displacement, but its immediate practical effect was negligible. The resident representatives' line of work was economic development, not humanitarian assistance. Not only did few have humanitarian experience, they had no authority to initiate actions to assist the internally displaced, and the secretary-general's designation of them as "focal points" gave them none; they had to wait for governments to ask for help. And they had no authority whatsoever to act to protect the internally displaced from killing and other abuses that governments and insurgent movements frequently inflicted. Perhaps most importantly, drawing the attention of governments to human rights abuses was awkward, to say the least. It would have impeded the kind of good diplomatic relations on which UNDP technical cooperation depends. In short, it was not in the bureaucratic interests of officials based within a country even to raise the issue.

Still, Pérez de Cuéllar's instruction kept the subject alive. It nudged the UNDP's Governing Council to ask, in June 1990, for a survey of the UN system's ability to assist refugees, displaced persons, and returnees. That request in turn generated a resolution in the Economic and Social Council (ECOSOC) the following month asking the secretary-general for a survey of the UN system to "assess the experience and capacity of various organizations in assisting all categories of refugees, displaced persons and returnees."[10] Jacques Cuénod, a recently retired UNHCR official, was hired. His 1991 report concluded by recognizing the obvious reality that "within the United Nations system there is no entity entrusted with the responsibility of ensuring that aid is provided to needy internally displaced persons."[11] The problem, Cuénod wrote, was the lack of international protection:

> Assistance to internally displaced persons raises delicate issues for the United Nations system which has to respect the national sovereignty of its members. In some situations, an offer of assistance by the United Nations may be interpreted as an interference in the internal affairs of the State or an implicit judgment on the way some nationals have been treated or not protected by their Government. The Secretary General has little room to act because the United Nations Charter recognizes explicitly the concept of domestic jurisdiction in its Article 2(7).[12]

Humanitarian and human rights advocates hoped, somewhat prematurely as it turned out, that the Security Council's authorization for U.S. and allied intervention in Iraq to protect the Kurds, in the spring of 1991, would mark a turning point, a breach that would show the way to shake off the shibboleth of state sovereignty when large numbers of persons were at risk.[13] Even earlier, in 1989, Operation Lifeline Sudan (OLS) had established a precedent for UN action to provide food and medicine for displaced persons, albeit in that instance with reluctant agreement from Khartoum.[14] Nonetheless, governments remained hesitant to challenge the notion that state sovereignty in most instances barred the United Nations from assisting people uprooted and abused within their own countries. When France proposed, in ECOSOC, a right of intervention in humanitarian crises, the resolution failed.

In the end, nongovernmental organizations would push the issue of internal displacement onto the agenda at the UN's Commission on Human Rights. By the 1980s, NGOs had become a powerful force both in the shaping of public opinion and in the delivery of relief and development assistance worldwide.[15] In 1986 NGOs spent over $3 billion for development-related activities,[16] and UN operational agencies increasingly sought them out as implementing partners for their programs.

Church groups were among the first to feel the impact of the growing number of internally displaced persons. By the late 1980s those affiliated with the World Council of Churches (WCC) were finding their resources strained to the limit in providing food, shelter, and protection to southern Sudanese who had fled to camps on the outskirts of Khartoum to escape the ravages of the civil war in that country, and to similarly displaced populations in El Salvador and Sri Lanka.

The link between human rights and refugee and IDP issues was under discussion both at the WCC's Geneva UN office and in

Washington at the Refugee Policy Group, a think-tank set up in 1982 by Dennis Gallagher. A former Carter administration political appointee, Gallagher had big ideas for RPG and the entrepreneurial talent to make them happen. The board of trustees that he organized included prominent names in the refugee field: Alice Henkin, Doris Meissner, Robert Nathan, former Canadian secretary of state for foreign affairs Flora MacDonald, and Kitty Dukakis, wife of the 1998 Democratic Party's presidential candidate; and later Francis M. Deng who had left Sudanese government service and in 1988 became a senior fellow at the Brookings Institution and director of its Africa Program.

Gallagher and his deputy Susan Martin gathered a team of energetic professionals researching and writing on a broad range of refugee and migration issues. The main focus at first was on refugee resettlement in the United States and asylum and protection. Some initial work on refugee problems in developing countries suggested that there was little difference in the problems on both sides of a border, but that there was a real hole in the international institutional fabric because IDPs were largely outside of everyone's purview.

As the number of IDPs grew in the late 1980s nearly to match that of refugees, the issue came in for serious notice. In 1988 Lance Clark, a young staff associate who had been hired to expand RPG's work in the Third World, wrote a reflection for USCR's annual *World Refugee Survey* entitled "Internal Refugees—The Hidden Half."[17] In both Cambodia and Afghanistan, for instance, repatriation involved as many internally displaced as refugees. Gallagher himself raised internal displacement at a conference on refugee problems organized by the ICRC in San Remo in 1989. The issue clearly had a strong human rights component, and for some time he had been looking for ways to integrate human rights into RPG's work. As Susan Martin remembered: "There was a real disconnect between humanitarian and human rights agencies and issues."[18] While she was referring specifically to the U.S. government and American NGOs, her generalization applied more broadly.

To this purpose, in the spring of 1989 Gallagher enlisted Roberta Cohen, a former executive director of the New York-based International League for Human Rights and deputy assistant secretary in the State Department's Human Rights Bureau in the Carter administration. The plight of the displaced touched Cohen on a personal level both because of her Jewish roots and because living in Addis Ababa in 1984 and 1985 she had witnessed first-hand the misery of Ethiopians displaced by famine and civil war. She was a pioneer in the international human rights movement, and in 1977 was a *New York*

Times "quotation of the day" for saying that human rights had suddenly become "chic." And as a member of the U.S. delegation to the Commission on Human Rights in 1979 and 1980, she pushed for and helped win approval for the establishment of its working group on disappearances.

Cohen spent the late summer of 1989 drafting a 40-page paper published by RPG in January 1990, *Introducing Refugee Issues into the United Nations Human Rights Agenda*. She pointed out that NGOs could play an important role in helping to develop standards for the UN that "would clearly spell out the rights of those displaced internally by human rights violations and internal conflict and the responsibilities of governments to protect and assist them." Another of Cohen's recommendations was "for the UN to appoint a rapporteur to study the worldwide status of the internally displaced . . . and to make recommendations to ensure that internally displaced people receive the best protection possible from the international system."[19]

For Elizabeth Ferris, an American who headed the refugee service section at the WCC's Geneva office, the report was a catalyst. As she wrote to Gallagher in January 1990, churches and ecumenical groups in the constituency had long urged action on the issue, but "it wasn't until we saw the draft of Roberta Cohen's paper back in September [1989] that we were able to think strategically and practically about how to go about it."[20]

In the fall of 1989, Ferris and Martin Macpherson, a Briton at the Quaker United Nations Office in Geneva, began holding weekly meetings to map out a strategy for getting the UN more actively involved with the internally displaced. In a memorandum that Ferris drew up in November for circulation to church networks, she estimated the number of internally displaced at 30 to 40 million. "This large group," she wrote, "has been virtually ignored by the international community and particularly by the United Nations system."[21] In the early years, the division of labor was worked out with the WCC and the Quakers responsible for the lobbying and the RPG and for substance.

The UN Commission on Human Rights seemed to offer the best prospect to lobby for intergovernmental action. The alternatives were the General Assembly or ECOSOC, but both were in New York while the majority of humanitarian NGO voices were in Geneva. More importantly, NGOs had too little standing with the General Assembly, whose universal membership also made it an unwieldy body in which to operate; and ECOSOC accredited only some NGOs and with limited access. The CHR's membership changed from year to year, but stood at 53 in 1992. Its detractors liked to call it the "human rights violators commission," as much in seriousness as in jest, because so many of its member states had dismal human rights records. But it allowed wide access to NGOs, both in lobbying and in the presentation of formal statements; and it had a strong Western group that fairly consistently supported human rights initiatives.

And there was a further consideration. ECOSOC would have been the place to raise internal displacement viewed solely as a humanitarian issue—a matter of food, shelter, and medical care. Bringing it onto the agenda of the Commission on Human Rights would be a step beyond, which would clearly mark it as also having important human rights implications; and international responsibility for protecting IDPs clearly was the essence of a solution.

The goal that the Geneva-based NGOs set for themselves was to get the commission to appoint a rapporteur or working group on internally displaced persons. In UN parlance, rapporteurs and working groups that focus on issues that cut across borders are "thematic mechanisms," because their work focuses on a topic that is global in scope. Rapporteurs are individuals, often former senior government officials or prominent academics, chosen for their expertise on a particular issue. Working groups are composed of four or five such persons representing as many geographic areas. In 1989 the commission had only one working group, on enforced or involuntary disappearances (it was the first of the thematic mechanisms, set up in 1980) and four rapporteurs (on summary or arbitrary executions, torture, religious intolerance and discrimination, and mercenaries). The commission's 1990 session would add a rapporteur on the sale of children, and in 1991 a working group would be appointed on arbitrary detention. In addition, there were rapporteurs on particularly egregious country situations.

Both rapporteurs and working groups are considered independent. Their experts report only to the CHR, at its yearly sessions, though they can issue statements at other times. The commission does not always give their prose close attention, but the thematic mechanisms enjoy wide latitude and few if any political constraints. Already by the late 1980s, they had become one of the commission's most visible instruments—they provided a pulpit with an amplification system of sorts to broadcast abuses of human rights at higher decibel levels than otherwise would have been the case. They at times issued scathing reports about states that, owing to their sheer weight on the international scene or their ability to enlist allies, managed to elude the opprobrium of a CHR resolution. Those on human rights violations in China and Sudan consistently failed, for example, but both countries were regularly cited in reports by the thematic mechanisms. The violators of course did not like this at all, and they tried to get rapporteur mandates foreshortened or discontinued altogether to avoid the unwanted publicity. The Western group regularly foiled these efforts. Macpherson and Ferris realized that winning the commission's approval for a rapporteur or working group on IDPs would be a monumental task, and so they eagerly sought allies.

The Geneva offices of Caritas Internationalis and the International Council of Voluntary Agencies (ICVA) quickly joined the collective effort. Help came also from the Refugee Policy Group in Washington. Dennis Gallagher sent Roberta Cohen to Geneva in February 1990, as the commission opened its annual session. The coalition organized a lunch meeting on displaced persons at the Quaker UN Office, inviting delegates from member governments as well as officials from UNHCR and ICRC, and asked Cohen to give the keynote address. With delegates from some 30 governments in attendance, Cohen sketched out the dramatic numbers of IDPs and the dire situation in which many found themselves, and then went to the crux of dealing with the phenomenon:

> Internally displaced persons are first and foremost the responsibility of national governments. But what is important for human rights bodies to address is what should happen when governments do not meet their responsibilities to internally displaced people. The U.N. can not assign responsibility for the protection of such people to the very authorities that may have been the cause of their problems. The fact that they are displaced internally does not mean that the international community does not have a major responsibility to protect them.[22]

Cohen warmly endorsed a call by the World Council of Churches for the commission to appoint a rapporteur on internally displaced people. A rapporteur, Cohen said, could "put a spotlight on the problem, identify its human rights dimension and find ways to protect" IDPs. A rapporteur could also recommend drafting international standards that "could spell out the rights of those internally displaced, the responsibilities of governments to protect and assist them and the role human rights, refugee and humanitarian organizations could play when government assistance breaks down."

Despite vigorous lobbying at the commission's February–March 1990 session, the Geneva NGOs were unable to push through a resolution of any kind on internal displacement, much less muster adequate support for the creation of a mandate for a new rapporteur. Martin

Macpherson canvassed all five regional groups and found "a general interest in the subject but also a lot of caution." He was disappointed by the insistence of Western countries that protection for the internally displaced should be "cost free"—that is, it should entail no additional expense for donors. He found Third World delegations interested mainly in talking about assistance while ignoring the human rights dimensions. Efforts to mobilize delegates from the smaller African countries in support of a resolution "were not a great success"; those delegations simply did not have the physical means to seek and get quick approval from their capitals. And the more important delegations from Latin America, Africa, and Asia were already committed to a large number of agenda items and unprepared to take on sponsorship of a new and controversial resolution.[23]

Macpherson and others in the Geneva coalition realized that if they were to be successful at the 1991 session, they would have to scale back their objective and try a more gradual approach. In the CHR as in the UN system generally, the first step toward getting action is a study to raise the visibility of an issue. Macpherson prepared a draft of a resolution calling on the commission to request the secretary-general to prepare "an analytical report on internally displaced persons taking into account information submitted by Governments, specialized agencies, relevant United Nations organs, regional intergovernmental organizations and non-governmental organizations in consultative status." The WCC and the Quakers submitted the document to the commission at the end of November 1990, and it was circulated to member delegations on 15 December of that year.[24]

But even more than a scaled-back strategy, the Geneva NGOs needed a respected and willing ally among the states seated on the commission. They sought a delegation that would champion the cause of internal displacement, sponsor a resolution, and energetically promote it with other governments. Macpherson raised the issue of internal displacement at a luncheon of Western European delegations hosted by the French ambassador in January 1991; and Christian Strohal, the Austrian delegate to the CHR, seized it. Macpherson was delighted, for he knew Strohal was well liked and had a solid reputation for "good networking" in the local diplomatic community.[25]

Strohal knew it was not going to be easy to push through a resolution on internal displacement at the commission. In looking back, he commented, "We were talking about what was at the time considered an internal issue, something people were not comfortable with." If progress were to be made, the subject had to be moved forward incrementally; there was no chance that the CHR would simply start off by giving approval for a rapporteur. For that reason, he liked Macpherson's idea of calling first for an analytical report.[26]

After getting approval from his foreign ministry, Strohal took Macpherson's resolution and floated it among Western and other delegations and lined up 16 co-sponsors; the United States was notably absent but the Union of Soviet Socialist Republics, soon to be the Russian Federation, joined as a co-sponsor. Strohal strengthened the operative paragraph of Macpherson's resolution by adding that the secretary-general's analytical report should also take into account "the protection of human rights of internally displaced persons."

The goal was to have the resolution adopted "by consensus"—that is, without a vote, a maneuver perfected in UN circles to suggest more agreement than actually exists. At each of its sessions, the commission approved dozens of resolutions in this manner. A resolution could be approved with the support of no more than a simple majority, but any negative vote weakened its standing, and the objection of only one member state was sufficient to trigger a vote. Consensus approval also had the advantage of silencing later critics, who could be reminded that the commission already had endorsed without reservation the very ideas to which they objected. That was particularly important for supporters of a resolution on internal displacement, for their main purpose was to build a basis to expand over time the scope of the CHR's action on the issue.

Backed by intensive lobbying by the Geneva NGO coalition, the Austrian resolution won consensus approval on 5 March 1991. Resolution 1991/25 with the title of "Internally Displaced Persons" was a tentative but critically important first step. It meant that no longer would internal displacement be considered within the UN system to be exclusively a humanitarian issue, a matter of nothing other than food, shelter, and medical care. Now, for the first time, it was front and center on the human rights agenda as well.

That the phenomenon of internal displacement was as much a human rights as a humanitarian problem was a concept that Roberta Cohen and Dennis Gallagher had been working to promote ever since Cohen's address at the Geneva Quaker House in February 1990. Neither they nor anyone else denied the importance of the humanitarian aspects. At the same time, food and shelter would be of little avail if those uprooted from their homes had no protection from murder, rape, or forced labor. The ICRC had come under criticism for having visited camps in France during the Second World War after which inmates were shipped to gas chambers.[27] ICRC's Urs Boegli noted the recurrence of this ugly reality in Bosnia where "the only thing you can do for them is to make sure they are fed before they are shot."[28] Cohen and Deng would later help popularize what were to be called "the well-fed dead" in the Balkans, a term attributed to the late Fred Cuny.[29]

But in the early 1990s, protection for IDPs was an issue for which the UN system was wholly unprepared and institutionally ill-equipped. Dealing with it meant confronting the limits of the domestic jurisdiction of states. Gallagher sensed that here was a cutting edge to the issue, one that offered the Refugee Policy Group an opportunity and the possibility to raise the requisite resources to do so. In the fall of 1990, he asked Cohen to organize an international conference on human rights protection for internally displaced persons. Cohen turned to the Jacob Blaustein Institute for the Advancement of Human Rights and the European Foundation for Human Rights for funding and drafted a 47-page paper that served as a blueprint for the conference when it convened in Washington in June 1991.[30] Cohen argued that "there is an integral relationship between protection and assistance" and that "providing relief also has to involve dealing with the security needs of aid recipients."[31] She urged human rights groups to take a more active role in monitoring situations of internal displacement and humanitarian organizations to press for greater protection for the IDPs, and she also pointed out the need for new international legal standards and remedies for them.

Cohen's paper introduced into the literature on internal displacement a concept that had been developed by Francis Deng, William Zartman, and other scholars in their work on governance in Africa.[32] "Sovereignty," she wrote, "carries with it a responsibility on the part of governments to protect their citizens." Deng explained that it was the "culmination of work begun in the late 1980s to see how the end of the Cold War changed the way conflict and conflict resolution were perceived in Africa."[33] It was a new way of thinking about an issue that was central to the problem of assistance and protection for the internally displaced.[34] It was a way of squaring the circle, to reconcile the seemingly clashing principles of state sovereignty and nonintervention, on the one hand, with the need to halt the worst kinds of abuse of human rights, on the other hand, and even to intervene militarily in the most egregious of cases.

"Thinking was a bit ahead of events," Susan Martin recalled, "but not that far."[35] In particular, the U.S.-led intervention on behalf of the Kurds in northern Iraq in April 1991 was the first post-Cold War test of the meaning of responsible sovereignty. The massive military intervention to protect and assist both refugees and IDPs meant that in its most traditional sense, as one of us wrote, "sovereignty was no longer sacrosanct."[36] For the newly appointed high commissioner for refugees, Sadako Ogata, her baptism by fire in northern Iraq necessitated dealing with IDPs as much as, and eventually more than, refugees.

The confluence of post-Cold War politics and thinking about the phenomenon of internal displacement, in particular, was revolutionary in its implications. Deng would later amplify and make sovereignty as responsibility the centerpiece of his mandate as representative of the secretary-general on IDPs.[37] It provided an overarching conceptual framework for the Brookings Project on Internal Displacement throughout the 12 years of Deng's tenure, and beyond. Patenting an idea, of course, is impossible. But the effective dissemination of sovereignty as responsibility, including its international protection dimensions, is a key legacy of Deng's discharge of his mandate and of the Brookings project.

The June 1991 conference was the first broad forum on internal displacement. Its 40 participants came from the senior ranks of the human rights and humanitarian worlds. It opened with former Canadian secretary of state Flora MacDonald in the chair with addresses by Sadako Ogata, James P. Grant, the UN Children's Fund's (UNICEF) executive director, and Tony Hall, chairman of the U.S. Congress Select Committee on Hunger. There followed panels chaired by Martin Ennals, former secretary-general of Amnesty International, Roger Winter, director of the USCR, Larry Minear, Nigel Rodley, Jerome Shestack, Francis Deng, and Dennis Gallagher. Issues ranged from protection for the internally displaced to sovereignty, new international standards, sanctions, and enhanced cooperation by human rights and humanitarian relief organizations. Martin Macpherson came from Geneva as did Georg Mautner-Markoff, who had left the Austrian Foreign Ministry and joined the UN's human rights unit working on such special mechanisms. Among others there were Adama Dieng, secretary-general of the International Commission of Jurists, Robert Goldman from the American University's Law School, and Bertram Ramcharan, later to become deputy and then acting high commissioner for human rights. Competing priorities and distractions often caused participants to fade away from meetings held in Washington, but this time there was an air of excitement, a sense of something new and important that kept the conference room filled right up to the close of the two-day meeting. Many of the participants would later look back on the conference as "the place where it all began." Ramcharan, shortly after retiring from the UN, looked back at the "imaginative solution" of those first moments. He commented, "It would not have worked had it not been for Roberta Cohen."[38]

RPG's concluding report noted that the participants had "strongly recommended" a compilation of existing human rights and humanitarian law and UN resolutions applicable to internally displaced persons. Also strongly endorsed was the creation of special machinery to deal with human rights and humanitarian emergencies, though opinion was divided over whether this should be a rapporteur of the CHR or some other mechanism. Oftentimes, people in operational and lobbying jobs look askance upon research. In this case, however, Elizabeth Ferris congratulated Dennis Gallagher: "As a former academic researcher, I know that sometimes you wonder whether or not your research has any impact and I wanted to let you know how useful your work on human rights has been to us in our work with refugees and displaced persons."[39]

The report and the conference set the stage for an intensive lobbying effort by RPG, the Geneva NGO coalition, and others that stretched from late summer 1991 up to and through the commission's January–March 1992 session. The goal was to win support for a resolution creating a rapporteur or working group on internally displaced persons. Launching this effort in August, Macpherson addressed a letter to John Bolton, then the State Department's assistant secretary of state for international organization affairs, soliciting U.S. support. The reply Macpherson received from Bolton the following month might have come from the government of a repressive Third World dictatorship fearful of international ignominy and sanctions. The United States, Bolton wrote, wished to avoid "anything which could be construed as authorizing one country to invade another country under pretext of protecting minorities in that country."

Nevertheless, under unrelenting lobbying during the fall and winter, the U.S. position gradually shifted to one of cautious support for action on internal displacement at the commission's 1992 session. Cohen developed a "lobbying plan," and Gallagher and Hall sent letters to Bolton, Morris Abram, the U.S. ambassador in Geneva, and J. Kenneth Blackwell, the U.S. representative to the commission's session. Gallagher and Cohen followed up these letters with one-on-one meetings with all three, and Cohen walked the State Department halls rounding up support at other levels, finding allies in particular in Alan Kreczco and Michelle Solomon of the legal adviser's office. RPG likewise sent letters to the ambassadors of 33 states represented at the commission, urging their support for steps to strengthen human rights protection for the internally displaced.

Despite the efforts of the Geneva NGO coalition, Cohen wrote toward the end of 1991 that "prospects for strong Commission action this year may not be overly promising."[40] Debates in the UN's General Assembly about a coordinator for humanitarian assistance had brought to the fore considerable Third World opposition to possible intrusion by humanitarian agencies into their countries in order to provide assistance to war victims; and such states constituted almost three-quarters of the commission's membership in 1992. Knee-jerk hostility was present during debates of General Assembly resolutions 43/131 and 46/182, which eventually ended with the establishment of the Department of Humanitarian Affairs (DHA).[41]

It is sometimes difficult to recall in this first decade of the twenty-first century that the end of the Cold War had initially led to a period of optimism and UN activism before it also erupted in new forms of violence. In what subsequently became known as the "new wars," even if many of their characteristics were old,[42] sensitivity to the sovereign prerogatives of states was, if anything, ever more acute—some would say "sacrosanct." Those with vivid memories of misuse of the adjective "humanitarian" during the colonial period and more recently as a justification for military involvement in Iraq may feel an understand-able skepticism about the motivations of outsiders. However, many states simply cling to traditional sovereignty as an effective camouflage for repression with acquiescence from outsiders.

The CHR's session opened on 27 January 1992. On 5 February, Jacques Cuénod, who in the meantime had become RPG's Geneva representative, attended a meeting that Austria convened for Western countries interested in the issue of internal displacement. Cuénod reported to Gallagher that the feeling at the meeting was that "it will not be possible, at this session, to pass a resolution establishing a mechanism." Austria had been the moving force behind the 1991 reso-lution but now seemed to be giving higher priority to other issues. Moreover, the analytical report ordered by the 1991 resolution was "blocked on the 38th floor" of the UN Secretariat in New York—that is, the top floor housing the secretary-general and his closest political advisers. Either it might not come out in time for the session or be issued so late as to make it easy for delegations to argue that more time would be needed to study it. Cuénod noted that at their meeting the Austrians had, apparently deliberately, not distributed a resolution drafted by the Quakers calling for the appointment of an "indepen-dent expert" (a term the NGOs believed might be more palatable to some commission members than "rapporteur") on internally displaced persons.[43]

But by 12 February, Cuénod reported that the outlook had brightened. The analytical report was released that day by the UN Secretariat following a direct appeal to Secretary-General Boutros-Ghali by the head of the World Council of Churches. And the Western group, in a meeting the previous day, had begun "moving toward the creation of a working group thanks to the efforts of Norway, a more positive attitude of Austria and a less negative attitude of the USA." Cuénod reported that although Mexico's position was in doubt, the Latin American group now was "apparently in favor of a working group with a 'soft' resolution." He estimated that even China, which along with India and Mexico was known to be unfriendly toward action by the commission on internal displacement, "would not oppose the creation of a working group based on soft terms of reference." The strategy, Cuénod concluded, was therefore "to propose to establish a working group to examine the issue and to make recommendations to the Commission at its next session."[44]

Roberta Cohen was in Geneva during the week of 17–22 February to deliver a statement to the CHR and join the Geneva NGOs in lobbying for the appointment of a working group. On returning to Washington, she reported that it "looked as if the Commission might create machinery, if not the preferred working group then an independent expert."[45] But on 5 March, two days before the scheduled conclusion of the session, the Philippines, Mexico, Cuba, and others threatened to bring the Austrian resolution to a vote, thereby effectively blocking a consensus resolution. They offered a counter-proposal that made no mention of a working group or an independent expert; the commission would simply take note of the analytical report and ask the secretary-general "to again solicit views of member states on this subject."

But after several hours of discussion in the corridors, a compromise was reached and adopted by consensus that same day as resolution 1992/73. Gone from it was any mention of a working group or an independent expert. Instead as a compromise, the secretary-general was asked to designate a representative "to seek again views and information from all governments on the human rights issues related to internally displaced persons." Included in the representative's mandate was "an examination of existing international human rights, humanitarian and refugee law and standards and their applicability to the protection of and relief assistance to internally displaced persons." And there was a second operative paragraph that called on the secretary-general "to present a comprehensive study . . . identifying existing laws and mechanisms for the protection of the internally displaced, possible additional measures to strengthen implementation of these laws and mechanisms and alternatives for addressing protection needs not adequately covered by existing instruments." To opponents all this may have looked innocuous at the time—just more studies, and what better way to kill an issue than burying it in paper? But soon it would open up prospects for an even broader mandate for international action to confront the phenomenon of internal displacement.

Interviewed more than a decade later, Christian Strohal, Austria's delegate, had no detailed recollection of the negotiations that led to the adoption of resolution 1992/73. The dropping of any reference to a "working group" or "rapporteur" and substituting "representative of the secretary-general"—that is, an individual supposedly more subject to the political restraints inherent in the UN system—must have been critical to gaining the acquiescence of governments that feared the scrutiny of a panel of independent experts or even of a single one. Even with that concession, Austria and the other co-sponsors—the list by then included both Washington and Moscow—had to exert considerable effort to overcome the opposition that any UN mechanism for reaching inside borders and confronting sovereignty aroused at the time.

Norway's intervention must have been a factor in persuading Austria and the Western group to press forward with the resolution despite early reservations. That year Oslo had only observer status at the CHR and therefore no vote to trade, but its voice carried weight in the Western group. Its entry on the scene marked the beginning of both a partnership and a rivalry between Austria and Norway as prime sponsors within the UN system of what was to become the mandate of the representative of the secretary-general on internally displaced persons.

In a fax to Cohen the day that resolution 1992/73 was adopted, Macpherson commented that "it was the best we could get without a vote." But he was heartened some months later when he learned that Francis M. Deng had been chosen to be the representative. Deng, he wrote, was "a serious person, someone with standing who could make an impact."[46]

The potential impact of these decisions was underestimated at the time, certainly by the recalcitrant states that went along thinking that the issue would soon fade from the international radar screen. Deng was later told by an Egyptian diplomat who participated in the session that the general expectation among those who were unenthusiastic about the mandate was that it would die after a year. Instead, a number of governmental and nongovernmental analysts and activists had managed to explore what was *terra incognita* and place the issue of internal displacement squarely on the UN's map. It is to the initial steps to shape the new mandate that we now turn.

2   Shaping the mandate in the early years, 1992–1993

Francis Deng had known Boutros Boutros-Ghali for many years, but the call he received at his home in Washington, D.C., from the secretary-general one afternoon late in July 1992 came as a surprise. Deng had no idea that he was being considered as a candidate to take on the task of pulling together the UN's tentative efforts to assist and protect the internally displaced.[1]

Deng first met Boutros-Ghali in the early 1970s at a conference in Khartoum. They then got reacquainted in 1977, the year the latter became minister of state for foreign affairs in Egyptian president Anwar Sadat's government and a year after Deng's appointment to that same position in the government of Sudanese president Jaafar al-Nimeiry. Relations between Sudan and Egypt traditionally were close, and that closeness brought the two men together often in a friendly relationship. Boutros-Ghali was almost two decades Deng's senior, but their backgrounds and roles and status in their respective governments ran parallel. Both had brilliant academic records in the study of the law, each graduating first in his law school class, Boutros-Ghali from Cairo University and Deng from Khartoum University. Boutros-Ghali earned a doctorate in international law from the Sorbonne in 1949 and then became professor of law and international relations at Cairo University, over the years compiling a record of publications and honors that filled several pages. Deng won a scholarship and was awarded his doctorate in law from Yale University in 1968. In 1967 he joined the UN's human rights office in New York and was given permission to teach legal anthropology at New York University and African law at Columbia. He returned to Yale Law School on a leave of absence from the UN on a fellowship in the Program of Law and Development to write a book on Sudan's identity crisis. While on leave at Yale, he was appointed in 1972 as Sudan's ambassador to the Scandinavian countries and to the United States in 1974.

Even though they were among the most talented professionals in their respective countries, both men hit a glass ceiling—ethnic and religious discrimination—which blocked their ascent to the very top of the public administration hierarchy. Boutros-Ghali was a Coptic Christian, a sect that constituted only some 5 percent of Egypt's otherwise Muslim population. Deng was a Christian southern Sudanese, the son of a prominent chief of the powerful Dinka tribe, serving in a Muslim-dominated government in a time of reprieve from civil war and the periodic efforts by the Muslim majority to impose its faith and practices on the Christian and animist south. Boutros-Ghali remained minister of state, subordinate to younger and less experienced and, according to many, less able foreign ministers until shortly before his election as UN secretary-general in December 1991. In 1980, as Nimeiry began his shift toward Islamic government, Deng wanted to leave government service but was persuaded by Nimeiry to continue for a time by stepping down from his job as the second ranking official in the Sudanese foreign ministry to become ambassador to Canada, keeping his rank of state minister. In 1983 as Khartoum's policies reignited the civil war, Deng left the Sudanese diplomatic service and took up residence in the United States. After a series of fellowships at various places, he joined the Brookings Institution late in 1988 to head its Africa Program.

So when Francis Deng's name came across Boutros Boutros-Ghali's desk, the UN's top official picked up the phone to speak personally to his former counterpart. He informed Deng that he was going to be his representative on internally displaced persons. Deng was honored but he required time to think about it because he was working at Brookings on Africa and had little involvement with the issue of internal displacement outside of Africa. The secretary-general would not take "no" for an answer. He insisted, pointing to the suffering of Deng's continent, country, and people, the Dinka, who were driven from their villages and pasture lands during Sudan's civil wars. Boutros-Ghali also praised Deng's credentials as a diplomat. The secretary-general closed the conversation by stating that he was going to announce Deng's appointment that very day but specified that he could reconsider if he really were unhappy with the job description after he learned more.[2]

Deng felt that he could not refuse, but he had virtually no idea what the appointment entailed. To find out, he called Georg Mautner-Markoff in Geneva, chief of the Special Procedures Section at the UN Centre for Human Rights, the office of the Commission on Human Rights that serviced its rapporteurs and working groups.

Mautner-Markoff had met Deng at RPG's conference on internal displacement in June of the previous year and had been impressed. After the CHR approved resolution 1992/73, it had fallen to Mautner-Markoff to compose a short list of candidates for the job, with the usual necessity for senior UN positions to place geographic representation at the top of the list of criteria. The word from on high was that "an African was wanted for the job," and Deng fit the bill perfectly— competent *and* of appropriate origin. After consulting with Gallagher, Cohen, and others, Mautner-Markoff narrowed the list down to three; and with Deng's name prominently featured, he sent it to UN headquarters in New York. He was not surprised when Boutros-Ghali chose Deng, though he was surprised to learn of the appointment first from Deng, rather than through the normal official channels from the secretary-general's office.[3]

Deng learned that the position of RSG was "voluntary"—that is, unsalaried—and that the center would be able to offer only minimal resources in support of his mandate. As Mautner-Markoff explained, the money simply was not there. For the entirety of its operations in support of the commission and its many mandates, the center got about half a percent of the UN's overall budget. Some thought the center was deliberately left starved of resources so as to prevent it and the CHR from pursuing initiatives too energetically. But budgetary constraints notwithstanding, the commission continued at each of its sessions to add more rapporteurs, working groups, and representatives. Mautner-Markoff worried that the scant backing the center could offer his burgeoning number of investigators would affect negatively the quality of their reports, to the discredit of the center and the UN's human rights work generally. As for others, right from the start he encouraged Deng to seek support outside the UN system, from governments and from private institutions; and when it materialized, he welcomed the input into the center's work.[4] After Mautner-Markoff left in 1998, his successors at times would adopt a more defensive and rigid attitude toward the collaboration with private institutions in support of Deng's work. But the precedent was set of relying upon sympathetic sources of finance, including governments, to circumvent the UN's onerous political as well as financial and administrative constraints.

Mautner-Markoff's warning about the center's lack of resources made the assignment doubly challenging: there were barely six months left before the next session of the Commission on Human Rights. To do the study and write the report called for in the 1992 resolution, it would be essential to enlist very substantial outside support, and to do so quickly.

Deng turned first to John Steinbruner, the director of foreign policy studies at the Brookings Institution. Steinbruner's main concern was whether the appointment as representative of the secretary-general would require Deng to carry out UN instructions that could compromise the Brookings reputation as a research institution built on in-depth and independent analysis, not politically correct claptrap. Once satisfied that Deng would be free to develop his own program and that "there was a reasonable overlap between his duties as representative of the Secretary-General and at Brookings," Steinbruner warmly endorsed Deng's taking on the UN mandate. He sought and readily obtained approval from Bruce MacLaury, the president of the Brookings Institution. Steinbruner did not establish for Deng any kind of percentage of time to be divided between his direct work for his salary and his work as representative. As he put it later, the two went together; and what Deng would do for the UN would be "good for Brookings and good for the world."[5]

Steinbruner's decision cleared the way for Deng to devote the fall of 1992 and early winter of 1992–93 to the job of shaping his mandate. The CHR's resolution called for the RSG to seek "views and information" from governments and conduct an "examination of existing international human rights, humanitarian and refugee law and standards and their applicability to the protection of and relief assistance to internally displaced persons." The resolution called on the secretary-general to do the same with UN agencies as well as regional and nongovernmental organizations, and to submit a "comprehensive study" to the commission on the legal aspects of the issue. The UN secretariat, deciding that "the Secretary General and his Representative could not have been intended to operate separately," handed over the entire job to Deng. There would be a single report, prepared by him.[6]

At the center, Mautner-Markoff assigned a staff member, Daniel O'Donnell, to draft a letter soliciting the views of governments, UN agencies, and NGOs. Deng signed it early in August and asked for replies before 15 October. For help in preparing other parts of the report, Deng turned to Roberta Cohen and Jacques Cuénod at the Refugee Policy Group's Washington and Geneva offices, respectively, and to former colleagues at the Yale and Harvard Law Schools. To Cohen and Cuénod, he assigned the "institutional" side of the report—that is, the analysis of what UN agencies were, were not, and should be doing in regard to internal displacement. Teams from Yale and Harvard were asked to draft papers on existing international legal standards applicable to the internally displaced.

But there was also a need for a first-hand look at the problem. Mautner-Markoff was able to stretch the center's budget to allow for Deng to travel to five countries with serious problems of internal displacement: Yugoslavia (then in the process of imploding), Russia, Somalia (as it was unraveling), Sudan, and El Salvador. This set the precedent of country missions—direct encounters with the harsh world of the displaced and the governments that oppressed or were unable to help them. As the concrete basis that would inform his advocacy as well as legal and institutional recommendations, the quasi-official UN "voice" of the RSG pronouncing his findings on countries was essential to raise the visibility and credibility of the phenomenon of displacement.

Early in October, before departing for his trip to Yugoslavia, Deng went to see Boutros-Ghali. What specifically, he asked, did the secretary-general expect of him? Boutros-Ghali replied that he wanted Deng to give the UN "ideas and guidance" on what it should do to protect IDPs. Legal and scholarly analyses were interesting, but the important thing was to think in practical terms. As for what the mandate should be after the initial one-year appointment, Boutros-Ghali remarked that he did not think the Commission on Human Rights was a particularly effective body when it came to practical action. He made clear that he favored Deng's retaining a connection with the secretary-general's office rather than relying exclusively on his appointment by the commission.[7]

That accorded with Deng's personal preferences. The alternative, favored in particular by several NGOs, was for Deng to become a rapporteur on internal displacement. But that job would have been, according to the CHR's tradition, to investigate and expose, to point a finger at offending governments. Deng did not think that was the way to make progress, and in any event he did not see himself in that role. The 1992 resolution called on him to undertake "dialogues" with governments. His experience as a diplomat and his own personal inclinations led him to the conclusion that such give-and-take conversations were more likely than confrontation to produce results. Dialogue did not rule out exposing abuses, but it did not mean doing so in ways that would automatically antagonize governments and make them more resistant to change.

Indeed, the voice of the RSG was heard in part precisely because of the style. Elisabeth Rasmusson of the Norwegian Refugee Council (NRC) remarked: "Deng had far better access to governments than NGOs, and he opened up space for them to pursue their own type of more aggressive and visible advocacy . . . It is a misunderstanding to think that effective advocacy requires being in the media spotlight."[8] Part of the problem in appreciating the impact of Deng's country reports may result from a limited notion of the approaches considered most effective. Many NGOs as well as national governments and activist scholars have a single "model" for human rights monitoring. This consists of a highly visible advocate who employs high-decibel levels for public denunciations and seeks large headlines. If this is the standard, then the representative does not really measure up. At the same time, behind-the-scenes lobbying and discreet work with governments can lead to breakthroughs as the ICRC has demonstrated for the last century and a half. Deng represents a hybrid between a free-wheeling NGO and a more reserved UN or ICRC staff member. One-size-fits-all is hardly applicable to successful advocacy; on the contrary, a range of complementary styles is most effective.

Anticipating what governments will find unacceptable and avoiding the topic is a widespread shortcoming throughout the UN system, where it is difficult to surpass what governments construe as acceptable criticism. A number of NGOs have leveled criticism at Deng over the years for not speaking out more forthrightly and for his natural inclination, as a former senior government official himself, to want to be accepted and even liked by governments. There undoubtedly were times when more candid public pronouncements would have been appropriate. The criticisms of Deng's style, however, resemble those lodged against the ICRC whose discretion often, if not always, has advantages for access and credibility when acting as an interlocutor for a target government.

It is more sensible to think about the impact of the RSG's country missions and reports by more outspoken NGOs working on human rights as complementary and reinforcing rather than as antithetical or mutually exclusive. Whether justified or not, criticism undoubtedly had the healthy effect of encouraging Deng to become progressively bolder in his public statements and conversations with governments, which became apparent during his first five country missions.

These country missions took up most of October and November. For the trip to Yugoslavia, Deng accompanied Poland's former prime minister and Solidarity activist Tadeusz Mazoweicki—the outspoken and controversial special rapporteur whom the commission designated for that country at its first-ever special session, held in August 1992. The civil war that broke out in the summer of 1991 entailed the forcible expulsion of hundreds of thousands of people. Together with Mazoweicki and other rapporteurs from the commission, Deng visited Belgrade and Zaghreb to confer with government officials and then went on to towns in Serbia, Croatia, and Bosnia most affected by the conflict.

The visit to Russia came at Moscow's invitation. The collapse of the Soviet Union caused the displacement of more than a million persons as fighting broke out within and between some of its newly independent former components. Ethnic Russians in Moldova, the Baltic states, and the central Asian republics suddenly found themselves unwelcome in lands that they had called home for generations. In sharp contrast to his later experience, in 1992 Deng found officials in Moscow "unusually candid about the internal problems of their country." One Foreign Ministry official went so far as to comment that "the international community should intervene by force to protect the internally displaced where conditions make such intervention necessary."9

In Somalia, the collapse of the central government would soon lead to a humanitarian intervention authorized under the UN Charter's Chapter VII provisions for the use of force with an international blessing. Chaos in the fall of 1992 was such that Deng could do little more than meet with UN officials and General Mohammed Farah Aideed, the factional leader who controlled the largest part of Mogadishu and uncompromisingly opposed international intervention.

Sudan was Deng's home and also the country with the largest number of IDPs, some 4 million at that time. In 1988 about 250,000 persons internally displaced from southern Sudan by the civil war had died of starvation while the Khartoum government fended off pleas by international humanitarian agencies to assist them. The following year international pressure compelled it to open its doors to Operation Lifeline Sudan.10 Deng argued in his talks with senior government officials that the lesson was twofold: first, that Sudan needed to address the crisis of displacement and needed international cooperation in resolving it; and second that the Khartoum government stood to gain diplomatically by supporting initiatives on internal displacement at the Commission on Human Rights. Deng won a pledge of support for his mandate and authorization to visit two large camps for the displaced near Khartoum and another at Abyei on the border between northern and southern Sudan.11

He chose El Salvador because it was a prime example of cooperation between the United Nations and a member government in bringing a civil war to an end, consolidating peace, and launching reconstruction. By the fall of 1992, Deng was able to confirm that internal displacement, which at the height of that country's civil war had affected approximately one-quarter of the population, was on its way to being resolved. NGOs and displaced and resettled populations nonetheless remained distrustful of the government's intentions and strongly in favor of a continued UN presence. Government officials, although confirming that their country was "a model of international cooperation on a domestic problem," made clear that they looked forward to an early end to the world organization's mission there.[12]

For Deng the purpose of these initial visits was not to undertake formal monitoring and reporting on conditions affecting IDPs, as later he would do, but to acquire insights into the problem, consult with governments, and gain their support for his mandate. Nonetheless, he hoped the visits would help give concrete meaning to his mandate by establishing a precedent for direct dialogue with state authorities and the displaced themselves.[13] This precedent was set and would be built upon over the coming decade.

Deng's annual reports to the Commission on Human Rights are published as official ECOSOC documents, and biennial reports are submitted to the General Assembly. They contain analyses of the political, legal, and institutional conundrum of internal displacement. Country reports, with tailored and in-depth recommendations to governments and international agencies, are published separately (as annexes) but summarized in the main reports. Like all human rights efforts, those on behalf of IDPs are difficult to evaluate because of the inherent difficulties in separating the impact of discrete efforts from local and global geopolitical developments. However, Deng's visits raised awareness of an acute problem, empowered local and outside actors to engage in the issues, and stimulated improvements in the treatment of IDPs by governments and aid agencies.

The contents and language of the country reports suggest an intricate blend of circumlocutions in "UNese" and more hard-hitting prose. Merely getting agreement from a government to explore human rights and IDPs may actually be considered an achievement of sorts for an intergovernmental organization. Moreover, there are important subtleties that are apparent to specialized readers of these reports over the years—for example, a willingness to examine closely a government's rationale in allowing assistance into areas not under its control (Sri Lanka), or solidarity between a government and its internally displaced population (Azerbaijan), or the relative obscurity of IDPs absorbed by local populations (Armenia).

At Deng's request, toward the end of November 1992, Roberta Cohen took on the task of editing a first draft of the report that Deng was to submit to the Commission on Human Rights at the opening of its 1993 session at the end of January. The UN set a deadline of mid-December for receipt of the text for printing. Cohen spent the morning of Thanksgiving cutting, pasting, and joining together elements of research already done by herself and Cuénod as well as by the Yale—Harvard team working on the international legal aspects of internal displacement. Cohen had no formal legal training, but she knew international human rights law. She struck out large sections of the draft from the law schools and substituted pages from the secretary-general's 1991 analytical report which, she wrote in a covering letter to Deng, "is much more sophisticated in legal analysis."[14]

The report had also to include comments by governments, UN agencies, other IGOs, and NGOs. Governmental responses were at best unenthusiastic. By the mid-December deadline, only 16 governments had replied to the questionnaire that Deng had sent out the previous August. Most offered hardly more than *pro forma* acknowledgments. The Pakistani mission in Geneva advised laconically that "Pakistan is not confronted with the problem of internal displaced persons and as such it has no comments to offer in this matter."[15] The Chinese note dismissed the problem of IDPs (which it said "do not exist in China") as "chiefly a question of humanitarian aid."[16] Cyprus, Jordan, Egypt, and Armenia highlighted foreign aggression as the prime cause of internal displacement. Replying for the United States, Ambassador Morris Abram in Geneva expressed concern over the problem of internal displacement and wished Deng success but cautioned: "At this time we are not prepared to suggest that new mechanisms or laws are, a priori, necessary to address the needs of the internally displaced."[17] Estonia chimed in, declaring itself "of the position that the United Nations Commission on Human Rights should assume a greater role in promoting and protecting the human rights of internally displaced persons but in our opinion this can be carried out most effectively within the framework of already existing United Nations organs."[18] Among the Western European states, only Austria and Norway, the two main supporters of action on internal displacement, replied with any seriousness to the questionnaire. Both stressed the need for "standards or more specific principles or guidelines concerning the treatment of internally displaced persons in order to ensure effective protection of their basic human rights."[19]

By 1992 the number of internally displaced persons was such that it affected all UN humanitarian and development organizations in one way or another. As good bureaucrats who saw a growth industry in the offing, their comments emphasized the work that their institutions were already doing to assist IDPs and commented on aspects of the issue that particularly affected their field of competence with an eye toward expansion. With varying degrees of enthusiasm, UN agencies endorsed the creation by the Commission on Human Rights of a thematic mechanism to monitor internal displacement. The only serious expressions of reserve came from two agencies outside the UN system but closely associated with it on humanitarian issues, the International Committee of the Red Cross and the International Organization for Migration (IOM). The ICRC in particular objected to creating a new and separate category, arguing that the 1949 Geneva Conventions and the 1977 Additional Protocols gave it authority to protect all those affected by armed conflict, whether displaced or not, and that preference should not be given to those who are displaced over others whose needs are similar. The IOM's mandate focused on orderly migration, inside a country and internationally, and so it also saw no need for a new category in its work.

The replies from NGOs again showed them to be the main champions of human rights protection for IDPs.[20] Caritas, Catholic Migration, the WCC, the Lawyers Committee for Human Rights, RPG, and the USCR all offered detailed responses to Deng's questionnaire together with strong expressions of support for the establishment of a mechanism on internal displacement.

In his report to the commission, Deng had recommended that:

> Given the magnitude of the problem and the likely increase in the numbers of the internally displaced the United Nations is called upon to create some mechanism, whether a Representative, Rapporteur or Working Group, that can serve as a focal point for international protection, help mobilize the efforts of existing United Nations bodies involved with assistance and protection, and can act to dialogue and advocate on behalf of internally displaced persons.

Without stating his own preference, Deng added that his position would permit him to pursue two goals. One would be to "monitor conditions and alert the international community as necessary to initiate actions." The other would be an operational role that would include "interceding with States and other concerned parties to alleviate problems and assist in protection and assistance."[21]

The phrasing could hardly have been more felicitous. Whatever reservations some states continued to harbor about empowering the commission to lift the cover of sovereignty, it was hard to raise serious objections to a mandate whose purpose was to "alleviate problems and assist," the more so in a year in which the number of IDPs worldwide was soaring toward 30 million. And who could oppose a representative whose role would be to sound the international alert when people were in dire need? On 11 March 1993, the commission adopted without a vote a resolution sponsored by Austria. Resolution 1993/95 requested the secretary-general "to mandate his representative for a period of two years to continue his work aimed at a better understanding of the general problems faced by internally displaced persons and their long-term solutions." Three-year mandates were the norm for the CHR's thematic mechanisms, but, as a further gesture to those in doubt, the Austrian sponsor agreed to limit the representative's first term to two years.

The mandate gave Deng a "voice" to address the full UN membership but at the same time provided a relatively independent platform to broaden the scope of his work on internal displacement. At his urging, the Austrians inserted a provision in the 1993 resolution authorizing him to report on his work to the General Assembly as well as to the Commission on Human Rights. The provision substantially broadened Deng's reach and opened up a new avenue, through General Assembly resolutions, for the gradual expansion of his mandate. As Roger Winter, who headed the USCR at the time, recalled: "There was no master plan. Francis and Roberta were in the right place at the right time."[22]

The resolution likewise offered a division of labor for Austria and Norway, the mandate's two main state sponsors: Norway took the lead in the General Assembly and Austria in the CHR. The role of these two countries is essential to the story in the next chapter. Now that we have the historical back-drop for putting the issue on the map and the initial shaping of the mandate, we can explore the creation of a back-stopping capacity for the representative outside the United Nations proper.

3 Creating the project on internal displacement and improving the knowledge base and awareness, 1993–1998

The text of the resolution "Internally Displaced Persons," adopted by the Commission on Human Rights in March 1993, was cast in very general terms. The end of the preambular section of resolution 1993/95 noted that the representative of the secretary-general had identified the compilation of existing rules and norms and the question of general guiding principles to govern the treatment of internally displaced persons as a task requiring further attention and study. But the only request made of the representative was that he continue his work with a view to identifying, where required, ways and means of improving protection for and assistance to internally displaced persons.

The concluding paragraph of Francis Deng's 1993 report to the commission had set out a far more ambitious agenda for action to help those internally displaced by political persecution, inter- and intra-state wars, and other disasters. It called for:

- United Nations bodies to be pragmatically mobilized and coordinated to provide effective protection and assistance
- Monitoring and early warning systems or the detection of impending or prevailing crises of displacement
- Procedures for the consolidation of existing international instruments into a code, a declaration or a convention and
- Diplomatic initiatives to avert, alleviate, or correct humanitarian tragedies or human rights violations.[1]

Even had it been assigned to a fully staffed UN organization, this program would have been truly challenging, if not utterly unrealistic. The resolution that asked him to continue his work and presumably address his own agenda also extended Deng's mandate as RSG for two years; but it offered him virtually nothing in the way of back-stopping or financial resources. He was still a single individual, without salary or support personnel of any kind. In the Brookings Institution, he had the good fortune of an understanding employer that subsidized his voluntary position as RSG, but alongside his work as representative he still bore responsibility for Brookings's Africa Program. The Geneva Centre for Human Rights, Deng's official base within the UN system, had money for some official travel but even that was tightly limited. In due course a budget was drawn up that allowed Deng, for 1994, five trips from his home base in Washington, D.C., to New York for consultations at UN headquarters, three to Geneva for meetings at the commission and the center, and three for country missions. But owing to chronic budgetary restrictions, the center was unable to assign even one full-time staff member to the problem of internal displacement.

Outsiders often find such UN lapses baffling. How could a "decision" be made to move ahead but with no resources to give it operational meaning? Over a decade later, the situation remained the same. In February 2005, a multi-volume evaluation of projects for refugees and IDPs financed by the UK's Department for International Development (DfID) commented on Deng's continuing lack of back-up: "The RSG-IDP also lacks the political clout to insist on implementation of recommendations or, indeed, the operational capacity to follow up."[2]

Such is the nature of UN decision-making by consensus and often its only approach to governance, operations, and programming. It permits states that are against an initiative but embarrassed to say "no" instead to say "yes," while being almost guaranteed that nothing will happen. In this respect, the CHR's March 1993 decision to start work on IDPs resembled a host of Security Council "decisions" to ensure security in Somalia or halt Serbian aggression. *The Economist* described the latter as "confetti resolutions," a useful description for many so-called UN decisions.[3] Among other shortcomings, this quali-fies as one of the institutional "pathologies" analyzed by Michael Barnett and Martha Finnemore.[4] This is also why at the outset of this volume we described the soon-to-be-established Project on Internal Displacement as a possible model for circumventing the UN's busi-ness-as-usual politics and bureaucracy.

Securing staff support at the center became Deng's first priority. He found an ally in Georg Mautner-Markoff, chief of the Special Procedures Section, who agreed to accept an intern for the job. Deng persuaded Harvard Law School to fund a summer internship for Maria Stavropoulou, a promising young student from Greece who was a member of the team that had drafted legal language for Deng's 1993 report to the commission and who went to the center in July 1993. And when her Harvard-sponsored internship ran out, Mautner-Markoff was able to extend her by using a grant by the government of Norway specifically earmarked to support the mandate of the RSG to secure a series of short-term renewable contracts. The grant also paid for the assignment to the center of a young Norwegian lawyer, Daniel Helle, as back-up for Deng's mandate.

This rather ad hoc back-stopping was essential even for the country missions, which were only a portion of the work program. It remained essential for purposes of reporting to the United Nations. The missions from 1992 to 1998 accelerated and are listed in Box 3.1.

For everything else, for both staff support and program, Deng had to look outside the UN system. Already in 1992 the Refugee Policy Group had raised funds for staff support in the preparation of Deng's first report to the commission. The Norwegian Refugee Council, based in Oslo, also volunteered. In February 1993, as the Commission on Human Rights opened its yearly session, the Norwegian government

---

Box 3.1 RSG country missions, 1992–1998

1992   Former Yugoslavia, visited 12–22 October (Report E/CN.4/1993/35, annex, paragraphs 157-174).
        Russian Federation, visited November (Report E/CN.4/1993/35, annex, paragraphs 175–187).
        Somalia (Report E/CN.4/1993/35, annex, paragraphs 188–201).
        Sudan (Report E/CN.4/1993/35, annex, paragraphs 202–235).
        El Salvador, visited 24–27 November (Report E/CN.4/1993/35, annex, paragraphs 236–244).

1993   Sri Lanka, visited 10–17 November (Report E/CN.4/1994/44/Add.1).

1994   Colombia, visited 10–18 June (E/CN.4/1995/50/Add.1).
        Burundi, visited 30 August – 4 September (E/CN.4/1995/50/Add.2).
        Rwanda, visited 7–11 December (E/CN.4/1995/50/Add.4).

1995   Peru, visited 12–25 August (E/CN.4/1996/52/Add.1).

1996   Tajikistan, visited 1–12 June (A/51/483/Add.1).
        Mozambique, visited 21 Nov – 3 December (E/CN.4/1997/43/Add.1).

1998   Azerbaijan, visited 21 May – 1 June (E/CN.4/1999/79/Add.1.).

together with the NRC and RPG convened a "Roundtable Discussion on United Nations Human Rights Protection for Internally Displaced Persons" in Nyon, a suburb of Geneva. With ambassadors and other representatives from 19 of the commission's member states in attendance, Deng addressed the roundtable along with Jan Egeland (Norway's state secretary for foreign affairs, who a decade later became emergency relief coordinator (ERC)), Sadako Ogata (UN high commissioner for refugees), Jan Eliasson (UN under-secretary-general for humanitarian affairs), and Antoine Blanca (UN under-secretary-general for human rights and director-general of the center). The meeting helped smooth the way to extend Deng's mandate. One of its main themes was the expressed need for a coherent set of legal standards for the protection of the internally displaced, the focus of the next chapter.

But neither that nor any of the other objectives set out in Deng's 1993 report to the commission could be accomplished solely with the aid of two junior staff members in Geneva; all the more as Stavropoulou and Helle found themselves called on by the center to perform duties other than those for IDPs. Through the spring and summer of 1993, Deng worked on a book that incorporated and expanded upon the findings in his report to the commission on four of his five country visits during 1992, excluding the joint one to Yugoslavia with Mazoweicki. The RPG and the Brookings Foreign Policy Program organized working groups to help with the project, while Terrence Lyons at Brookings and Roberta Cohen at RPG lent assistance. *Protecting the Dispossessed* was published by the Brookings Institution Press in fall 1993, the first book-length treatment of internal displacement.

Looking back at his experience, Francis Deng ruminated: "I defined an original niche beyond the usual role of rapporteur, dealing not only with symptoms but increasingly with the underlying problems."[5] He recalled that his country visits had mostly followed a pattern. The program would begin with a briefing by the UN's resident representative. There followed meetings or group briefings to encounter the following constituencies: the highest level of the official government hierarchy, including the head of state or government, relevant ministers, officials with responsibilities for the internally displaced; representatives of UN organizations; the donor community; human rights bodies and other NGOs. Field visits to IDP camps and visits with civilian and military officials at the district and local levels to hear their views were then followed by debriefings back in the capital.

In a later address to an academic audience in Germany, Deng explained how he had always dealt with the ever sensitive issue of sovereignty in his meetings with senior government officials:

> The first five minutes are crucial for trying to impress upon the president or the minister of foreign affairs or other relevant authorities that I recognize the problem as internal and falling under the sovereignty of the state; that my task is to see how the international community can assist the government to help its own people. And then, once I notice a level of comfort and see that the dynamics of interaction are becoming more harmonious, I go on to explain politely, but affirmatively, that I don't interpret sovereignty negatively. Sovereignty is not a way of closing doors against the international community. In this world of intense interaction and interdependence, sovereignty is to me a positive concept, which stipulates state responsibility to provide protection and assistance for its people . . . Given an appropriate level of comfort, one can even add that the best way to protect sovereignty is to discharge the responsibilities of sovereignty and to call on the international community to assist in carrying out these responsibilities.[6]

The meetings with the displaced were at times the most problematic segment of Deng's missions. According to the UN rules governing his mandate and common intergovernmental practice, he could only travel where governments permitted, where the presence of officials and interpreters could seriously inhibit people in the camps from freely expressing their views. In one camp in Sudan, for instance, people who were too afraid to speak out stuffed written complaints into his pockets without his even noticing.[7]

That the overwhelming majority of the displaced are women and children was made starkly apparent to Deng during a visit to one camp where out of some 7,000 IDPs all but 25 were women and children:

> After I addressed the whole community in the camp, I asked for a smaller number of people, 10 to 15, to discuss in depth what the needs of the people in the camp were. All those who came were men. I said: "I thought you said there were only 25 men in the camp?" I was told, "Well you asked for leaders." What this small sample shows is if you have that large a group constituting mostly women and children, and those you want to discuss the problems with are 10 out of the 25 men, then you begin to realize that you

don't have anywhere near the insight needed into the needs of women and children.[8]

That particular aspect notwithstanding, meetings with IDPs would at times offer other insights into some of the deeper causes of displacement. In one Latin American country, for example, Deng asked a displaced community what they wanted him to report to their leaders in the government:

> The response I got was, "We have no leaders. Those are not our leaders. To those people we are criminals, and our only crime is that we are poor." They were thinking in socioeconomic class terms. In another, in central Asia, I asked the same question. There, thinking in ethnic terms, they said: "Those people are not our people. We don't have any of our people among those people." They felt totally excluded or marginalized.

Remarks of this sort, heard frequently in his talks with the displaced, reflected a crisis of identity that Deng pinpointed as one of the fundamental causes of internal displacement. In the competition for power and resources, one group shut out others and exploited that leverage. Often this cleavage was more grounded in race, ethnicity, language, religion, or culture than in socioeconomic class. But it could be felt just as strongly by the rulers as by the ruled, as Deng recounted:

> In an African country the Prime Minister complained to a UN official that they were not providing enough food for refugees who had become a burden on his country. The UN official explained, "We have limited resources, and we are helping your own people who are affected by the war." Then the Prime Minister said, "Those are not my people. The food you give to those people actually is killing my soldiers." These were his citizens, nationals of his country and yet he said, "They are not my people." His people were the soldiers who were killing "these people."

Deng's choice of persuasion through diplomacy did not rule out speaking candidly about what he found during his country visits. At the end of each mission, he prepared a detailed report of findings, including criticisms of government actions either in dealings with the displaced or in programs for them. Usually he offered recommendations for action by political authorities as well as by international humanitarian and human rights agencies. He presented his findings and his recommendations directly to the government and to the agencies on the ground, and over the years to the UN's Inter-Agency Standing Committee (IASC) and its working group, the Commission on Human Rights, the General Assembly, and the secretary-general.

Although he advocated vigorously for action with UN organizations, once he left a country, however, the decision to act or not to act was largely out of his hands. As RSG he had no operational authority, and no means of regular follow-up. UNDP resident representatives, in their role as UN resident coordinators, were supposed to send Deng reports on actions taken as a result of his recommendations, but many did not or sent only the most perfunctory reports. It would be rare for such a UN official to call into question his or her overall ability to negotiate development projects in order to pursue a human rights agenda.

Moreover, the UN rarely had resources for Deng to make repeat visits, and he himself hardly had the time with so many countries with serious problems of internal displacement; in addition, he had a host of other commitments unrelated to his voluntary IDP mandate. The first follow-up to a country mission that Deng was able to make did not come until 1999. It was to Colombia, which he had visited five years earlier, and in 2000 he visited Burundi for a second time (his earlier visit was also in 1994) at the specific request of the IASC in response to forced relocations of people carried out by the government of that country. In 2000 and 2001, Deng made additional visits to Sudan, where his first visit as representative had taken place in 1992. And in 2003, he returned to Russia (first visited in 1992), including Chechnya.

So while meetings with the displaced themselves gave Deng critical insights into their problems, they also left him with a degree of anguish and doubt about his own role:

> You come ... bearing the flag of the UN. You represent the Secretary General, the United Nations and the international community. And you go to these masses of people who are in desperate need for everything. By going there you bring them hope. They feel elated that the world cares and will do something. And then as you leave, you wonder, "What if the world doesn't do something? What if the world doesn't deliver and prove that it really cares?" The hope that these people had then turns to despair.

His disturbing encounters and reflections provided the impetus for writing *Protecting the Dispossessed*, another example with significance for others trying to advance an issue that has low priority on the international agenda. Deng chose to put down in black and white his relatively unvarnished views rather than use exclusively the vehicle of official UN reports with all of the associated problems of packaging, diplomatic niceties, and political correctness. This approach was essential not just because the Brookings Institution has a deserved reputation for autonomous research, but also because the phenomenon of internal displacement needed to move from the wings to center stage. A decade later the outspoken ERC Jan Egeland told us that there is, at least in his view, far more room for critical commentary from the United Nations than is commonly believed: "In general, we overestimate the fall-out from telling the truth."[9] As a UN official, albeit part-time, Deng on occasion called some spades spades.

The next step was to embark upon a much more ambitious and comprehensive study. Internal displacement had only recently emerged on the international public policy agenda, and in academia as well it was relatively unexplored. While *Protecting the Dispossessed* was a good beginning, it did not sufficiently address a number of critical issues. Deng felt strongly that the subject had to be explored in much greater depth. In the fall of 1993, he returned to New York to see the secretary-general, who earlier had been enthusiastic about supporting Deng's research. With some difficulty, Deng was able to persuade him to at least commit $25,000 from secretariat funds, inadequate but a start nonetheless. Boutros-Ghali telephoned later and apologized for the paucity of resources—after all, he himself had made a living with scholarship—but promised to write a foreword for the volume.[10]

Protecting the Dispossessed had confirmed John Steinbruner's view of the productive overlap between Deng's work as a Brookings senior fellow and as RSG. The proposed comprehensive study was a sensible and desirable next step, and the eventual product added further confirmation to Steinbruner's original view. Policy-relevant analyses were what the Brookings Institution was set up to do, and he enthusiastically endorsed the idea.

Roberta Cohen, however, was skeptical. Why, she asked, was yet another study needed? As a consultant to the Refugee Policy Group, she had been writing papers on the phenomenon of internal displacement for over three years. But the idea of a major research effort appealed to Dennis Gallagher, RPG's founder and executive director. He knew that studies were one way to get things accomplished, a necessary if insufficient step toward successfully advocating policy change. They were also the way to raise visibility and money, and even the best of causes could not thrive without a solid funding base. To carry out the work,

Gallagher proposed a partnership between RPG and Brookings; and to finance it, he drafted a proposal for the McKnight Foundation.

Deng also raised resources from the governments of Norway, Sweden, and the Netherlands. To carry the study out, and to help him operationally in his work as RSG, he proposed to bring Cohen to the Brookings Institution. In addition to having contributed to Deng's book and reports, she had demonstrated her effectiveness in dealing with the UN system and the U.S. government. An opportunity opened up early in 1994 when a vacancy became available at Brookings for an Africa scholar to join Deng's program. Deng recommended Cohen for the job, notwithstanding the fact that she did not have the requisite academic background.

John Steinbruner had his eye on a scholar from Yale University with a specialty in military affairs in Africa, but he agreed to interview Cohen. Concerned that her human rights background and reputation as an advocate might be at odds with the Brookings Institution's practice of detached scholarship, he opened the meeting with the comment that "at Brookings we do not overthrow governments." Cohen replied that his image was an inaccurate stereotype. Human rights work could be based as much on serious scholarship as values and ideology. In fact, she pointed out, there were scholarly journals devoted exclusively to human rights, and her articles had appeared in several of them. When Steinbruner asked Cohen about her academic credentials in African studies, she readily acknowledged that she had none. She had, however, lived nearly five years in Africa and had written articles on Ethiopia. Her work on internal displacement, a new issue and one of growing importance, related closely to the continent with the majority of the world's IDPs. It was a subject that she knew well, and one to which she felt she could make an original contribution. Cohen gave Steinbruner a copy of her article that had just been published by the American Society of International Law (ASIL) along with her curriculum vitae including a list of her other articles and book chapters.

At the close of the interview, Steinbruner walked down the hall to Deng's office to tell him that the fellowship could go to Cohen. Deng had almost concluded that he would have to find another way to associate Cohen with his work. Incredulous, he called Cohen to ask good naturedly, "What did you say to him?" A productive partnership was thus put on a firm institutional foundation, one that continues for the rest of our story. The complementary styles and personalities of the two partners may be one explanation for why the relationship was fruitful— "an odd couple but a perfect match," according to Elisabeth Rasmusson of the Norwegian Refugee Council.[11] Virtually everyone interviewed, including the two principals themselves, recognized the value of their good-cop-bad-cop routine. Deng is diplomatic, cautious, erudite, wily, and a Dinka son of a leading chief from southern Sudan. Cohen is what many would see as a stereotypical New Yorker—straightforward, some-times brash, smart, irreverent, and with little patience for the diplomatic niceties associated with the United Nations.[12]

Those who worked closely with them are worth citing here. What William Zartman would affectionately call the "Brookings doctrine" to describe their conceptualization of sovereignty as responsibility—essentially that IDPs as individuals have rights that transcend frontiers and governments—represented the creative push and pull from both partners.[13] In short, Cohen pushed harder than Deng would have liked, but he stopped her from antagonizing unnecessarily many people. As Gimena Sanchez-Garzoli, a PID staffer who worked on IDP problems in the Americas, pointed out: "Roberta pushed to the limit. She asked what everyone would like to but was afraid to ask. And Francis could somehow tell someone that he was totally wrong but without completely offending him."[14] Or as Susan Martin remarked, "On their own, neither would have been as effective."[15]

The fact that Deng was "non-threatening to governments," in the words of Human Rights Watch's Bill Frelick, provided many NGOs and advocates with fodder for criticism.[16] Deng reflected on this fact in his "farewell" letter to Secretary-General Kofi Annan:

> The main principle that guided me in my work on the mandate has been to balance between allaying the fears of Governments about national sovereignty while impressing upon them the compelling humanitarian and human rights concerns of the international community with the plight of the internally displaced . . . I believe the soft approach was crucial to winning the cooperation of the Governments on an issue of great sensitivity. On the other hand, I have been encouraged in recent years to be more outspoken and assertive.[17]

Nevertheless, most people share the judgment that his diplomatic style was effective in combination with what Joel Charny described as "the fox terrier Roberta Cohen with her links to the NGOs and her eyes on the news and visibility."[18]

Cohen joined Brookings as a visiting fellow at the beginning of September 1994. The Brookings-RPG Project on Internal Displacement came into being after formal approval by Brookings's president and board of trustees later that autumn. In a report published jointly by the RPG and the UN's Department of Humanitarian Affairs in December 1994, Deng described the newly established project as having been "developed at the request of the UN Secretary-General in recognition of the magnitude of the crisis of internal displacement worldwide and the need for developing an appropriate international response." The Project on Internal Displacement, he said, "aims at developing a comprehensive global strategy for providing more effective protection of and assistance to the estimated 30 million internally displaced persons around the world."[19]

The formal establishment of the PID provided a critical institutional underpinning for Deng's RSG mandate. The project would become the vehicle for bringing in financial support from governments and foundations, help that the UN system itself was unable to provide and that Boutros-Ghali himself recognized was essential for the work of his representative. It is worth repeating here the close link between the RSG and the project, which was set up specifically to support the mandate of the representative. Without the resources and intellectual firepower of the PID, the work called for by specific UN resolutions or other directives from donors and UN bodies would have been impossible.

Over the coming decade the PID would enable Deng and Cohen to address, with substantial degrees of progress, the four agenda items set out in the closing paragraph of Deng's 1993 report to the Commission on Human Rights. Of his main pillars, two—raising awareness of the issue and improving the knowledge base as a means to conduct advocacy to improve protection and assistance of IDPs—were already well underway. In 1998 Brookings published the two lengthy volumes that put the Project on Internal Displacement on the map: Cohen and Deng's *Masses in Flight*, a 400-page authored manuscript, and their 500-page edited set of 12 case studies, *The Forsaken People*.

The former was especially important as the first comprehensive overview of the problem of internal displacement, going well beyond *Protecting the Dispossessed*, Deng's initial foray five years earlier. Though Cohen and Deng wrote the book, their work was based on a carefully organized cooperative effort, each chapter reflecting inputs and commentaries from selected staff members working for international human rights and humanitarian organizations and other NGOs as well as from independent experts. The U.S. Committee for Refugees contributed several policy papers from what Roger Winter described as his "brain trust."[20] Cohen later commented that "it was as much a process as a book," one in which individuals and groups from around the world had participated. And the case studies in the latter volume were written by a well-known and eclectic group of authors who put between two covers an academically respectable overview of the major geographical areas producing IDPs.

While activists often dismiss research and data-gathering as the preoccupation of those with the luxury of residing in ivory towers, the phenomenon of internal displacement lacked even the most basic of data, let alone an authoritative interpretation. As a result of assiduous badgering by Deng and Cohen, a helpful spin-off was also established at the Norwegian Refugee Council.

The development of this data-gathering capacity is worth examining as it illustrates not only the kind of "catalytic" role that Deng pursued as RSG but also the relationship between the mandate and the PID's efforts. From the very outset, he had insisted on the establishment of such an information-gathering mechanism in order to monitor situations of internal displacement. This major information gap was not unlike the one for refugees—UNHCR with a budget of $1 billion regularly used second-hand statistics, and only devoted one-half a staff line to a statistician. However, Deng still felt that overcoming this lack of basic information was essential to fulfilling his mandate.

He envisaged the creation of an office with personnel assigned to monitor and report on each major group of countries and make their findings available to the public as well as to UN agencies and NGOs. In 1996 Deng and the ERC signed a memorandum of understanding in which they made a "shared commitment" to develop an IDP information system. The original idea was that DHA would undertake to set up and manage the data system with whatever assistance that the Brookings project and other outside institutions could offer.

Whether the task was too daunting or out of fear of antagonizing UN member states that would be the subject of the data gathering, DHA's successor—the Office for the Coordination of Humanitarian Affairs (OCHA)—decided that the job should be outsourced beyond the UN system. As the Brookings project did not have the resources or expertise to take on the task itself, Deng and Cohen turned to the U.S. Committee for Refugees, which had first published data on IDPs in its annual *World Refugee Survey* in 1982. Indeed, from 1986 onward and with nudging from the PID, it included IDPs in its annual reports. While the USCR was prepared to expand reporting on IDPs in the framework of its well-regarded annual refugee surveys, it was not ready to develop the kind of full-blown global database about IDPs that Deng and Cohen sought.

The Norwegian Refugee Council, a nongovernmental organization that had been one of the early supporters of the RSG's mandate, offered to undertake the job. In the human rights arena, this kind of spin-off is fairly typical. If the UN cannot or will not do it, some NGO may.[21] Deng and Cohen had worked closely with both the USCR and the NRC, and they did not want to appear to favor either one over the other. At the same time, they were concerned that implementing the mandate would not be made easier if competing studies by USCR and NRC were to offer significantly differing sets of statistics. To settle these and other turf issues, the Brookings PID hosted meetings in Washington and Geneva between USCR and NRC that led to agreement that the two would work more closely together: the USCR would continue to expand its annual coverage of IDPs, but NRC would do the IDP database and set up an office in Geneva for that purpose.

Beyond the meeting in Washington, however, this agreement had to gain UN approval, which required the PID team to make a pitch to the IASC. This creative arrangement, so necessary to the fulfillment of the mandate, met some initial resistance because such sub-contracting raised concerns about confidentiality of information provided by UN agencies in the field and sensitivity of governments that could be embarrassed by the data.

This is not to say that IDP data were or are uncontested. Bill Frelick, who was a researcher at the USCR at the time and later its executive head, stated: "Counting refugees is hard but counting IDPs is even more difficult, not least because of problems of definition and when an IDP ceases to be an IDP."[22] Roger Winter was the director of USCR then and recalled that his institution "was a small NGO. We were not looking to be competitive, and the government of Norway was ready to fund the NRC."[23] Both Frelick and Winter commented that one of the problems and points of dispute was that the NRC took figures from various sources at face value and was reluctant to remove countries and IDPs from their compilation so that the numbers kept continuously growing even if a war—in Guatemala or South Africa, for instance—ended and a more critical approach might have reduced the global figures.

In spite of these criticisms and of similar shortcomings that exist for all statistics about war victims and disputes over who should be included,[24] the NRC has since become a key source for such data. The Global IDP Project brought out a first comprehensive global survey in 1998 in published form,[25] and the internet version appeared in December 1999 at www.idpproject.org. The initial posting of reports on 14 countries now has grown to almost 50.

Meanwhile, the Brookings project, itself consisting until 1999 only of Deng and Cohen, slowly became the recognized source of analysis and policy development about internal displacement. In addition to the 1998 books, a host of refereed articles and book chapters along with op-eds and publications designed for public consumption have appeared.[26] Most persons interviewed for this history praised the overall quality of the analyses and certainly PID's productivity. What would qualify as a solid production for full-time scholars was done often between flights and in addition to other duties. The back-stopping capacity outside of the United Nations proper was essential to improving the knowledge base about internal displacement and awareness of the issue among policy- and decision-making elites.

This chapter ends with the year of the publication of *Masses in Flight* and *The Forsaken People*, 1998. This was also the same year that Deng and his network achieved another first when he presented to the General Assembly the Guiding Principles on Internal Displacement.[27] This first compilation of international legal principles applying to the protection of the world's IDPs covered the pre-displacement phase, the situation during displacement, and return or resettlement. We now turn our attention to that story.

4 Giving birth to the Guiding Principles, 1993–1998

Right from the start, the development of a set of international legal standards was one of the main goals of those who sought action by the United Nations to assist and protect the internally displaced. Even if not in the form of what lawyers would call "hard" law binding upon state signatories, such a framework would provide at least a "soft" form of guidance to agencies trying to help and protect such war victims and a constraint of sorts on their oppressors. NGOs, in particular, considered the elaboration of legal standards to be a fundamental requirement. The idea also found early support from those in UN organizations increasingly called on to assist IDPs, especially the high commissioner for refugees Sadako Ogata and officials of the World Food Program (WFP) and UNICEF—the other two main UN institutions helping in humanitarian disasters.

There was, as the 1992 *Analytical Report of the Secretary-General on Internally Displaced Persons* observed, "no clear statement of the human rights of internally displaced persons." International law was "a patchwork of customary and conventional standards." Those charged with helping the internally displaced needed a compass for the human rights of such populations, "guidelines which could be applied to all internally displaced persons regardless of the cause of their displacement, the country concerned, or the legal, social, political or military situation prevailing therein." The report suggested that "one comprehensive, universally applicable body of principles" be fashioned from existing standards. States, however, were wary. Most of those that submitted comments for the analytical report and for Deng's 1993 report to the CHR did not even allude to the issue of legal standards. Others (for example, Sri Lanka and Mexico) predictably emphasized the primacy of the principle of noninterference and nonintervention in the internal affairs of states, a code for no new legal standards.[1]

Nonetheless, Deng from the outset of his mandate envisioned the gradual development of a defined normative base, or a pillar consisting of an international legal framework to govern the situation of IDPs before, during, and after they became forced migrants. States were not the only parties dragging their feet. The early reactions by the International Committee of the Red Cross were defensive, almost as if Deng, in proposing to explore the issue of legal standards, were treading on sacred Swiss territory. The ICRC considered itself "the custodian and promoter" of international humanitarian law and the "neutral and independent humanitarian organization that provides protection and assistance to all victims of armed conflict and disturbances without discrimination." Fearful apparently that its Geneva Conventions and Additional Protocols would be undermined, initially the ICRC opposed a special mandate for IDPs. In its view, states had only to ratify and respect the 1977 Additional Protocols. However, the ICRC conceded that a "code of conduct" could be useful "provided that there is a consensus among governments in favour of it and that it does not weaken existing law."[2]

The International Organization for Migration also initially opposed creating a special category for the internally displaced, arguing that it helped resettle all migrants equally, whether internally or externally displaced, and required nothing additional. Article 1 of the IOM Constitution states a primary function is "to concern itself with the organized transfer of refugees, displaced persons and other individuals in need of migration services." As a subsequent policy document argued, for instance, "IOM is widely considered as being competent to address IDP issues."[3]

Deng realized that ICRC and IOM opposition could be at least as much an obstacle to achieving his mandate as the reticence or hostility of governments. On each of his visits to Geneva, therefore, he made a point of meeting with senior officials of both organizations. Over time his talks at ICRC and IOM headquarters helped smooth the way for their acceptance and even active collaboration in elaborating standards for the internally displaced. At the outset, however, Deng realized that both procedural and political considerations suggested a step-by-step approach. The time was not yet ripe for drawing up a set of rules. The first task was to find out what protections existing international law offered the internally displaced.

In his February 1993 report to the Commission on Human Rights, Deng recommended that "it would be useful to prepare a compilation of the existing international standards which are most relevant to the protection of the rights of internally displaced persons . . . Such a compilation would be of great value to governments and international bodies."[4] The CHR responded by giving Deng an amber rather than a green light. Proceeding with caution, it limited itself to "noting," in a preambular paragraph to its March 1993 resolution, that Deng had singled out the "compilation of existing rules and norms and the question of general guiding principles to govern the treatment of internally displaced persons" as a "task requiring further attention and study."

The resolution, like its predecessors and successors, was the product of a careful gauging of what the political traffic would bear. In 1993, as they would in each of the commission's sessions over the coming years, Deng and Cohen sat down with Christian Strohal, the Austrian delegate, and his staff members—Bert Theuermann, Richard Kuehnel, and Martin Oelz—to work out language to move the mandate forward. Strohal would then take that language to the resolution's co-sponsors and float a draft with other sympathetic and less-so delegations with the aim of coming up with a text that could be adopted without a formal vote. The draft Strohal started out with in 1993 spoke of a "compilation of existing legal rules and norms." The sensitivity to potential infringements on sovereignty was such that in the resolution adopted by consensus the word "legal" had to be eliminated in order to mobilize the consensus.

Austria did not limit its role to shepherding the 1993 resolution through the commission. In the summer of that year, the Foreign Ministry assigned a member of its staff to search through international human rights law for rules and norms that might apply specifically to IDPs. When that initial effort was completed, it turned the job over to the Ludwig Boltzmann Institute of Human Rights in Vienna, headed by Professor Manfred Nowak, a respected legal scholar.

Deng welcomed the Austrian initiative, but he also wanted other contributions. In Washington, he turned over the task of organizing the American side to Roberta Cohen. She was a member of the board of the Washington-based International Human Rights Law Group. She won the support of the group, headed by Gay McDougall, and enlisted Robert Goldman, a fellow board member and a professor at the American University's Washington College of Law. Goldman was an expert in international humanitarian and human rights law and had long been involved in the promotion of human rights law in Latin America. Cohen also won the backing of the professional staff of the ASIL, headed by Lawrence Hargrove and later by Charlotte Ku. Both the International Human Rights Law Group and the ASIL organized sessions with legal experts to identify issues and debate alternatives.

The result was two substantial but also very different approaches. Under Nowak's direction, Otto Linher, a member of the Boltzmann Institute, produced a 75-page document, *A Compilation of International*

Legal Norms Applicable to Internally Displaced Persons. As Linher
wrote, the Boltzmann Institute study was "a collection and evaluation
of existing rules and norms that are of particular relevance to the situation of internally displaced persons."[5] Goldman's first-hand experience
in Latin America taught him that it was not enough to look solely from
that limited angle. Everyone had rights, it was true, but the situations of
the IDPs were different from those of the general population. They had
special needs, and so it was necessary to look at what the law offered to
meet them. The 190-page U.S. study was prepared under the joint
auspices of the ASIL and the International Human Rights Law Group
and written by Goldman, together with Janelle Diller and Cecile
Meijer, and entitled *Internally Displaced Persons and International Law:
A Legal Analysis Based on the Needs of Internally Displaced Persons.*

The Austrian study was rights-based, a straightforward look at
what treaty and other hard international human rights and humanitarian law had to offer. The more extensive and innovative American
study turned the issue around and examined it from the perspective of
the needs of IDPs and then considered what international law corre-
sponded to them. These needs were defined as personal safety and
liberty, subsistence, movement-related, personal identification, documentation and registration, property-related, maintenance of
community and cultural values, self-reliance, special protection and
assistance for vulnerable groups, and international protection and
assistance. The U.S. study also broadened its reach to bring in—alongside international human rights and humanitarian law and refugee law
by analogy—regional conventions as well as General Assembly and
Security Council resolutions and standards enunciated by UN organizations that deal with the administration of justice.

The two studies were presented at a "Legal Roundtable" hosted in
Vienna by the Austrian government in October 1994. The meeting was
the first in a long series, and it initiated a practice of inclusiveness that
would be a key element in the ultimate success of the undertaking.
Deng and Cohen understood that no text, no matter how learned or
esteemed its authors, would ever be accepted without wide international debate and input. In looking back, Roberta Cohen observed:
"Deng and I recognized that principles developed in a closed room by
a team of lawyers would never see the light of day unless there was
international understanding and support for those principles."[6] To the
October 1994 meeting they invited 22 experts, including the chief legal
officers of UNHCR, ICRC, and IOM, as well as international legal
scholars from the United States, Austria, Switzerland, Africa, Sweden,
and Finland.

The Vienna meeting brought to the fore the differences between the two approaches, which in turn were accentuated by the sharply differing personalities of their principal architects: Manfred Nowak, formal and with an old world reserve that some thought suggested haughtiness; Robert Goldman, direct, down-to-earth, and outspoken. Goldman considered the Boltzmann Institute study too restrictive while Nowak questioned the methodological soundness of the needs approach. How had the needs been identified, Nowak asked, and what empirical data supported that identification?[7] The inclusion of "soft law" in the U.S. study, based on UN resolutions and related texts, also troubled Nowak.

Deng required a text that would attract widespread support. The American and Austrian documents would have to be merged, but it was clear that neither Goldman nor Nowak would be able to do that job to the satisfaction of the other. Personal relations were strained, and the gap between their two approaches threatened deadlock. To break it, Deng turned to Walter Kälin, a professor of constitutional and international law at the University of Bern and a former UN rapporteur who, though still only in his forties, had won international recognition for his work and insights. Already in the course of the Vienna meeting, Kälin had shown exceptional skill in reconciling differences. His background included training in the law both in Europe and in the United States, and he was one of the few whose expertise extended to refugee law as well as to international human rights and humanitarian law. Kälin readily agreed to take on the task. Citing his own national origins and the Swiss experience in mediating linguistic and regional disputes, he sought a solution from which, as he put it, "everyone gets something." Looking back at the experience, he recalled that the differences reflected not politics or judgments but "two different academic cultures" in which "U.S. lawyers see custom everywhere" whereas their European counterparts "are more positivists" who seek "super solid precedents."[8] He chaired a meeting of the American and Austrian legal teams in Geneva in May 1995 and proceeded during the summer of that year to do the merger. Accepting the needs-based approach, he took the U.S. text as the basis for merged compilation, but he then filled in the treaty and other "hard law" from the Austrian text as well as reinforced it with "soft law" provisions cited in the American text.[9]

Kälin's work saved the day. His text was reviewed and approved at a meeting in Washington in September, albeit with one caveat. The text did not address the issue of a right not to be arbitrarily displaced, which Deng believed was essential. UN high commissioner for refugees Ogata, in particular, urged that a "right to remain" should be articulated; and Deng himself regarded prevention as an essential component of dealing with displacement. The top legal experts initially were dismissive. Their compilations were based on law that applied once people were already displaced; evoking a right not to be displaced would, they felt, be breaking new ground. Deng, however, insisted. Maria Stavropoulou was assigned the task of digging into the law to see what she could find.

The merged document (minus Stavropoulou's contribution on the right not to be displaced, which would be completed later) was finalized in December 1995. It ran to over 100 pages, excluding the lengthy footnotes. Deng presented it to the commission at its spring 1996 session under the heading "Compilation and Analysis of Legal Norms." Its basic finding was that while existing law covered many aspects of relevance to IDPs, there were areas in which the law failed to provide sufficient protection. The compilation identified 17 areas in which the law was imprecise and eight areas with clear gaps. It concluded with the recommendation that an international instrument be drafted to restate the general principles of protection in a more specific form and to address both the areas of inexplicit articulation as well as actual holes in the law. Kälin himself later observed that international law protected IDPs "but in a way that is too complicated and in many regards incomplete." The rights of internally displaced persons were often disregarded "simply because of a lack of awareness." He argued for "a declaration or a body of principles" that would restate and reinforce the rights of IDPs "in a manner which would facilitate their application."[10]

Drafting that document would be the next step, but first Deng wanted an unambiguous endorsement from the Commission on Human Rights. Christian Strohal had inserted language in an operative paragraph of the commission's 1995 resolution encouraging Deng to continue work on his compilation and analysis of existing norms. What was needed was a straightforward call for the RSG to develop a legal framework for the protection of the internally displaced. Deng and Cohen were ready to aggressively lobby at the CHR's 1996 session. Cohen prepared a briefing paper for talks with delegations. She and Goldman used it in lobbying the Latin Americans, who had 11 members on the commission, at a meeting of the Inter-American Institute of Human Rights in San José, Costa Rica. NGOs were alerted to pitch in. And Deng and Cohen enlisted the support of Adama Dieng, a Senegalese national who was president of the Geneva-based International Commission of Jurists, to lobby African delegates.

The original draft of the Austrian resolution reinserted the call for a "legal framework" that would consolidate "in one document" the rights for the protection of the internally displaced.[11] To gain approval, the words "one document" and "legal framework" had to be excised once again from the resolution that finally emerged from the commission—as always adopted by consensus. Nonetheless, resolution 1996/52 called upon the representative of the secretary-general "to continue, on the basis of his compilation and analysis of legal norms, to develop an appropriate framework in this regard for the protection of internally displaced persons."

Well before the CHR convened for its 1996 session, Deng and the legal team had decided upon the form for the final document. In several of his reports to the commission, Deng had already spoken of the need to develop a "body of principles" or "guiding principles" that would stand on their own as standards to be observed by all parties. "I come down in favour of developing a legal framework that would consolidate the norms, focus attention, and, by so doing, serve an educational purpose," Deng declared in his 9 April address to the commission. "It is also my belief that the momentum which has built up over the last several years would justify the preparation of principles in a document that would help create at least a moral and political climate for improved protection and assistance for the internally displaced."[12]

The alternative, a convention to be submitted for signature and ratification by governments, obviously would have had greater force but also multiple drawbacks. Walter Kälin warned that it could take years, even decades, to negotiate a convention or similar document, and the process of doing so would open up endless opportunities for governments to weaken already existing rights.[13] Even if states were favorably inclined toward a convention—most definitely were not—IDPs could not wait years for the process to unfold. They and those who helped them needed something immediately.

Not everyone was persuaded by these arguments. Among Deng's strongest backers, the Nordic governments seemed prepared suddenly to throw a spanner into his plans. At the commission in 1995 and 1996, they pushed for formal approval of an alternative document, the Declaration on Minimum Humanitarian Standards. Drafted by Professor Theodore Meron of New York University School of Law and finalized at a meeting of international legal experts in Finland in December 1990, the declaration sought to establish minimum legal humanitarian standards to be followed in conflict situations of all kinds, including internal violence "in the gray zone between war and peace."[14] The Norwegians argued that these more general standards should be considered first by the commission before attention was given to principles that addressed only the internally displaced; and they questioned whether standards for IDPs would even be necessary. The ICRC, in line with its unease over establishing categories of vulnerable people, backed the proposed minimum standards declaration.

Deng, Cohen, and the members of the legal team looked on with considerable apprehension. They did not want to oppose an initiative supported by states that along with Austria had been their main supporters, both politically and financially. Yet they did not feel that an overall minimum standards declaration could replace an instrument specific to the needs of IDPs; and they feared that any effort to gain formal state approval for new legal norms would drag on forever and might never succeed. Their unease that the declaration's introduction into the machinery of the Commission on Human Rights would throw off track their own more pragmatic effort subsided when the draft was circulated for comment and few states besides the Nordics were prepared to back it. Moreover, UNHCR opposed it, believing that putting any new text up for state ratification could end up weakening already existing law, as did the International Commission of Jurists. With the declaration languishing at the bottom of the commission's agenda, Deng met with the Nordic representatives who gradually came around to casting their support unreservedly behind Deng's proposal for principles geared specifically to IDPs.

The CHR's 1996 resolution cleared the way for Deng and the team of lawyers to move forward. They faced a double problem: to reduce the 100 pages of text to some two dozen principles, and to rally a consensus around a final document. In April the American team produced a first draft consisting of 27 principles. With presentation of the final document to the commission's 1998 session as the goal, the Brookings project convened a series of meetings. In June, the core working group of Goldman, Kälin, and Nowak met in Geneva together with Jean François Durieux of UNHCR and Toni Pfanner of ICRC. Then in October, the PID pulled together a larger group of 22 who included, in addition to the core working group, representatives from DHA, the Centre for Human Rights, the World Health Organization (WHO), IOM, the International Commission of Jurists, and the Quaker UN Office in Geneva. This pattern of alternate meetings of the core working group to draft and make revisions and the larger forum to seek comments and rally broad support from international and regional organizations, NGOs, and independent experts continued through 1997.

The process culminated in an "Expert Consultation on the Guiding Principles on Internal Displacement," hosted by the Austrian government in Vienna in January 1998. That meeting brought together 50 participants from the main UN organizations together with the Organization of African Unity (OAU), the Inter-American Institute of Human Rights, the Organization for Security and Co-operation in Europe (OSCE), NGOs, and scholars in the field of international human rights, humanitarian, and refugee law from Europe, the Americas, and Africa. The document before the group comprised 30 principles together with an expanded definition of the term "internally displaced persons."

The definition proposed in the secretary-general's 1992 analytical report was: "Persons who have been forced to flee their homes suddenly or unexpectedly in large numbers as a result of armed conflict, internal strife, systematic violations of human rights or natural or man-made disasters and who are within the territory of their own country."[15] That language was deemed too restrictive on several counts. Not all IDPs left their homes suddenly or unexpectedly, nor did they all necessarily leave in large numbers. For example, many Iraqi Kurds forcibly displaced by Saddam Hussein's government in 1989 following the conclusion of the Iran–Iraq war were given long advance notices of their displacement. And rural Colombians subjected to death threats by drug lords or large landowners often fled an individual or a family at a time. The Guiding Principles sought to remedy these defects in defining IDPs as:

> Persons or groups of persons who have been forced or obliged to flee or to leave their homes or places of habitual residence, in particular as a result of or in order to avoid the effects of armed conflict, situations of generalized violence, violations of human rights or natural or human-made disasters, and who have not crossed an internationally recognized border.[16]

Drafting the definition occasioned considerable debate between those who believed that only persons caught up in wars—either international or intra-national—or major human rights violations should be considered internally displaced, and those who wanted the category broadened. The latter won out with the specific mention of "natural or human-made disasters" but the words "in particular" left open the possibility that still broader categories might also be deemed to be internally displaced and eligible for specific international attention. The focus, however, remained on war victims. War-induced IDPs account for the vast majority of acute crises in areas where politics are problematic and political authorities are resistant to the intrusion of outsiders into their domestic affairs. These IDPs were also the main motivation behind enthusiastic donor support for the PID and for the Guiding Principles. The horrific situations in Darfur, the Democratic Republic of the Congo (DRC), Russia, Afghanistan, and Iraq demonstrate the wisdom of having added "in particular" to clearly indicate the priority for war-related IDPs.

At the same time, the language left room for other causes of displacement—especially development-induced displacement, or even causes that could not be foreseen at that moment. The inclusion of "in particular" was not intended to emphasize war victims but rather to convey that the list of causes in the definition was not exhaustive, and it reflected the PID staff's position that many needs of IDPs were analytically comparable. Erin Mooney, for instance, recalls that "in recognition that internal displacement was not necessarily limited to these causes alone, the definition in the Principles prefaces the list of causes with the qualifier 'in particular' so as not to exclude the possibility of other situations that meet the key core criteria of involuntary movement within one's country."[17]

Other tensions arose between the core legal team and representatives of some international agencies who wanted more specific measures to give practical effect to a particular right for which the legal team considered there to be insufficient basis in law.[18] Such differences were common throughout the negotiating process.

The decisions regarding language about women are illustrative. Participation by staff from the Women's Commission for Refugee Women and Children at the final meeting in Vienna was instrumental in ensuring that women and children's issues were specifically addressed. Their representative was pressing for the inclusion of female genital mutilation (FGM). Roberta Cohen too sought inclusion in "Section III, Principles Relating to Protection During Displacement" of a specific prohibition against FGM. But the legal team argued that, however laudable the intent, it could not be supported by existing law. Several UNICEF proposals were turned down for the same reason. The best Cohen could get was the naming of "mutilation" and "gender specific violence" along with rape, torture, cruel, inhuman or degrading treatment as acts against which the internally displaced should be protected.

The Vienna roundtable wrapped up a two-year drafting effort. A statement issued by the Austrian Federal Ministry for Foreign Affairs at the close of the meeting announced that "participants . . . voiced strong support for the Guiding Principles and made valuable suggestions for their refinement." It added that "the meeting concluded with a commitment on the part of participants to undertake efforts to disseminate, promote and apply the Guiding Principles in order to address the needs of the internally displaced in a more effective and comprehensive manner."[19]

Now that the Guiding Principles on Internal Displacement were blessed by UN organizations, regional bodies, NGOs, and many jurists, the next step was to seek some type of recognition from the Commission on Human Rights at its March–April 1998 session. Without early acknowledgment by the commission, the consensus that Deng and the legal team had mobilized could be put into question, and four years of effort undermined. Adding to the delicacy of the situation was the fact that Deng's mandate would come up for renewal at the same session.

Before it opened, Deng and the principles got a boost from the appointment of Sergio Vieira de Mello as UN under-secretary-general for humanitarian affairs, who had risen through the UN system as a career official of UNHCR where he supported the agency's expansion to help IDPs. Vieira de Mello had all along been an enthusiastic backer of Deng's mandate and of the effort to bring together legal principles governing the status of the internally displaced. Only weeks after the conclusion of the Vienna roundtable, he put the Guiding Principles before the Inter-Agency Standing Committee—which brings together the heads of the UN's humanitarian organizations along with the ICRC, IOM, and the two NGO consortiums of InterAction and ICVA—and got its endorsement.

The IASC's action was not something the commission could ignore, but neither was this collective institutional judgment sufficient to force the hand of UN member states. Although the undertaking had been endorsed by governments sitting on the commission, the actual drafting and finalization of the principles had been done outside the framework of states. "It is not the substance but the process of drafting that is disputed by governments," summarized Simon Bagshaw.[20] Governments are accustomed to thinking of themselves as the sole legitimate font of international law. To some, therefore, a quasi-legal text that states had had no hand in formulating was truly threatening, as OCHA's Mark Bowden stated: "The real problem is that the Guiding Principles were drafted by non-governmental actors."[21] The principles were presented as a compendium of existing law, but even some states that liked the Guiding Principles wondered whether they went beyond established law. Might the unorthodox process that led to their drafting itself establish a dangerous precedent wherein nonstate actors could legislate for states?

In short, another intense lobbying effort was required for the commission's 1998 session. Robert Goldman, who in the meantime had been appointed to the Inter-American Commission on Human Rights, volunteered to press the Latin American states in their capitals. Adama Dieng was again brought in to work on the African delegations in Geneva, and the lobbying skills of NRC and other NGOs were put into play as well. Francis Deng spent two weeks in Geneva during the session. And then by fortunate coincidence, Roberta Cohen was asked to join the official U.S. delegation to the session as a public member. The invitation to Cohen came from Nancy Rubin, a board member of the International Human Rights Law Group and contributor to the Democratic Party, whom the Clinton White House appointed to head the American delegation that year. Rubin had limited experience with the commission, and she wanted Cohen, her fellow Law Group board member, on her delegation. Cohen agreed on condition that she be given the portfolio for the commission's annual resolution on internal displacement and that she be allowed to address the CHR directly on that issue.

Cohen's arrival in Geneva as a member of the U.S. delegation gave her leverage that she would not have had as an NGO representative. The United States had joined in co-sponsoring the 1992 resolution that launched Deng's mandate, but afterward had shown little interest in issues related to internal displacement. Given the Senate's distaste for ratification, State Department lawyers harbored an almost pathological fear of new international legal instruments. They pondered every word of any proposed new text to make sure it was in compliance with U.S. law. Before flying to Geneva, Cohen met with Princeton Lyman, the department's assistant secretary of state for international organization affairs, to lobby for U.S. support for the Guiding Principles. One of her main requests to Lyman was, "Please call off your lawyers." Lyman smiled but offered no commitment.

It was with the lawyers that Cohen had to negotiate in drafting the statement that she would deliver to the commission. She wanted to say that the United States "welcomes" the Guiding Principles. To the attorney at the U.S. delegation, that sounded too much like a straightforward endorsement, something that could get him into trouble back in Washington. After much back and forth, he offered a compromise of a kind that only a legal mind could find meaningful. Cohen would be authorized to say that the United States "welcomes *the completion* of the Guiding Principles."

Regardless of whether other delegations caught this subtlety, the very fact that the United States spoke on the Guiding Principles on Internal Displacement gave the advocacy effort a boost. And membership in the American delegation gave Cohen ample opportunity to lobby other delegations in meetings and in the corridors, and not just those who might be favorably inclined toward endorsing them. Russian delegation members questioned whether the principles went beyond the law; and Mexico, India, China, Cuba, and Sudan regularly mounted the ramparts at the commission and elsewhere in defense of traditional interpretations of state sovereignty. Her presence as a representative of the U.S. government meant that her explanations were at least registered by other government delegates rather than being dismissed as NGO palaver.

Mexico took the lead in raising objections to the Guiding Principles. As it happened, alongside Cohen's portfolio on internal displacement, the U.S. delegation had assigned her responsibility for the commission's annual resolution on the treatment of migrants, a top priority for Mexico. Cohen did not have to tell the Mexican delegate that the commission's rules offered more than enough opportunities for her to forestall his efforts to promote a resolution on migrants so that moving it to adoption could take a very long time. The Mexican delegate groused about the danger of "standard setting by the back door," but he posed no obstacle to consensus adoption of that year's resolution acknowledging the Guiding Principles and renewing Deng's mandate.

Even before the session began, the Austrians judged that getting a strong endorsement for the principles would be unrealistic. The draft resolution submitted by the delegation called for the commission to take note of the principles "with appreciation."[22] Deng's and Cohen's greatest fear was that opponents would insist on sending them out for comment by governments, a procedure that could have seriously undermined them. But in the end that did not happen, and only the words "with appreciation" had to come out of the resolution, stricken from it at the insistence of the Russian and Mexican delegates.[23] The resolution did, however, retain its "takes note" phrasing in regard to the Guiding Principles. It also "noted" Deng's stated intention to make use of them in his dialogue with governments, IGOs, and NGOs; and it "noted with interest" the IASC's welcoming the principles. The resolution garnered 55 co-sponsors, including the United States; and it was adopted by the commission by consensus on 17 April.[24] For Deng, Kälin, Goldman, and all those who worked with them, the Guiding Principles on Internal Displacement were an impressive achievement. They essentially constitute a bill of rights for IDPs covering prevention, assistance, protection, and return. Based on extant human rights and international humanitarian law, they are comparable to the bill of rights for refugees under the 1951 Refugee Convention.

In reflecting later on the decision to take this route, Roberta Cohen summarized the three reasons why the Guiding Principles represented a sensible step forward:

> First, there was no governmental support for the development of a legally binding treaty on a subject as sensitive as internal displacement. Second, treaty making could take decades, whereas there was urgent need for a document *now* to address the emergency needs of IDPs. Third, sufficient international law existed to make it possible to bring together in one document, adapted to the needs of the internally displaced, the myriad of provisions dispersed in a large number of instruments.[25]

Deng guided the process through from inception to completion and on to early international acknowledgment, but he clearly acknowledged that "Without Roberta, I could not have done it."[26] Refugees International president Ken Bacon, who was the Pentagon spokesman and assistant secretary of defense at the time, summarized: "Francis was the road show and Roberta stayed back at the ranch. Neither would take 'no' for an answer. They treated the Guiding Principles as if they were law . . . and created a self-fulfilling prophecy."[27]

The final draft of the principles themselves represented chiefly the work of Robert Goldman and Walter Kälin. Although many others, including Nowak, made significant contributions along the way, Goldman and Kälin were architect and builder. Goldman used his innovative design of a needs-driven search of the law, and Kälin employed his skill and persistence in bringing the pieces together, testing them for soundness, and making them fit.

As soon as the principles were finished, staff from such agencies as UNHCR pointed out that lawyers in the field would need to see the law on which they were based but in less dense form than the two huge legal studies. Walter Kälin quickly began work on what would become the *Annotations*.[28] But that is getting ahead of the story. Over the preceding four years, both he and Robert Goldman gave large portions of their time without receiving, or asking for, monetary compensation of any kind. Goldman would later—only partly in jest—recall the time as "voluntary servitude."

But Deng, Kälin, Goldman, and the others who assisted them could not have succeeded without support from the governments of Austria and Norway as well as Georg Mautner-Markoff of the Centre for Human Rights in Geneva. Austria managed the resolutions of the commission that gave the process its legitimacy and hosted in Vienna several of the key meetings that shaped the outcome. Norway organized meetings in Geneva in support of Deng's mandate and the principles at the beginning of each of the commission's sessions and contributed financially. The Centre for Human Rights provided what assistance Mautner-Markoff could squeeze from its limited resources.

In the background, pulling together all the strands of the overall financial and operational support, was the Brookings Institution's Project on Internal Displacement. Convening meetings cost money and required logistical support. Someone had to raise the funds, to make the case for the gatherings, to draw up lists of participants, contact them, arrange and pay for travel and lodging, foot the bill for printing and distribution of documents, and write the meeting report. Even when Austria, Norway, or the Centre for Human Rights was the host, the PID carried a substantial part of the burden of financial and operational support. Francis Deng as director of the project raised money from Norway, the Netherlands, and Sweden; and Roberta Cohen raised funds from the European Human Rights Foundation and the Jacob Blaustein Institute and got an initial grant from the Ford Foundation. When that money ran out, she and Deng leveraged additional funding from the McKnight Foundation and the John D. and Catherine T. MacArthur Foundation. From her office at the Brookings Institution in Washington, Cohen orchestrated the effort.

The Project on Internal Displacement initially was conceived as a joint effort by the Brookings Institution and the Refugee Policy Group, but its center of gravity shifted gradually to Brookings after Cohen joined in the fall of 1994. In name it remained the Brookings-RPG Project until 1997 when the Refugee Policy Group closed its doors, and Brookings took exclusive title. With the 1998 publication of the Guiding Principles and of their two-volume study, *Masses in Flight* and *The Forsaken People*, Cohen and Deng became co-directors of the PID.[29]

Beginning in 1999, with the construction of the pillars of better knowledge and legal standards, the Project on Internal Displacement expanded substantially as the mandate of the RSG took on new directions. But before turning to that next phase in Chapter 6, we need to look at how Francis Deng approached, and what he achieved in, the other main task assigned him by his mandate: the dialogue with governments and UN agencies to lay institutional foundations for operational activities on behalf of IDPs. This pillar of activities is critical because

embedding such an idea and its ramifications within organizations—
governmental, intergovernmental, and nongovernmental—is a concrete
way that the actual impact of advocacy efforts on the lives of IDPs can
be observed. Once bureaucracies have specific mandates to work on the
phenomenon of internal displacement, once careers are advanced by
concentrating on such victims, and once donors begin allocating
substantial resources for programming on their behalf, the consequences
of conceptualizing IDPs take recognizable organizational form.

Indeed, this eventuality was the worry of the governments in the
Commission on Human Rights that had sought to minimize the IDP
issue and sovereignty as responsibility from the outset. It is to this part
of the story that we now turn.

5 Laying institutional foundations, 1993–1998

The idea that sustained Francis Deng's quest for better information, increased awareness, and more specific legal standards for IDPs as well as dialogue with governments, was sovereignty as responsibility. As we see later, this idea subsequently took on a life of its own—as the logic that underlay the efforts to define "two sovereignties," "humanitarian intervention," and the "responsibility to protect" by the secretary-general in 1999 and thereafter, the International Commission on Intervention and State Sovereignty (ICISS) in 2001, and by the High-level Panel on Threats, Challenges and Change in 2004.[1] This modification to the sacrosanct notion of state sovereignty was then endorsed by Kofi Annan in his proposals to the General Assembly for the 60th anniversary and endorsed by the heads of state and government who met in New York in September 2005.[2] Before turning to these developments, we first need to understand how the notion evolved and what it meant for aid and human rights agencies.

Essentially, the notion amounts to adding a new dimension to the traditional interpretation of state sovereignty, which "is not just a protection for the state against coercion by other states," writes one set of analysts. "It is also the means of locating responsibility for the protection of people and property and for the exercise of governance in a territory."[3] There is an awareness, even among nongovernmental human rights agencies, of the legal and practical reality that domestic authorities are best positioned to protect fundamental rights. However, when they are unwilling or unable to do so, their claim to sovereignty weakens, and international protection assumes priority. In brief, the three recognized characteristics of a sovereign state since the Peace of Westphalia and also spelled out in the 1934 Montevideo Convention on the Rights and Duties of States (territory, authority, and population) are supplemented by a fourth: a modest respect for human rights.

This notion is not without its critics. The reluctance and hostility of governments is also present in the scholarly community. Mohammed

Ayoob, for one, looks upon humanitarian intervention as a contemporary version of colonial Britain's "white man's burden" or the French equivalent, *mission civilisatrice*. At the same time, even as one of the concept's harshest opponents, Ayoob admits the "considerable moral force" of sovereignty as responsibility.[4]

In the Introduction, we suggested that the power of this conceptualization of internal displacement would be illustrated in several ways.[5] The four previous chapters have suggested how sovereignty as responsibility has reshaped international discourse about internally displaced persons, redefined state and nonstate interests and goals, and facilitated the formation of new coalitions to begin codifying international law as well as improve assistance and protection for IDPs.

The fourth way to observe the relevance of Deng and Cohen's conceptualization of internal displacement—when and how it becomes embedded in institutions—has always been the most problematic of Deng's original pillars.[6] It confronts head-on the decentralized United Nations and its private counterpart, "the NGO scramble,"[7] with their combined turf-consciousness and preoccupation with market shares.[8]

Sovereignty as responsibility offers no utopian vision of world government. In one way, at least, it is profoundly conservative. Deng recognized categorically that there is "no presumptive, let alone adequate, replacement for the state." The state remains "the locus of responsibility for promoting citizens' welfare and liberty, for organizing cooperation and managing conflict." So his challenge as RSG was not to replace state sovereignty but reaffirm it "to meet the challenges of the times in accordance with accepted standards of human dignity."[9] At the same time, when national protection fails, international protection begins.

In many ways, the conceptualization of internal displacement brought balance back into the debate spearheaded by NGOs, some of which came perilously close to arguing that intergovernmental and nongovernmental organizations were the best guarantors of human rights, not states. Deng insisted that it was a state's responsibility to protect populations within its borders. For those who chart changes in international discourse, the evolution toward recognizing the centrality of state capacity is insightful and practical. This is not nostalgia for the repressive national security state of the past—many of which were and are responsible for massive abuses of rights—but recognition, even among committed advocates of human rights and robust humanitarian intervention, that state authority is elementary to enduring peace and reconciliation. Human rights can really only be defended by states with the authority and the monopoly of force to sustain such norms. The remedy thus is not to rely on international trusteeships and transnational NGOs but rather to fortify failed, collapsed, or weak states.[10]

In pursuing his mandate, Deng was careful to walk a fine line. His was not the customary interpretation of sovereignty by which the ruler, embodying the absolute authority of the state, was above the law. Deng suggested that this view of sovereignty, in which the state was allowed to do whatever it wanted within its borders without accountability to anyone, was no longer tenable in the contemporary international system.

While he would not disagree that in many ways the notion has been violated repeatedly, Deng also had a particular interpretation of the 1648 Peace of Westphalia. For him, the modern state system implied "both responsibility and an international system which imposes accountability on the state in the mutual interest of the state and the international community." In other words, right from the beginning states were supposedly responsible to one another for "promoting conditions of domestic law and order . . . so as to facilitate peaceful international and commercial relations." The advent of democratic government and, over the second half of the twentieth century, of a system of human and humanitarian rights agreements returned sovereignty to its true course by obliging governments to protect the human rights and welfare of their citizens and requiring them to allow others to scrutinize their records. If states did not measure up, they opened themselves to various forms of international intrusion, ranging from criticism and demands for access to forced delivery of humanitarian assistance and, in extreme cases, even to military intervention. The legitimacy of a government would depend on its discharging the responsibilities of sovereignty. For states, Deng wrote, "living up to the responsibilities of sovereignty becomes the best guarantee of sovereignty."[11]

Actually, the topic is more problematic than Deng implies, and respect for human rights is not viewed by all governments or observers as part and parcel of sovereignty. The UN Charter, like all good international compromises, mobilized consensus for its signing and ratification by fudging what would happen when values clash. The UN's constitution thus embodies a definite tension—some would say "schizophrenia"—in its dual emphases on both sovereignty and noninterference in domestic affairs in Article 2, and human rights, especially in Articles 1 and 55.[12] Kofi Annan put it diplomatically in his "Preface" to *Masses in Flight*: "Internal Displacement has emerged as one of the great human tragedies of our time. It has also created a challenge for the international community: to find ways to respond to what is essentially an internal crisis."[13]

In pursuing his mandate, what in practice did Deng's interpretation mean for the domestic politics of countries in which there are IDPs? Responsibility for their welfare resides first and foremost in their own governments—a straightforward if controversial affirmation that IDPs have human rights. If a government is willing and able to take care of them, the community of states looks on to verify that the government is doing its job properly. If a government is willing to help but does not have adequate resources, it would be expected to seek international assistance. And even if it does not seek international assistance, it would be expected to allow it when humanitarians come to the rescue.

Folding in Roberta Cohen's concern with international protection of human rights, Deng was ready to assert a legal right for the states to intervene when masses of people were starving or otherwise threatened with extermination. Deng and Cohen would not go so far as to argue that the community of states has a corresponding legal duty or obligation to intervene on behalf of threatened populations—that is, they saw a moral one but stopped short of the French call for a duty (*devoir*) to intervene[14]—because there was no standard for enforcement. But the existence of sovereignty as responsibility means that without respect for human rights a state loses sovereignty temporarily, which then sets up the right of outsiders to assist and protect IDPs. As mentioned earlier and is detailed in the next chapter, the next normative step was taken by the International Commission on Intervention and State Sovereignty in formulating the "responsibility to protect."

Deng's own intellectual framework reflected his training as a lawyer and diplomat. His conciliatory style as RSG—some NGOs and analysts described him as trying too hard to be accepted and acceptable to governments—represented his own personality and training.[15] In this context, he admitted that "Roberta usefully pushed the tougher line."[16] Nonetheless, the standard operating procedure for the Commission on Human Rights and its rapporteurs, indeed of the UN system as a whole, is invariably to seek official permission to visit a country. But if the government of a country afflicted by internal displacement did not issue a formal invitation, Deng considered his hands more or less tied. Efforts to elicit an invitation continued, but the invitation *per se* was essential.

His first country mission following his confirmation in 1993 as representative of the secretary-general was to Sri Lanka, where a 10-year civil war had displaced an estimated 1 million persons. Between then and 1998, he mounted missions to Colombia, Burundi, Rwanda, Peru, Tajikistan, Mozambique, and Azerbaijan. It was a roster that together with Deng's 1992 visits to the former Yugoslavia, the Russian

Federation, Somalia, Sudan, and El Salvador comprised most of the world's states with substantial problems of internal displacement.

There remained some countries that refused formal permission and that harbored substantial IDP populations—including Turkey, Burma, and Algeria.[17] In his reports, Deng specifically noted the constraint of formal host-country approval. The Turkey case is interesting in that over years Deng engaged doggedly the government—especially through many sessions with its ambassadors in Geneva—and eventually an invitation was forthcoming and a mission undertaken in 2002.

But Deng was at a loss when it came to solving the touchiest problem of all, and which became a broken-record theme in his reports. There was no operational agency with specific overall responsibility for assisting and protecting the world's internally displaced persons when there was insufficient capacity or willingness at the national level. International attention might be necessary, but there was no magic wand to make disappear the institutional lacuna that had been made starkly apparent in Jacques Cuénod's 1991 background document, the secretary-general's 1992 analytical report, Deng's 1993 report to the commission, and Cohen's early articles and statements. Most agencies helped in one way or another, but this ad hoc system left millions falling between institutional stools.

The RSG could recommend action, but he certainly could not require it. He had no institutional bureaucracy behind him or regular budget allocation that would make it possible to influence matters on an ongoing basis. Each of the CHR's yearly resolutions called on UN agencies to cooperate with the RSG, and all politely heard him out. But the resolutions did not confer on Deng the authority to do more than sound the alert.

Deng defined his role as that of a catalyst, "serving both to raise awareness to the plight of the internally displaced and to stimulate effective action on their behalf."[18] His credibility in evaluating the system as a whole was strengthened because he himself had no connection to a specific operational agency; he had no institutional interests in ongoing turf-battles. The mandate established for him in the commission's 1993 resolution was limited to dialogues with governments and, very tentatively, exploring the issue of legal standards. It did not include reviewing how the UN itself responded to crises of internal displacement, but the Austrians saw to it that the 1994 resolution closed that gap. Resolution 1994/68 invited the RSG "to make suggestions and recommendations with regard to ways and means, including the institutional aspects, of providing adequate and effective protection of and assistance to internally displaced persons."

In theory, the creation of a new agency specifically mandated to respond to crises of internal displacement would have been a straight-forward solution, but there was neither political support nor money to back it. The next best thing would have been to endow an existing agency with the mandate for IDPs. And finally, there was the possibility of enhanced coordination. It was in response to such directives that Deng presented these three institutional options and kept hammering away at them over the years.

Given the similarity between the needs of refugees and IDPs, Deng and Cohen, as well as a number of other observers, considered UNHCR to be the best choice. As they wrote in *Masses in Flight*, "UNHCR plays the broadest role in addressing the problems of the internally displaced: it offers protection, assistance and initial support for reintegration."[19] What made UNHCR the best fit for the job was that, unlike other UN agencies and the IOM, it had both a human rights and a humanitarian mandate. It also had a distinguished half-century of hands-on field experience in succoring uprooted people and protecting them from abuse both by governments and by insurgent groups.

UNHCR itself was divided over the issue of adding the internally displaced to its agenda. Some staff favored it, pointing out that IDPs already substantially exceeded refugees in numbers, and that the agency on numerous occasions had helped IDPs because they were in "refugee-like conditions" and mixed with refugee populations. Others objected, arguing that the assumption of responsibility for persons in their countries of origin would alter the character of UNHCR and undermine its ability to protect and assist refugees, its primary mission.

Serious criticisms came from those who might be called "refugee fundamentalists" who tried to keep UNHCR's focus away from IDPs. They warned that any shift in emphasis would play into the hands, and were perhaps even driven by the interests, of asylum countries that sought to keep large numbers of potential refugees away.[20] And they feared that UNHCR's involvement with IDPs would lead to conflicts with host countries and jeopardize its refugee protection mandate— for example, a conflict with Khartoum over its IDPs could hurt activities in Sudan on behalf of Somali and Ethiopian refugees. In any case, the agency's efforts in the Balkans certainly had mixed results, and the dangers of in-country protection became obvious. Indeed, "Srebrenica" became a conversation-stopper on this topic.

Although he describes himself as more of a "skeptic" than a "fundamentalist," Human Rights Watch refugee policy director Bill

Frelick recalls why he wrote critically about UNHCR's possible expansion.[21] On the one hand, he saw the "paradox of IDPs as valid—they are exactly like refugees, and they are exactly not like refugees." He resisted, however, task expansion by UNHCR because in northern Iraq and the Balkans "the creation of so-called safe havens and safe areas coincided with the doors closing on asylum." Srebrenica provided a perfect illustration as to why "in contrast to the popular theme at the time, assistance does not necessarily equal protection." While he and other critics supported expanded efforts for IDPs, they nonetheless judged that Mrs. Ogata's policies of "preventive protection" and "the right to stay" played into the hands of asylum countries—both neighbors and those farther away—to close borders in violation of Article 14 of the Universal Declaration of Human Rights.[22]

Jeff Crisp, who spent most of the tumultuous decade as an analyst and evaluator of UNHCR activities, remembered that "Mrs. Ogata's ambiguity toward the IDP issue grew from the Gulf War."[23] The crisis in northern Iraq with the flight of Kurds led to a vast infusion of funds, enhanced exposure and visibility from the media, and praise from the United States (the main donor). At the same time, much of her staff was upset that the agency had lost its soul while massive management problems were evident for the overextended organization in actually delivering quality assistance and protection.[24]

On the other hand, the logical result of keeping IDPs away from the UN agency best equipped to deal with them amounted to callously shunting aside the obvious needs of the internally displaced in exchange for the dubious advantage of purity by respecting a narrow mandate. This "let them suffer" approach was deemed "unacceptable" by Deng and Cohen. It would be difficult to take issue with Susan Martin's characterization of the approach as "morally bankrupt."[25] The argument by the "containment theorists" was built upon avoiding any dilution of UNHCR's mandate, but one could make the opposite case in many instances—namely, that by adopting the internally displaced UNHCR could reinforce it. The agency would be in a better position to defend asylum with potential host asylum countries if they were effectively doing their utmost to prevent IDPs from migrating by good-faith efforts to assist and protect them in the home countries. In the case of a competitor in the intergovernmental system, moreover, "international assistance has long been explicitly recognized by IOM member states to include assistance in countries of origin as well as outside them."[26] Why would UNHCR also not be in a better position to find creative solutions if the agency were working on both sides of a border?

The clash between organizational purists and IDP proponents—both within the agency itself and outside—perhaps explains why UN high commissioner for refugees Sadako Ogata was herself so ambivalent. In her public addresses she frequently described internal displacement as one of the most serious crises of the times, and she strongly supported Deng's mandate. She also repeatedly said that "UNHCR could do more." And in the Balkans the agency took the lead for refugees, IDPs, and civilians who had not moved.[27] Yet she was cautious and concerned about undermining UNHCR's statute. Some of the agency's protection staff had second thoughts about further watering down UNHCR's legal work with yet more assistance, which had already dwarfed and hence diluted its efforts to protect refugees and prevent non-refoulement. Moreover, she was apprehensive that taking on such a large additional burden could stretch the agency's financial and personnel resources to the breaking point.

These substantive concerns, however, were not to prove the most decisive objections. What truly killed the idea of putting responsibility for the internally displaced in the hands of UNHCR were the bureaucratic objections of other UN organizations and NGOs. After he took over from Boutros Boutros-Ghali as secretary-general in January 1997, Kofi Annan ordered a system-wide review of the world organization with especial attention to humanitarian and human rights operations. Put in charge was Maurice Strong, a Canadian businessman and old UN hand who had first made his mark as secretary-general of the 1972 Stockholm Conference on the Human Environment. Strong's penultimate draft of the proposals for reform recommended handing responsibility for internally displaced persons over to UNHCR, and an appendix even fleshed out the possibility of creating over the longer run a consolidated UN humanitarian agency.

Other UN agencies—especially UNICEF and WFP—as well as NGOs in the guise of their consortium InterAction sensed a threat to their territory.[28] They feared that UNHCR would come to loom over them in size and authority. Facing fierce opposition, which was backed by donors who preached coordination but had their own agendas as well—including protecting the territory and budget allocations of their favorite intergovernmental and nongovernmental organizations in quintessential patron–client relationships—Annan backed off. The final version of his 1997 reorganization was largely a repackaging of the DHA as OCHA.[29] The quintessential old-wine-in-a-new-bottle routine meant that coordination was reaffirmed as the UN's mechanism of choice for dealing with crises of internal displacement.

Eyes glaze over, as they should, at the mere mention of "coordination" because there is no power of the purse to compel working together—resulting in a low-level of actual collaboration, which Antonio Donini dubbed "coordination by default."[30] Prospects for successful coordination depend on getting the main UN operational agencies that play a role with internally displaced persons (UNHCR, UNICEF, UNDP, WFP) and those outside the UN framework (ICRC and IOM and also the largest international NGOs) to pull together. Coordination thus depends on good faith and is voluntary wherever the United Nations orchestrates an overall humanitarian response.

But the IDP situation is especially problematic because no single agency is responsible and no legal statute guides state or agency behavior. Georgetown's Susan Martin, who has argued in favor of a new agency for some time, explained her rationale: "Accountability is the bottom-line. And no one is accountable."[31] Not one of the many organizations that flock to emergencies has the ability to meet all the needs of IDPs. But with proper overall guidance—or so goes the theory—they could respond effectively. In practice, "coordination lite" rarely works as hoped, if it works at all. As numerous NGO and UN officials have remarked: "Everyone is for coordination but nobody wants to be coordinated."

The UN is the logical choice for orchestrating international humanitarian responses and has been trying to do so not just for the internally displaced but for all its humanitarian operations ever since the position of emergency relief coordinator was created in 1991 and the DHA, which a half-decade later was renamed OCHA, was set up in 1992. But the resolution that created the ERC and the DHA gave them a mandate only for assistance, not for protection, and in any case without resources or a field presence. Those gaps seriously limited their reach when it came to dealing with IDP problems. In many cases, protection was just as critical as assistance, but providing it involved usurping a central function of state sovereignty. IDPs are a domestic human rights issue, and so repressive governments are even less likely to welcome international protection during a civil war.[32]

Another problem is a purely bureaucratic one. The ERC, an under-secretary-general, has the same rank as the heads of UN organizations. He chairs the IASC and has control over its agenda, but he has neither a cadre of operational staff at his disposal nor the power of the purse and hence the authority to oblige agency heads to respect directives or even consensus decisions. Without either carrots or sticks, the most that the ERC can do is plead and recommend. UN agencies are like feudal fiefs, symbolically operating under the authority of the secretary-general but with their own separate boards of directors and funders, jealously guarding their independence and taking orders only when they come directly from the secretary-general, if then. And secretaries-general rarely, if ever, were ready to give their ERCs the kind of backing that they would require if they were genuinely to be able to coordinate agencies. The rapid turnover of early ERCs—three between 1992 and 1997—also further reduced effectiveness.

One of the IASC's first actions after it was set up in 1992 was to create an IDP task force, the UN's first real institutional attempt at coordination specifically designed to respond to the phenomenon of the internally displaced. It was not a standing body but rather brought together in ad hoc meetings representatives of the major UN humanitarian and development agencies—the RSG, the Office of the High Commissioner for Human Rights (OHCHR), the ICRC, and the IOM—and NGOs also often were invited. Among its first actions was to recommend that the ERC be designated as "reference point" for requests for assistance and protection in situations of internal displacement. But as originally constituted, the task force did not even have the authority to discuss specific situations of internal displacement. In 1995, on the recommendation of the task force itself, its mandate was broadened to include not only the review of specific country situations but also the analysis of assistance and protection needs of IDPs and the examination of national and international institutions to deal with them.

The task force was never able to fulfill this expanded mandate. It acted with a mixture of extreme caution and impulsive daring that proved to be its undoing. It failed to make recommendations about specific situations in which UN agencies might become more involved, as in Sierra Leone which reportedly had 1 million internally displaced persons in dire need; or in the great lakes region of Africa where a well-funded assistance operation for refugees existed alongside an under-funded and ill-coordinated response for IDPs. But when Burma, a country with hundreds of thousands of such persons whose government rejected any international oversight, was placed on its agenda for discussion, UN headquarters in New York ordered the task force to withdraw the item lest it interfere with talks that the UN's Department of Political Affairs (DPA) was organizing in Rangoon. And when reports of IDPs being subjected to widespread abuses in Angola prompted the task force to propose to visit that country to review protection programs in the field, both senior DHA officials and the staffs of operational agencies on the ground objected. Task force members complained that its actions were both too timid and too forceful. Some were ready to blame the task force's failings on its chair, although its difficulties stemmed mainly from the fact that the UN system simply was not yet ready to come to grips with the institutional problems raised by internal displacement.

In 1997, the IASC quietly shut down the task force and transferred the issue to the agenda of its working group, a senior to mid-level body charged with coordination of the UN's humanitarian and developmental operations. Deng was made a "standing invitee" of the IASC, where previously he was listed to attend only when issues involving the internally displaced were to be discussed. His inclusion in this forum gave him a platform from which to broaden his and Cohen's campaign for integrating (or "mainstreaming," as it is called) internal displacement into the work of all UN organizations. The IASC's working group was given detailed and comprehensive terms of reference for dealing with IDPs. At the outset, its members looked askance at this new and unfamiliar item that raised the uncomfortable issue of protecting people within the borders of their own countries. Deng recalled one irony within this turf-conscious interagency forum: "Sometimes UN agencies lagged behind the times and were unaware of the actual changes in government policies. Governments often complained to me of agencies being behind the curve."[33] But gradually the working group came to accept internal displacement as a routine part of its discussions.

The result was, at least on paper, an impressive organizational chart for coordinating assistance and protection for IDPs. At its summit sat the ERC assisted by DHA (OCHA from 1998), with a line running down to the IASC and its working group. From there lines ran to the right and left to the operational agencies and then down to the UN resident coordinators in each country who reported back up to the ERC. In 1998, at Deng's suggestion and with strong support from Sergio Viera de Mello—the newly appointed ERC—the IASC directed its member agencies to appoint "focal points" (customarily mid-level UN officials) to facilitate collaboration. The resulting network of interagency focal points was to be coordinated in turn by a senior official in OCHA. This coordination mechanism led to the eventual establishment within OCHA of an interagency IDP network in 2000 followed by the Internal Displacement Unit (IDU) in January 2002, which was upgraded to the Internal Displacement Division (IDD) in July 2004.

Like many organizational concoctions, the organigram did not necessarily translate into better performance in the field. Field officials for the most part continued to do what they thought that their headquarters required, regardless of the needs of IDPs or the views of those sitting around conference tables in New York or Geneva. The resident coordinators sometimes tried to coordinate the country programs, and sometimes they did not.

When Richard Holbrooke, the U.S. permanent representative to the United Nations, visited Angola in December 1999, he found the UN's so-called coordination mechanism sorely deficient. There were more than a million internally displaced persons in camps in Angola, victims of that country's long-running civil war. But for the most part, Holbrooke declared, they were "out of reach of the international community's assistance."[34] Not one to mince words, Holbrooke called the UN's programs in Angola "ill organized and unable to provide adequate support." He observed that "what's decided in New York or Geneva does not translate into real follow-up in the field, or vice versa. And the Office for the Coordination of Humanitarian Affairs, or OCHA, the organization entrusted with overall coordination responsibility, has neither the authority nor the resources to drive the system."[35]

Speaking at a session of the Security Council that he chaired in January 2000, Holbrooke held aloft a copy of Cohen and Deng's *Masses in Flight* and commended it to the assembled delegates as "a very important book." Like the two authors, Holbrooke argued that responsibility for IDPs should be vested in UNHCR. But the outcome of the 2000 elections in the United States (he was a leading candidate for secretary of state in a Democratic administration) left him without a government platform from which to press that proposal.

Earlier Deng also had proposed designating UNHCR as the agency to deal with internal displacement. But as RSG, he did not see it as his place to contest his boss's choice of a looser coordination framework. So after Annan backed away from Strong's proposal to put internal displacement in the hands of UNHCR, Deng and Cohen once again directed their efforts toward finding other ways to improve coordination. Deng urged agencies to sign a memorandum of understanding (MOU) to divide up responsibility according to the institutional expertise of each, and several did. Deng and Cohen assiduously visited all the major UN agencies and NGOs, one by one, to emphasize the critical importance of focusing more institutional attention and programming on the phenomenon of internal displacement.

Yet another proposal promoted by Deng and Cohen called on the Office of the UN High Commissioner for Human Rights to establish a field presence to promote protection for internally displaced persons as well as help create conditions for return and reintegration. Others also, most notably Sadako Ogata, called for the deployment of human rights monitors in field operations. This had been done in the former Yugoslavia in the early 1990s and in Rwanda in 1994, albeit with mixed results. José Ayala Lasso, the first UN high commissioner for human rights appointed following the 1993 Vienna world conference, was prepared to pursue the effort to deploy field monitors. But when Mary Robinson took over from him in 1998, she drew down the program and emphasized instead technical assistance to governments in developing systems of justice and human rights, except in Colombia and a few other countries where OHCHR continued to deploy monitors.

After Robinson came aboard, Georg Mautner-Markoff resigned from the Centre for Human Rights and rejoined the Austrian Foreign Ministry. As director of the office of special programs, he had been involved in fielding OHCHR staff in emergency situations and, more significant for this discussion, had given unstinting support to Deng's mandate and to the Brookings project. Mautner-Markoff recognized the mandate as being different from that of most of the center's other mechanisms, with a broader humanitarian reach. He encouraged that coverage and along with it Deng's bringing in outside support. In his new position as director for human rights and international humanitarian law in the Foreign Ministry in Vienna, Mautner-Markoff continued to give critical backing to Deng's mandate. However, his departure from the UN marked a significant shift in attitude in Geneva toward the mandate of the RSG—one more intent on respecting bureaucratic procedures than on finding pragmatic ways to avoid delays and move forward.

Another idea advanced by Deng and Cohen for improving coordination was the "lead agency" arrangement, a method that has worked elsewhere—indeed, UNHCR's performance as lead agency in the former Yugoslavia was one reason why many analysts and agency staff wanted UNHCR to take over the mandate for IDPs,[36] and why Strong had proposed it in the draft of the 1997 reform. It consisted in conferring primary responsibility for IDPs upon a single agency in each major displacement crisis. Which agency should be chosen to take the lead would be decided on the basis of the specific needs of an affected population in a given crisis. If protection were paramount, UNHCR would play the main role. If material or development needs were the main concern, the job might be given to WFP, UNDP, or UNICEF. UNHCR had taken on the role of lead agency both in the former Yugoslavia and in Tajikistan. Deng had visited both countries and was impressed.

Nonetheless, the lead agency concept for IDPs never gained widespread acceptance within the UN system, though it came to be a *de facto* solution on occasion. OCHA considered it a challenge to its own authority to coordinate the actions of the various agencies. And it was joined by the operational agencies that saw such an arrangement as a back door for handing IDPs over to UNHCR, which as the provider of both assistance and protection was likely to be the only fitting choice to take the lead in virtually every war.

Thus, the most difficult and controversial item on the IDP agenda remained making their protection a routine responsibility of the UN's humanitarian agencies and ensuring a comprehensive attack on the problem. Deng, Cohen, and others—inside and outside the UN system—had been hammering away at this necessity for the better part of a decade. While Deng's preoccupation was the propagation of sovereignty as responsibility in his dialogues with governments, international protection was Cohen's issue, one might even say her obsession. Her original 40-page paper, *Human Rights Protection for Internally Displaced Persons*, was the keynote presentation at the Refugee Policy Group's June 1991 conference, and it came down hard on international protection. It offered the first detailed study of the need for humanitarian *and* human rights organizations to address the human rights dimension of internal displacement. In that paper and in *Human Rights and Humanitarian Emergencies: New Roles for U.N. Human Rights Bodies*, prepared for a seminar organized by the Life and Peace Institute of Uppsala, Sweden, in May 1992, she pointed out that international efforts had "focused mainly on the relief needs of internally displaced persons, with scant attention paid to the defense of human rights." The Commission on Human Rights, while "prompt to address the imprisonment of a few hundred on political grounds, [had been] slow to view the victims of war and famine as legitimate subjects of human rights concern."[37]

In their 1995 study, *Improving Institutional Arrangements for the Internally Displaced*, Cohen and Jacques Cuénod argued that "for humanitarian action to be effective, the provision of relief must be part of a larger and more integrated approach that includes protection."[38] In each of Francis Deng's reports to the CHR and to the General Assembly beginning in 1995, he made use of Cohen and Cuénod's work and pointed out that protection from abuse and killing was every bit as essential for the internally displaced as food and shelter.

Indeed, one of the hallmarks of the Brookings Project on Internal Displacement—and one of the reasons for solid donor support over the years—was the consistent call for a multidisciplinary approach that grouped together humanitarian assistance, human rights protection, and eventually development efforts for IDPs. In their 1998 book,

Masses in Flight, Cohen and Deng laid out both the international legal basis for providing physical and legal protection to the internally displaced and strategies for implementing protection as well as emergency aid. The Guiding Principles on Internal Displacement set out specific rules for protection both from displacement as well as during displacement. In short, in the PID's kitchen, the recipe was a comprehensive approach to the problems of IDPs.

While the lack of centralized treatment remains a definite source of frustration to fulfilling the mandate and to addressing comprehensively the phenomenon of internal displacement, nonetheless some institutional progress has been made. A variety of intergovernmental, regional, and nongovernmental organizations now routinely include IDPs in their plans, projects, and programs whereas at the beginning of the decade, there was even a question as to whether IDPs were a special category. By the time that *Masses in Flight* was published, Deng and Cohen had spoken with all important UN and private agencies as well as important donors. And over time most of them began to focus more of their attention on the phenomenon of internal displacement. As a result, ICRC as well as such major UN players as UNHCR, UNICEF, and WFP were obliged to publish reports to their governing bodies about how they were reorienting their programming. Donors began to allocate special funding for such efforts. UNHCR's revised guidelines on the protection of refugee women added IDPs to the categorization.

Thus, on the one hand, the mandate provided the cover and the Project on Internal Displacement provided the means to prod agencies to do more than they would otherwise have done. Starting from a point in the early 1990s when the category itself was disputed, the rate of institutional adaptation and change could be considered impressive—although as any mathematician would point out, the significance of the growth rate from such a low base may be misleading.

On the other hand, this visible institutional progress fell far short of what the size of the problem merited and IDP advocates would have liked. The institutional pillar for the mandate remained wobbly. "The international community has not yet acted in a systematic, concerted fashion to protect the world's internally displaced persons," Roberta Cohen summarized when commenting on UN agencies in her contribution to the *World Refugee Survey 1996*. "Protection has not been a central concern or function for many humanitarian and development agencies that are involved with the internally displaced . . . [T]he Inter-Agency Task Force on IDPs, which DHA chairs, has yet to focus on protection or to decide which institutions and organizations should address protection in the field."[39]

Coinciding as it did with the completion of the Guiding Principles, the appointment of Sergio Vieira de Mello as UN under-secretary-general for humanitarian affairs and ERC at the beginning of 1998 gave Cohen and Deng an opening to promote energetically the protection agenda. Vieira de Mello understood how essential it was to ensure protection for vulnerable populations. He came to prominence in the UN system through his career in UNHCR—an unusual institution, as noted above, among the UN's humanitarian agencies for having both protection and assistance in its mandate. But UNHCR's traditional work of protecting people outside the borders of their own country was a different challenge from protecting them inside their own country. The latter implied that people might need protection from their own governments, or that their governments be ignored because they were unable to protect them or uninterested in doing so. As international civil servants working for member states, such action was problematic.

Addressing the phenomenon of internal displacement necessarily involved intruding on state sovereignty. The Geneva Conventions gave the International Committee of the Red Cross a mandate to protect civilians in wartime, yet ICRC had only limited authority to do so in noninternational armed conflicts and none in other types of forced displacement. UN humanitarian and development agencies other than UNHCR had neither a mandate for nor experience in protecting the people whom they were assisting. WFP was the major provider of food to IDPs, but it had no protection role for those whom it fed. Neither did UNDP, which provided development aid and oversight, or WHO which provided medical training and assistance. UNICEF did have a protection role but its programs focused on health and sanitation problems and only for women and children. IOM helped refugees and IDPs, but it had no protection mandate and also was not a UN agency. The very idea that humanitarian and development agencies might be called upon to take on a protection role met with stiff resistance. It prompted initial responses bordering on panic from many in those organizations and elsewhere in the UN system. Merely raising the issue was considered provocative.

Sergio Vieira de Mello was deeply committed to helping IDPs. He remarked to Deng and Cohen that "internally displaced persons are dear to my heart." And he was not—as his death in the line of duty in Baghdad in August 2003 would testify—a run-of-the-mill UN bureaucrat cautiously waiting to test the political winds before making a move. Deng and Cohen met with Vieira de Mello and Mary Robinson in New York in March 1998 to talk about steps that agencies might take to assure the security of the displaced. Two decisions resulted. First, Deng suggested and Vieira de Mello agreed to establish a focal point in OCHA for the IDP issue. Second, after Deng and Cohen asked for a clarification of the operational meaning of international protection, Vieira de Mello asked them to develop a policy brief on the subject. Deng assigned the drafting task to Erin Mooney, then a young Canadian human rights officer who had been assisting him with his mandate in Geneva at the OHCHR since 1995, and who had also worked as a consultant for the PID.

In December 1999, shortly before being reassigned to head the UN interim government of East Timor in 2000, Vieira de Mello pushed the Inter-Agency Standing Committee to approve a 30-page policy paper entitled *Protection of Internally Displaced Persons* based on the text prepared by Mooney. Its opening paragraph stated: "The IASC emphasizes that the protection of internally displaced persons must be of concern to all humanitarian/development agencies." The paper went on to argue that while the primary responsibility for protection rests with state authorities, "humanitarian agencies have responsibilities of their own to ensure that protection features are integrated in their programmes and operations." The paper highlighted the Guiding Principles on Internal Displacement, stating that they "provide solid guidance on how protection activities should be oriented in order to be effective," but it also offered specific guidance for UNDP, UNICEF, WFP, WHO, and other UN and associated agencies for making protection an integral part of their work.[40]

That the IASC agreed upon a protection policy the following year was a reflection of just how far the IDP issue had come. Earlier both Deng and Cohen had been told repeatedly, "the UN does not do protection" and that the topic was "provocative."[41] Even a few years earlier, the idea of international protection of IDPs was anathema to the Inter-Agency Standing Committee. UN officials, in spite of the secretary-general's plea in his 1997 reform package to "mainstream human rights,"[42] were reluctant and even nervous about confronting directly the domestic human rights issues implicated when IDPs were involved. It took several years for protection to be taken seriously in headquarters, and in the field even more so. The PID draft was watered down and national protection was emphasized more than international efforts. Nonetheless the international nature of responsibility was clear. The 1999 agreement that protection of IDPs was a crucial issue for which UN organizations had a shared responsibility thus can be viewed as a major advance in collective thinking within the UN system on the phenomenon of internal displacement.

Enshrining the protection of IDPs in an IASC policy paper was a step in the right direction, but it obviously did not ensure compliance.

As Deng noted, "procedural agreements do not necessarily translate into practical action on the ground."[43] And so translating the IASC's directives into actual improved delivery and protection was to require continuing vigilance by Deng and Cohen who had written earlier: "Taken together, these initiatives represent an important progression toward developing mechanisms and policies within the UN system . . . Nonetheless, this global problem is still being addressed in a basically ad hoc manner."[44]

This chapter describes the first efforts, frustrating at best, to build the institutional pillar, so necessary to overcoming the organizational shortcomings of the UN system in dealing with internal displacement. As we saw in the previous chapter, compiling the Guiding Principles on Internal Displacement too was an arduous task and was a major achievement. But that achievement, like the IASC directives, had to be consolidated by winning broad acceptance from states and institutions everywhere, public and private. The 1998 resolution of the Commission on Human Rights took note of the principles and of Deng's intention to use them in his dialogues with governments; but this was only a very tentative and insufficient first step toward the integration of those principles into public policy and institutional programming.

Much more would need to be done on all fronts. In fact, from 1999 onwards Deng, as the RSG, and he and Cohen, as co-directors of the Brookings Project on Internal Displacement, would devote a substantial part of their time to lobbying for better operational coordination as well as gaining endorsements that would put the principles to work as guidance for all agencies involved with assistance and protection for IDPs. This evangelical effort in 1999–2005—which involved civil society and regional organizations in addition to governments and the UN system—is a topic to which we return in Chapter 7. First, however, we examine the evolution of the normative concepts and the project's operations in the same period.

6 Evolution of the concept and project, 1999–2005

Previous chapters detail how the foundations were laid and the construction begun on the pillars of Francis Deng's mandate as representative of the secretary-general on internally displaced persons. The intricate intertwining between the mandate and the Project on Internal Displacement makes it almost impossible to consider one in isolation from the other. As mentioned repeatedly, much of the work set out in UN resolutions was possible not only because of routine support by the PID, but also because it actually took the lead. In its second half-decade, thanks largely to a subtantial grant from the UK's DfID, the PID was able to expand the scope of its work and adapt to changes in the political and institutional landscapes.

The conceptualization of sovereignty as responsibility, including the various international dimensions of protection for IDPs, has not yet gained full formal adherence; but its acceptance is widespread, perhaps even close to being in the mainstream. Part of the story reflects how decisions to pursue research were calculated to influence international public policy. This chapter documents how in the last half of Deng's 12-year mandate two of his essential pillars were reinforced.

Knowledge base, advocacy, and awareness

As we saw in Chapter 3, the continual efforts to develop the knowledge base about IDPs and to make use of that information for advocacy and increased awareness about the phenomenon—two of Deng's pillars—represent some of the more successful consequences of the PID "model." Publications and research continued apace in 1999–2005.[1] Much of this work has been pioneering. Here we elaborate three critical developments.

First—and this point is obvious for a professional researcher—there are always new twists to be explored for almost any topic. The need to analyze the phenomenon of internal displacement is perhaps less pressing than a decade ago, but plenty of under-researched topics still exist that have a direct bearing on the lives of IDPs.

A recent one with direct consequences for those displaced by war, for instance, concerns the participation problems faced by the internally displaced in postwar elections. The Guiding Principles spell out that they are entitled to the same rights as non-displaced nationals, and elections clearly are an essential way for IDPs to have a say in decisions affecting their lives and livelihoods. Principle 22 states: "Internally displaced persons, whether or not they are living in camps, shall not be discriminated against as a result of their displacement in the enjoyment of . . . [t]he right to vote." In practice, however, they encounter numerous obstacles: lack of documentation; a host of discriminatory practices; insecurity and intimidation; restrictive residency requirements; problems with absentee voting; and lack of information.

An initial effort to probe these questions for the OSCE region was undertaken by Simon Bagshaw in 2000, and more in-depth analysis was pursued by Erin Mooney and Balkees Jarrah and published in 2004.[2] These studies explore not only how disenfranchisement infringes upon the rights of the internally displaced but also how it exacerbates social, political, ethnic, and economic marginalization. From our vantage point, similar studies would be useful additions to the literature in order to document the nature and range of obstacles in other parts of the world. If universal suffrage after wars is to have meaning, then special attention is required to alleviate and overcome the peculiar problems that IDPs confront in making their voices heard.

Another topic is the role of military and police—in some situations their presence is the only way that "protection" is meaningful for IDPs. As William O'Neill points out, this perspective is important to help stimulate new thinking about various protection coalitions and mobile protection teams as well as document best practices in different countries.[3] He continued this line of analysis with Violette Cassis in a later examination of the pluses and minuses of the African Union's military efforts in Darfur.[4] Given the threats and dangers to IDPs, the actual and potential role of peacekeepers, from the UN and regional organizations, in the protection of IDPs is of the utmost urgency. As one team of evaluators put it: "Where national government [*sic*] fail to protect IDPs, there is evidence of a continuing and substantial deficit in the protection work done by the international community."[5]

Other research is underway about the impact of natural disasters and development projects on IDPs, although many donors and analysts see these topics as a distraction from the most essential work of helping IDPs caught in the throes of such wars as in Sudan or Chechnya. With limited resources for research, the PID's clear comparative advantage is on conflict-induced displacement. Of course, there have always been links because natural disasters sometimes compound conflicts—in Zimbabwe, for instance, drought created IDPs as well as government policy just as it had in Ethiopia in the mid-1980s—and because war-induced IDPs often share the terrain with those from other kinds of disasters. As Paula Banarjee from the Calcutta Research Group reminds us, "[O]nce displaced, people are prone to multiple displacements."[6]

The December 2004 tsunami brought home that IDPs from whatever the cause often suffer from discrimination and persecution—for example, they do not have papers, sexual violations and exploitation occur in camps, and children are recruited as soldiers.[7] Walter Kälin sees the importance of inserting human rights into international responses to such crises as the tsunami and the October 2005 earthquake in Pakistan, but he also correctly observes that "the possibilities to act are very different . . . and easier."[8] Indeed, one could have applied parts of this logic to the "displacees" from New Orleans following the devastation from Hurricane Katrina in August and September 2005. The numbers of affected populations from such disasters are growing and undoubtedly will continue as weather conditions worsen and population concentrations grow in delicate and dangerous areas. Nonetheless, OCHA's Dennis McNamara points out that "protection is not part of our thinking for natural disasters."[9] To fill this gap, Kälin will be submitting guidelines for humanitarian and human rights organizations to use in natural disasters, in application of the Guiding Principles.

However, it can be argued that teasing out the similarities between war-induced and environmentally induced displacement in the Guiding Principles offers only modest opportunities for original analytical work by researchers, at the Brookings Project on Internal Displacement or elsewhere. With limited resources for analytical work, why pursue a problem that is better understood and relatively uncontroversial?

The emphasis, in any case, should be on situations where politics and consent of the host country are problematic. As Susan Martin notes, the value from an undiluted focus on war-induced IDPs results from asking "when we cannot and should not ask a government for permission."[10] Or in Roger Winter's words, "What do you do when a government is responsible for suffering because of a political decision?"[11] These thorny questions are the essence of the challenge of conflict-induced displacement and indicate the comparative advantage of emphasizing research on IDPs caught in the throes of war.

Distinctions between development-induced and conflict-induced displacement, however, may be less pronounced when those displaced by development have been compelled to move against their will and without adequate compensation.[12] On a spectrum of internal displacement that moves from the relative ease of responding to natural disasters and goes to the acute difficulties of dealing with international responses to war-induced internal displacement, the development-induced IDPs can be closer to the latter part of the spectrum. When that is the case, there are many similar difficulties in ensuring relief and protection. Their displacement is not caused by an act of nature but by a political decision from a government whose consent is then required to help, or whose refusal needs to be overcome by outside arm-twisting and even arm-breaking. The World Bank's lending, often made conditional upon "good governance" and standards on resettlement, provides an example of the former, and non-forcible sanctions and forcible military action examples of the latter.

Indeed, in Zimbabwe what was officially publicized as a development effort to "clean up" Harare was accomplished by dispersing slum residents who happened almost across-the-board to support the opposition. The needs and rights of these hundreds of thousands of repressed IDPs are analytically indistinguishable from those produced by wars elsewhere. Other situations—Saddam Hussein's forcible location of Kurds and Marsh Arabs or Myanmar's forced displacement—are war by other means. In much of the work on IDPs, a shift has occurred "away from simply responding to internal displacement through humanitarian assistance to encouraging responses that promote social justice, environmental responsibility and human rights."[13] As such, future research should avoid unnecessary distractions and tease out the precise differences between the requirements of persons displaced by war and the requirements of those displaced as a result of conscious decisions by their governments that are packaged as "development" but are simply disguised state repression.

Second, a good deal of the PID's commissioned research was carefully selected to influence international public policy. More than in the first half-decade of the project's activities, it was research with a purpose. For instance, at the PID's request James Kunder wrote an in-depth report on the U.S. Agency for International Development (USAID),[14] which resulted not only in the U.S. government's developing a policy on IDPs—the first donor government to do so—but also a specific request for Deng and Cohen to help draft it. Roger

Winter was at USAID at the time and stated that "it was all the consequence of Roberta and Francis."[15]

Other PID reports were designed to reach different audiences. One
by Mario Gomez on national human rights institutions in Asia, and
more especially the experience in Sri Lanka, became the basis of a
program to encourage national commissions to integrate internal
displacement into their work and funding for various follow-up activities.[16] An in-depth report by John Fawcett and Victor Tanner on the
eve of the 2003 war in Iraq broke new ground and brought international institutions up to speed for the task of assisting Iraqi IDPs in
the aftermath of the invasion.[17] The PID's work on voting mentioned
earlier has resulted in the OSCE's integrating IDPs into its work in
member countries. Another report by Kunder influenced a change at
the United Nations in the way that resource mobilization occurs for
IDPs within the UN's consolidated appeals process.[18] And the report
by Simon Bagshaw and Diane Paul, *Protect or Neglect?*, became the
basis for new procedures for in-country UN coordination.[19]

Third, because the source and ownership of research is important,
the PID began to support case studies on internal displacement by
research institutes in war-torn countries in Asia, the Caucasus, and
Latin America. As Paula Banarjee wrote: "Civil society organizations
such as the Calcutta Research Group have collaborated extensively
and profitably with the PID."[20] Other partnerships include the
Georgian Young Lawyers' Association, Colombia's Grupo de Apoyo y
Organizaciones de Desplazados (GAD), the Jadavpur University's
Center for Refugee Studies, and the Consortium of Humanitarian
Agencies in Sri Lanka. The resulting publications have fostered local
data-gathering and ownership of improved information. PID funding
for research by Third World partners has helped to make them viable
and provided first-hand information to the RSG and the PID.

Although the benefits of these partnerships may be more effective
as training and institution-building than cutting-edge research, one of
the more interesting aspects of these activities during this latter period
involved the increasing dissemination to and digestion by civil society
organizations in war zones of these research publications. The moti-
vating factor, as in all such undertakings, is to secure commitment
from the parties most interested in and capable of doing something
about the phenomenon of internal displacement. One type of genuine
local ownership is illustrated by the kinds of publications growing from
PID grants. The best examples include two books published in 2004
and 2005: *Forced Migration in the South Asian Region*; and *Internal
Displacement in South Asia*.[21] The healthy evolution is demonstrated

by contrasting them with *The Forsaken People*, the first set of case studies sponsored and published in 1998 by the Brookings project. Deng and Cohen were the editors of that collection, and the knowledgeable contributors were almost all, however, from outside the countries that were being compared. In contrast, the most recent volumes have editors from the regions in turmoil and were printed there; and the chapter contributors were mainly from the regions themselves and have begun to integrate the subject in their courses and NGO activities.

Part of the effort to elicit greater traction from the IDP idea with civil society revolved around an international awareness campaign. The 1999 publication of *Exodus Within Borders* was one of the PID's first sustained efforts at increasing international awareness among non-specialist publics.[22] This user-friendly book followed Secretary-General Kofi Annan's specific request for a publication that simplified the material presented in Deng and Cohen's *Masses in Flight* and *The Forsaken People*.[23] The Brookings Institution agreed that the PID could disseminate the shorter and more accessible volume in the Third World free of charge through the *Forced Migration Review* and the Human Rights Internet. This got the message out and also led to funding for a host of seminars worldwide at which the phenomenon of displacement and the Guiding Principles were discussed.

Moreover, the PID's own lengthy list of monographs, articles, and other publications has stimulated other analysts who have contributed to what is now an identifiable public policy concern; and it also has stimulated university and other courses on the problems of displacement. It is hard to list everything, but one example of a lecture series organized by PID in Skopje, Macedonia—which was then repeated in Albania and Bulgaria—is illustrative of getting government officials, international organizations, NGOs, and academics together. In this case, the motivation was to prevent in Macedonia the kinds of suffering that had occurred in Bosnia by highlighting the issue of internal displacement.[24] Such efforts are partially reflected in the PID's 2001 *Selected Bibliography on the Global Crisis of Internal Displacement*.[25]

We also saw earlier that the empirical basis for action was taken forward with the clear division of labor established with the Norwegian Refugee Council. Beginning with the 1998 publication of *Internally Displaced People: A Global Survey*, quantification has been the responsibility of the NRC.[26] While NRC statistics share with virtually all data about war populations the characteristic of being estimates—Elisabeth Rasmusson, who heads the NRC's Geneva office, was not defensive about calling them "guesstimates"—for the most part they are adequate for policy- and decision-making.[27]

Rasmusson agreed that a most pressing issue in terms of more reliable data was establishing criteria to answer the question, "When does displacement end?" The UN turned to Deng and the PID to provide operational guidance on this issue, another example of how the UN has come to rely on and recognize the role of the RSG and the PID's analytical capacities. The emergency relief coordinator once referred to the Project on Internal Displacement as the "research arm" of the UN system on IDPs.[28]

Much of the policy research and information has traditionally emerged from country missions, and these also continued apace between 1999 and 2004 by Deng and by Kälin afterwards. Part of the enhanced visibility came from first-time visits to East Timor, Georgia, Armenia, Angola, Sudan, Indonesia, Turkey, Mexico, the Philippines, Uganda, and Russia (Chechnya) along with follow-up visits to Colombia, Burundi, and Sudan. These country missions and dialogues with governments remained the basis for continued consciousness-raising and advocacy. The country missions are listed in Box 6.1 and also remained the basis for the RSG's official reporting to the United Nations.

In this context, it is worth recalling the standard operating procedure for the Commission on Human Rights and its rapporteurs and committees, indeed of the UN system as a whole: to seek official permission to visit a country afflicted by internal displacement before every mission. The Turkey country mission in 2002 came after almost a decade of pursuing such an invitation. Russia was another case where unrelenting conversations eventually led to obtaining access to discuss Chechnya in 2003. To be sure, possibilities for such engagement are often absent—for example, in Myanmar at present—but those successes demonstrate the importance of making aggressive efforts.

OCHA and the PID commissioned the study by Bagshaw and Paul, who examined the case of difficult countries in some depth. While acknowledging some breakthroughs and on-going diplomatic pressure on missions in New York and Geneva to extend invitations, they also wonder whether the RSG has erred on the side of caution, and whether it is time to "raise the level of his voice." If there is no shortage of countries denying access to the RSG and such situations require more public scrutiny, Bagshaw and Paul suggest that there is more room to speak out so that recalcitrant states cannot avoid scrutiny: "This is in many respects symptomatic of a broader system-wide problem

concerning the failure to exploit opportunities for advocacy and intervention due to poor risk assessment, i.e. unfounded or excessive fear
on the part of UN officials that a government or de facto authority
will react negatively to increased engagement."[29] This proposition may,
in fact, be tested. Both Secretary-General Kofi Annan and Emergency
Relief Coordinator Jan Egeland have expressed their wish for an
increase in decibel levels first to Francis Deng and later to Walter
Kälin.

Box 6.1 RSG Francis Deng's country missions, 1999–2005

1999   Colombia, visited 20–27 May (E/CN.4/2000/83/Add.1),
        first follow-up country mission.
2000   Burundi, visited 6–11 February (E/CN.4/2001/5/Add.1),
        follow-up mission at request of IASC in response to
        forced relocation.
        East Timor, visited 26 February–1 March (E/CN.4/2000/
        83/Add.3), at request of CHR Resolution 1999/S-4/1,
        Situation of Human Rights in East Timor.
        Georgia, visited 13–17 May (E/CN.4/2001/5/Add.4).
        Armenia, visited 18–19 May (E/CN.4/2001/5/Add.3).
        Angola, visited 31 Oct–9 November (E/CN.4/2001/5/Add.5).
2001   Sudan, visited 11–18 September (E/CN.4/2002/95/Add.1).
        Indonesia, visited 24–29 September (E/CN.4/2002/95/Add.2).
2002   Sudan, visited 22–25 May (E/CN.4/2003/86/Add.1).
        Turkey, visited 27–31 May (E/CN.4/2003/86/Add.2).
        Mexico, visited 18–27 August (E/CN.4/2003/86/Add.3).
        Philippines, visited 6–13 November (E.CN.4/2003/86/Add.4).
2003   Uganda, visited 10–16 August (E/CN.4/2004/77/Add.1).
        Russian Federation, visited 7–13 September (E/CN.4/
        2004/77/Add.2).
2004   Sudan-Darfur, visited 25 July–1 August (E/CN.4/2005/8).
2005   Missions of RSG Walter Kälin.
        Nepal, visited 13–22 April.
        Bosnia and Herzegovina, visited 9–15 June.
        Croatia, visited 6–8 June.
        Serbia and Montenegro, visited 16–24 June.
        Sudan, visited 3–13 October.

The responsibility to protect

The clearest way to gauge the impact of conceptualizing the phenomenon of internal displacement in terms of sovereignty as responsibility, including the international dimensions of protection, is to scrutinize the evolution of attitudes and awareness over the 1990s. This notion was somewhat eclipsed initially by the political brouhaha over "humanitarian intervention," including the secretary-general's own remarks and speeches in 1999. But the "Brookings doctrine" returned as the basis for compromise in the work of the Canadian government-orchestrated International Commission on Intervention and State Sovereignty whose final report opens with words that could have come directly from Deng's pen:

> State sovereignty implies responsibility, and the primary responsibility for the protection of its people lies with the state itself. Where a population is suffering serious harm, as a result of internal war, insurgency, repression or state failure, and the state in question is unwilling or unable to halt or avert it, the principle of non-intervention yields to the international responsibility to protect.[30]

This story is worth a closer look because the ICISS responded to two sets of events with direct pertinence for IDPs.[31] The first were several moral pleas in 1999 from the future Nobel laureate. Annan argued that human rights transcended claims of sovereignty, a theme that he put forward more delicately a year later at the Millennium Summit.[32] The reactions were loud, bitter, and predictable, especially from China, Russia, and much of the Third World. "Intervention," for whatever reasons—including humanitarian—remains taboo.[33] The chorus of complaints in the General Assembly after Annan's remarks in September 1999 had a remarkably similar tenor to negative reactions over the years voiced in the General Assembly and ECOSOC about many aspects of the RSG's mandate and initiatives.

The second set of events that motivated the ICISS concerned the divergent reactions—or rather, the non-reactions—by the Security Council to Rwanda and Kosovo, including the large numbers of IDPs in both crises. In 1994 intervention was too little and too late to halt or even slow the murder of what may have been as many as 800,000 people in the Great Lakes region of Africa and the forced displacement of a quarter of the country's population. In 1999 the formidable North Atlantic Treaty Organization (NATO) finessed the council and waged war for the first time in Kosovo. But many observers saw the 78-day bombing effort as being too much and too early, perhaps creating as much human suffering among IDPs and refugees as it relieved. In both cases, the Security Council was not in a position to act expeditiously and authorize the use of deadly force to protect vulnerable populations. In both cases, human rights advocates and humanitarian agencies supported the military protection of civilians whose lives were threatened, making the case for collective action clearer than it had been in the past.

As such, Kosovo and Rwanda represented examples of the widespread ugliness of civil wars in the post-Cold War era; and if the UN was going to be relevant, it had to engineer a basis for international involvement. The earlier debate about whether humanitarian disasters qualified as "threats to international peace and security" had resolved itself by the end of the 1990s. For example, in 1995 the Commission on Global Governance had proposed "an appropriate Charter amendment permitting such intervention." But by the end of the decade, so many humanitarian crises had been objects of council action that no such amendment was any longer necessary.[34]

Our own point of departure in reviewing the thrust of the ICISS, indeed of the thrust of work by the RSG and the Brookings project as well, should be made clear at the outset: the lack of reaction in Rwanda represents a far more serious threat to international order and justice than the Security Council's paralysis in Kosovo. At least in the latter NATO finally acted—although due to Washington's domestic political concerns, action was from an altitude of 15,000 feet.

Past or potential victims undoubtedly would agree. For instance, the most thorough survey to date of victims in war zones suggests that there is too little rather than too much humanitarian intervention. Fully two-thirds of civilians under siege who were interviewed in 12 war-torn societies by the International Committee of the Red Cross want more intervention and only 10 percent want none.[35] In addition, a 2005 mapping exercise of operational contexts for humanitarian agencies finds that recipients "are more concerned about *what* is provided than about *who* provides it."[36]

The ICISS mandate was to build a broader understanding of the problem of intervention and state sovereignty and to find common ground for military intervention in support of humanitarian action. The objective was for this independent commission to square the circle— to harmonize intervention and state sovereignty—much as the Brundtland Commission had merged the seemingly estranged notions of development and environmental protection and conservation through the concept of "sustainable development."[37]

Accordingly, humanitarian concerns and issues of sovereignty are reconciled through the ICISS's conception of "the responsibility to

Evolution of the concept and project   99

protect," a paraphrase of "sovereignty as responsibility." The 12-person group formulated its recommendations in less than a year after its establishment by then Canadian foreign minister Lloyd Axworthy. Although the commission never formally acknowledged the parentage of the idea, Axworthy himself did so in his book about his years in office: "The first time I heard the notion of 'responsibility to protect' was when Deng visited me in Ottawa and argued for a clear commitment by the international community to deal with the IDP issue."[38] Among individual commissioners and staff, however, there are individuals who are aware of the connection.

The Canadian government created the ICISS in September 2000 after Annan's poignant challenge: "If humanitarian intervention is, indeed, an unacceptable assault on sovereignty, how should we respond to a Rwanda, to a Srebrenica—to gross and systematic violations of human rights that offend every precept of our common humanity?"[39] Given the supposedly wide disparity of views across the North–South divide, it was co-chaired by persons from each camp, Gareth Evans and Mohamed Sahnoun, and it had a similar balance among the other 10 commissioners.[40] The new twist for independent commissions of this type was the behind-the-scenes role of a sympathetic government, Canada—a model replicated for a subsequent one on "human security" with Japan in the lead.[41] Furthermore, Ottawa continued to ensure follow-up so that this topic was not relegated exclusively to coffee tables and book-shelves.

Humanitarian intervention and sovereignty as responsibility are not really North-versus-South issues, but that is the way that they—like so many other international issues—are usually parsed. Ten consultations were held by ICISS in both the Northern and Southern Hemispheres to seek the views of governments, scholars, NGOs, and journalists. The cacophony cannot be summarized except to say that what was most notable, in historical perspective, is that nowhere did a substantial number of people argue that intervention to sustain humanitarian objectives is never justifiable.[42] After the genocide in Rwanda, very few policy makers, pundits, radical critics of Western imperialism, or practitioners exclude in principle humanitarian intervention as a policy option.

Moreover, as the UN prepared to celebrate its 60th anniversary, the High-level Panel on Threats, Challenges and Change endorsed the concept, and then the secretary-general wrote that "we must embrace the responsibility to protect."[43] The heads of state and government who gathered in New York in September at the 2005 World Summit followed suit and "stress[ed] the need for the General Assembly to continue consideration of the responsibility to protect populations from genocide, war crimes, ethnic cleansing, and crimes against humanity."[44]

These developments are not without critics among governments and analysts. A number of countries in the Third World (e.g., Algeria, Egypt, India, Sudan, Cuba, and Mexico) along with China and Russia are among the loudest critics. India, Algeria, and Russia together account for what may be 1.5 million IDPs and are clearly uneasy with any significant publicity of this reality.[45] They are joined by analytical critics ranging from Mohammed Ayoob who sees it as conjuring up "images of colonial domination under the guise of nineteenth-century 'standard of civilization' doctrine";[46] to David Rieff who questions whether "it has actually kept a single jackboot out of a single human face";[47] to Alex Bellamy who sees that the language itself has been "abused by states keen to avoid assuming any responsibility for saving some of the world's most vulnerable people."[48] And of course Washington categorically refuses to have its military committed by others. Moreover, skepticism emanates from practitioners like the Calcutta Research Group's Paula Banarjee who judges that sovereignty as responsibility "is of little importance as the government defines both sovereignty and responsibility . . . [and] often sovereignty means powerlessness of marginal groups and responsibility is only to the so-called majority."[49]

We are more sanguine about the necessity for humanitarian intervention and about its beneficial impacts even if the sun seems to have set for the moment.[50] The point here is that the emerging norm of sovereignty as responsibility represents a sea change in mainstream normative views over a few decades. It contrasts even more sharply with the experience of the 1970s. Three interventions with very substantial humanitarian payoffs were not even partially framed or justified by the interveners in such terms. At that time, the notion of humanitarian intervention when a sovereign state acted irresponsibly simply was too far from the mainstream of acceptable international relations. International order was firmly grounded in the inviolability of sovereignty, and therefore states were more attuned to their own unique political interests than to humanitarian concerns. Specifically, we can point to India's invasion of East Pakistan in 1971 as well as Tanzania's in Uganda and Vietnam's in Kampuchea later in the decade. All three were unilateral efforts geared to regime change and explicitly justified as self-defense. In retrospect, all three are frequently cited as evidence of an emerging right to humanitarian intervention. Yet, none was approved by the Security Council—and Vietnam's was actually condemned.

Clearly the international normative climate has changed dramatically, and in great measure along the lines recommended by Deng, Cohen, and their colleagues. On some occasions, the fundamental rights of civilians—including vulnerable IDPs—have assumed relatively more weight than the prerogatives of states to act with impunity and hide behind the formerly sacrosanct facade of sovereignty. UN authorization of military intervention is not an option against major powers as international tolerance for Russian and Chinese atrocities in Chechnya and Xinjiang aptly demonstrates. However, some international action, even if inconsistent, is better than none.

Like sovereignty as responsibility, the ICISS report argues that the relationship between sovereignty and intervention is complementary rather than contradictory. Sovereignty is conceived as a conditional right dependent upon respect for a minimum standard of human rights and upon each state's honoring an obligation to protect its citizens. If governments are unwilling or unable to protect them, the responsibility to protect them should be borne by the international community of states. Without so labeling it, the report employs a just war framework with respect to its "Principles for Military Intervention" and presents additional "Operational Principles" to guide decision-makers contemplating intervention for human protection purposes. Most notably, the ICISS insists that the criterion of "right intention" is only fulfilled if the primary motive of such a military action is to halt or avert human suffering. "Right authority" stipulates that the Security Council is the appropriate body to approve such interventions. Only if the council fails to act may authorization come either from the General Assembly or, more likely, from regional organizations under Chapter VIII of the UN Charter. The other criteria require that all non-military options be explored before military force is used ("last resort"); that the scale, duration, and intensity of an intervention be proportionate to the humanitarian objective ("proportional means"); and that the operation must have a reasonable chance of success ("reasonable prospects").

The change during the period covered by this book is remarkable. In 1992 there was little visibility for the notion of sovereignty as responsibility and only grudging acceptance of internally displaced persons as a category of victim requiring special attention. As vice-president of the Brookings Institution before becoming director of policy planning at the State Department, Richard Haass observed "the intellectual entrepreneurship" of Deng and Cohen and noted that "ideas and a couple of tenacious people can make a difference."[51] Looking back over the period, Ranabir Samaddar, the director of the Calcutta Research Group, recalled the attitude toward these vulnerable people at the beginning of the decade and the change over time: "Their facelessness results in zero liability and accountability on the part of governments or agencies . . . The recognition of IDPs as such and a category distinct from 'refugees' is a major development and has helped in highlighting their problems within the boundaries of nation states."[52]

Not only were specific aid allocations made for IDPs, but international organizations became involved on the ground. Moreover, countries like Sri Lanka that were initially reserved about the mandate became supporters after a country mission, and countries like Mexico also reversed their position and became active advocates. Other more politically visible actions took place as well. The Security Council, for instance, began to emphasize vulnerable groups whose numbers included IDPs—including resolution 1261 that condemns the targeting of children, resolution 1265 on the protection of civilians in armed conflict, resolution 1325 that specifically addresses the impact of war on women, and resolution 1400 that extends the UN mission in Sierra Leone mainly on the basis of IDPs. At a more global level, former *New York Times* columnist Anthony Lewis characterizes the ICISS's framing of issues as "the international state of the mind."[53]

It is impossible to prove that the work on the RSG mandate by the Project on Internal Displacement was the cause; but it is difficult not to draw the conclusion that improving the knowledge base for IDPs and related advocacy were essential in contributing to a growing awareness and a host of decisions that help protect them. At the end of his mandate, Deng summarized the impact in a letter to Secretary-General Kofi Annan:

> I found this balance in upholding respect for national sovereignty as entailing the responsibility of the state to protect and assist its needy citizens, if necessary with the support of the international community. This approach, which my colleagues and I initially developed at the Brookings Institution, has now been strengthened and mainstreamed by the report of the Canadian sponsored Commission on Intervention and State Sovereignty, *The Responsibility to Protect*. It remains, in my opinion, a promising tool for constructive engagement with Governments on this and related issues.[54]

This chapter reviewed the last half-decade of Francis Deng's tenure as RSG and the adaptation of the Project on Internal Displacement to new needs and demands that fostered improvements in the knowledge base, advocacy, and awareness about internal displacement along with mainstreaming of the emerging norm of the responsibility to protect. What happened in the legal and institutional arenas? It is to them that we now turn.

7 Evolution of the law and institutions, 1999–2005

In adapting from 1999 to 2005, the Project on Internal Displacement pursued the legal and institutional issues on the agenda from the outset. An essential new element was the engagement with civil society and the development of an energetic advocacy program to bring the Guiding Principles on Internal Displacement to a variety of groups and constituencies. While there is a broad consensus on the principles, and internal displacement is integrated better into the machinery of UN and regional organizations, NGOs, and donors, the coordination and predictability of international responses to internal displacement are still essentially nonexistent. This chapter documents how in the last half of Deng's 12-year mandate the legal pillar was put on firmer footings while the institutional one tottered.

The guiding principles

From the outset, one of the main barriers to addressing internal displacement was securing the recognition that this category of victim is automatically entitled to international protection under human rights law, which shields the human dignity inherent in all individuals. Unlike refugees, IDPs are citizens of the country within which they are displaced and are entitled to the same rights and freedoms as other citizens. State sovereignty is thus the defining factor distinguishing the differences between refugees and the internally displaced. "Protection is fundamentally a legal concept," writes Erin Mooney, "defined by the rights and entitlements of individuals as provided by law."[1] The lack of a binding convention was partially overcome by drafting the Guiding Principles, but they had to be disseminated and moved closer to becoming customary international law.

It should be recalled from an earlier discussion that the arrival of Sergio Vieira de Mello as the ERC placed an important ally of the RSG and the Brookings project at the top of the UN's humanitarian hierarchy. Even before Deng officially presented the Guiding Principles to the Commission on Human Rights, Vieira de Mello laid them before the IASC and got that body to adopt a decision welcoming them and calling on members to apply them in the field. His decision was facilitated by the fact that UNHCR, at Deng's urging, had already applied the principles in a manual for use by field staff, thereby proving that their application was useful in the most important operational agency's view.

Vieira de Mello had OCHA publish the Guiding Principles as an attractive pamphlet for wide "official" (that is, UN) distribution; and he followed this up with a letter to UN resident coordinators asking them to disseminate the principles to field staff as well as to governments and nongovernmental partners. In 1999 OCHA published two more booklets to promote use of the principles in field work: the *Handbook for Applying the Guiding Principles*, prepared by Susan Martin for the Brookings project, and the *Manual on Field Practice in Internal Displacement*, prepared by UNICEF for the IASC.[2]

Once again, the PID sought to ensure that these advances on constructing this pillar of Deng's mandate—the promulgation of international law, however soft—became part of operational as well as normative developments. Indeed, such practical tools give concrete meaning to what Martha Finnemore and Kathryn Sikkink label "dynamics and political change."[3] In short, the key publication found its way into practitioners' hands and often in their own working languages.

The Brookings team embarked on an ambitious effort to have the Guiding Principles translated into the UN's other five official languages (French, Spanish, Chinese, Russian, and Arabic) and into the local languages of many affected states. The UN translated the principles into the UN's working tongues but did not print up copies for dissemination. The PID mobilized funding for printing and dissemination in the major world languages and their translation and dissemination in local languages as well. At present, through a mixture of voluntary and commissioned translations, they now exist not only in the UN's six official working languages but also in 37 other ones.[4]

In a report to ECOSOC soon after the commission's resolution, Secretary-General Kofi Annan gave a boost to the Guiding Principles by calling them one of the "notable examples" of UN achievements in 1998 in strengthening emergency humanitarian assistance.[5] He also drew attention to the principles in a report to the Security Council in 1998; and the delegates of Canada, the United Kingdom, and Kenya took the floor to welcome their publication.

Worldwide dissemination activities became a staple of the PID's work in 1999–2005 (see Box 7.1) and reflected a commitment to get the Guiding Principles into national and regional dialogues and eventually translated into harder legal forms. Africa was a natural first geographical target for Deng's promoting the Guiding Principles. The Brookings project, in cooperation with UNHCR and the OAU, placed them before a Workshop on Internal Displacement in Africa, which they convened in Addis Ababa in October 1998. The Addis Ababa workshop was attended by representatives from the five member states of the OAU's Bureau of the Commission on Refugees (Algeria, Cameroon, Niger, Sudan, and Zambia) and recommended the dissemination and promotion of the Guiding Principles throughout Africa. The OAU's Commission on Refugees eventually took note of the principles, which then appeared in a compilation of legal instruments published by the organization.

Subsequently Deng returned with the principles to the OAU's Commission on Refugees in June 1999 to seek formal endorsement, and the OAU Council of Ministers considered them in July. Supportive statements from both bodies took note of the principles "with interest and appreciation."[6] From there, Deng and the PID took the principles to African sub-regional organizations—specifically, the Economic Community of West African States (ECOWAS) and the Horn of Africa's Inter-Governmental Authority on Development (IGAD).

Box 7.1 Regional and country workshops, seminars, and conferences organized by the Brookings Project on Internal Displacement, 1998-2005

October 1998 — Workshop on Internal Displacement in Africa, Addis Ababa, Ethiopia (cosponsored by Brookings Institution, UNHCR, Organization of African Unity) UN document E/CN.4/1999/79/Add.2.

May 1999 — Workshop on Implementing the Guiding Principles on Internal Displacement, Bogotá, Colombia (cosponsored by Brookings Institution, Grupo de Apoyo y Organizaciones de Desplazados, U.S. Committee for Refugees) UN document E/CN.4/2000/83/Add.2.

February 2000 – Regional Conference on Internal Displacement in Asia, Bangkok, Thailand (cosponsored by Asia Forum for Human Rights and Development, Brookings Institution Project on Internal Displacement, Chulalongkorn University, Norwegian Refugee Council, UNHCR, U.S. Committee for Refugees) UN document E/CN.4/2001/5.

May 2000 – Regional Workshop on Internal Displacement in the South Caucasus, Tbilisi, Georgia (cosponsored by Brookings Institution Project on Internal Displacement, Norwegian Refugee Council, OSCE Office for Democratic Institutions and Human Rights) UN document E/CN.4/2001/5/Add.2.

September 2000 – Colloquy on the Guiding Principles on Internal Displacement, Vienna Austria, (sponsored by Brookings Institution Project on Internal Displacement and hosted by the Government of Austria).

June 2001 – Seminar on Internal Displacement in Indonesia, Jakarta, Indonesia (cosponsored by Brookings-CUNY Project on Internal Displacement, Centre for Research on Inter-Group Relations and Conflict Resolution at the University of Indonesia, National Commission on Human Rights of Indonesia, OCHA, UNDP, UNHCR) UN document E/CN.4/2002/95/Add.3.

October 2001 – Seminar on the Compliance of the Legislation of Armenia with the Guiding Principles on Internal Displacement, Yerevan, Armenia (cosponsored by Brookings Institution Project on Internal Displacement, Georgian Young Lawyers' Association, OSCE Office for Democratic Institutions and Human Rights).

February 2002 – Seminar on the Compliance of the Legislation of Georgia with the Guiding Principles on Internal Displacement, Tbilisi, Georgia (cosponsored by Brookings Institution Project on Internal Displacement,

Georgian Young Lawyers' Association, OSCE Office for Democratic Institutions and Human Rights).

February 2002 – Seminar on the Compliance of the Legislation of Azerbaijan with the Guiding Principles on Internal Displacement, Baku, Azerbaijan (cosponsored by Brookings Institution Project on Internal Displacement, Center of Legal and Economic Education Azerbaijan, Georgian Young Lawyers' Association, OSCE Office for Democratic Institutions and Human Rights).

April 2002 – International Conference on Internal Displacement in the Russian Federation, Moscow, Russian Federation (cosponsored by Brookings-CUNY Project on Internal Displacement, Institute of State and Law of the Russian Academy of Sciences, Partnership on Migration) UN document E/CN.4/2003/86/Add.5.

October 2002 – Workshop on International Migration in West Africa: Concepts, Data Collection and Analysis, and Legislation (cosponsored by the Economic Community of West African States and International Organization for Migration, with the assistance and participation of Brookings Institution-SAIS Project on Internal Displacement).

November 2002 – Seminar on Internal Displacement inSouthern Sudan, Rumbek, Sudan (cosponsored byBrookings Institution-SAIS Project on Internal Displacement, UNICEF) UN document E/CN.4/2003/ 86/Add.6.

December 2002 – International Symposium on the Mandateof the Representative of the UN Secretary-General on Internally Displaced Persons: Taking Stock and Charting the Future, Vienna, Austria (hosted by the Governments of Austria and Norway, in collaboration with Brookings Institution-SAIS Project on Internal Displacement).

December 2002 – Conference on Development-Induced Displacement, Washington, D.C. (convened by Brookings Institution-SAIS Project on Internal Displacement).

August-September 2003 – Conference on Internal Displacement in the IGAD Sub-Region, Khartoum, Sudan (cosponsored by Brookings Institution-SAIS Project and UN Office for the Coordination of Humanitarian Affairs' IDP Unit, in collaboration with Inter-Governmental Authority on Development, and hosted by the Government of Sudan) UN document E/CN.4/2004/77.

February 2004 – Regional Seminar on Internal Displacement in the Americas, Mexico City, Mexico (cosponsored by Brookings Institution–SAIS Project and the representative of the UN secretary-general on internally displaced persons, and hosted by the Government of Mexico) UN document E/CN.4/2005/124.

August 2005 – Seminar on Internal Displacement in the SADC Region, Gaborone, Botswana (cosponsored by Brookings-Bern Project on Internal Displacement, the representative of the UN secretary-general on the human rights of internally displaced persons, UNHCR, and hosted by the Government of Botswana).

Other regions followed. Deng and the PID approached the Organization for Security and Co-operation in Europe, the Council of Europe, the Commonwealth, and the Organization of American States (OAS). The Guiding Principles won the unreserved support of the OAS's Inter-American Commission on Human Rights, one of whose members was their co-author, Robert Goldman. The commission called them "the most comprehensive restatement of norms applicable to the internally displaced" and said they provided "authoritative guidance to the Commission on how the law should be interpreted and applied during all phases of displacement."[7] As part of the effort to gain wider recognition and publicize their availability, Roberta Cohen published a series of articles on the Guiding Principles—which observers called a "blitz"—in leading NGO magazines and journals.[8]

In addition to the knowledge base and enhanced public awareness, Deng also used the principles as the key element in his advocacy campaign to put internal displacement on diverse international and national agendas. They became the centerpiece for his dialogues with governments, regional organizations, and UN humanitarian agencies. Routinely presented as a "package" in order to avoid exceptions being taken to particular articles, the principles were more palatable when promoted in each of his country missions. For his May 1998 visit to Azerbaijan, for instance, he got UNHCR to translate the Guiding Principles into Azeri in both Cyrillic and Roman scripts and vigorously promoted them with both national and local officials. He combined his May 1999 follow-up mission to Colombia with a seminar on them in Bogotá, organized by the Brookings project, the U.S. Committee for Refugees, and the Grupo de Apoyo y Organizaciones de Desplazados, a Colombian NGO.

Seminars and workshops seem a sensible way to disseminate the message in countries with large IDP populations. In 2000, the PID organized others in Bangkok, Thailand, for 16 Asian countries, and in Tbilisi, Georgia, for three South Caucasus countries—Georgia, Armenia, and Azerbaijan. By the time of his report to the UN Commission on Human Rights in January 2002, Deng was able to list seminars or workshops on the Guiding Principles organized by the Brookings project and local parties in Indonesia, Mexico (for the Americas), southern Sudan, Armenia, Georgia, Azerbaijan, Russia, Sudan (for the East Africa region), Senegal (for West Africa), Colombia, and Botswana (for southern Africa).

The field staff of UN organizations and NGOs have become increasingly aware of the provisions of the Guiding Principles, which have also served to empower some displaced populations themselves. Gimena Sanchez-Garzoli has worked in Colombia since the late 1990s—first for the PID and now with Peace Brigades International—and argues that "the Guiding Principles were more utilized by civil society than in any other country." In combination with Deng's 1994 and 1999 reports on his visits to Colombia, they "substantially influenced the writing of law 387 on IDPs as well as guiding the Constitutional Court on these issues."[9]

Indeed, one key indicator of the actual impact of such dissemination is the enactment of national legislation. Colombia took the lead and passed its own IDP legislation in 1997, the year before the official publication of the Guiding Principles. In 2000, Angola was the first country to use them as the basis for specific legislation on resettlement. Moreover, national legislation has been adopted in Uganda and Peru. Meanwhile Liberia, the Philippines, Sri Lanka, and Burundi have issued policies or declarations specifically pointing to the Guiding

Principles; however, as "sub-legislative policies or declarations," these do not have the force of law.[10] Moreover, in Sierra Leone representatives of IDPs used the principles to call upon UN agencies to improve education for their children. In Sri Lanka, those speaking for IDPs used them in negotiations with camp commanders when poor food, water, and security were problems. And the Southern People's Liberation Movement/Army (SPLM/A), working with the UN and the PID staff, used the Guiding Principles to draft a policy on IDPs.[11]

Obtaining approval by other governments and IGOs was also a major PID objective. For instance, the European Union and its member states have endorsed the Guiding Principles as have a number of African and Latin American states. UN humanitarian, development, and human rights agencies have taken the decision to incorporate the principles into their activities. For these organizations, however, there remains a lot to be done in terms of the actual implementation—but, as mentioned earlier, such a measurement is beyond the scope of this book.

As physical availability is an essential part of dissemination, another key objective has been to persuade others to simply print the Guiding Principles. In addition to the publication and distribution by the PID as well as OCHA and various UN agencies, a number of other outlets include: the *Internally Displaced People: A Global Survey* of the NRC; the *International Journal of Refugee Law*; the *Forced Migration Review* of Oxford's Refugee Studies Programme; the *International Review of the Red Cross*; and the *ICJ Review*. Moreover, a number of NGO newsletters have published the Guiding Principles including: *Uprooted People* of the Global Ecumenical Network of the World Council of Churches; *The Mustard Seed* of the Jesuit Refugee Service; *On the Record* of the Advocacy Group; *Human Rights Tribune* of Human Rights Internet; *Monday Developments* of InterAction; and the *RRN Newsletter* of the Overseas Development Institute. These sorts of publication efforts continue to proliferate.

The translation of the Guiding Principles from English into so many languages has meant that individuals as well as local, regional, and international organizations have begun to use them as a basis for assessing responses to particular situations. This includes the Inter-American Commission on Human Rights as well as such multi-country nongovernmental groups as Amnesty International and Human Rights Watch and such local NGOs as the Ecumenical Commission for Displaced Families and Communities (ECDFC) in the Philippines, the Consortium of Humanitarian Agencies in Sri Lanka, and the GAD in Colombia.

Indeed, one of the essential but often overlooked targets for outreach and training is nonstate actors,[12] including opposition movements as well as NGOs. Thus, in meeting with *de facto* political authorities in regions in armed conflict, Deng has sought to bring the message to diverse groups, from those in South Ossetia and Abkhazia to the Moro Islamic Liberation Front in the Philippines and the SPLM/A in his own country. Through a local Sri Lankan NGO, the PID also brought the principles to the Liberation Tigers of Tamil Eelam.

The late Arthur Helton publicly called the promotion of the Guiding Principles "one of the most sophisticated advocacy campaigns" that he had ever witnessed;[13] and Walter Kälin judged that their "marketing was a lasting contribution" of the PID.[14] Robert De Vecchi, the former president of the International Rescue Committee, was quoted as saying "that the work of Cohen and Deng has helped define the problem on the international stage and helped assist those who deal directly with the displaced." Their efforts "brought the problem to the attention of governments and made it obvious that something has to be done."[15] The campaign included the publication of Susan Martin's helpful and nontechnical *Handbook for Applying the Guiding Principles* and Kälin's *Annotations*.[16] The former has been thus far translated into Albanian, Arabic, Bahasa Indonesia, French, Macedonian, Portuguese, Russian, and Spanish; the far more voluminous but also authoritative *Annotations* has only been translated into Russian[17] and Turkish.

The PID has conducted 15 regional and country workshops on internal displacement, about two a year since the first one in 1998. The follow-up to these workshops by governments and certain armed opposition movements in Africa, Asia, and the Americas has been facilitated by the existence of documents in the languages of the parties themselves. A kind of "kit" is now available for future gatherings. A former staff member of one donor agency commented that the impact on local groups had been "phenomenal" in that many thought that they owned the principles. As she remarked, "the sincerest form of praise is that no one thanks you."[18]

It is difficult to gauge the exact frequency and impact of other meetings. While one critic sees the lack of firm legal grounding as "prevent[ing] citizens from raising concerns about state action,"[19] the Guiding Principles have been used practically in a host of ways within countries with IDPs. This type of expansion to the local level is an essential undertaking for the future because a modest project based in Washington, D.C., is limited in how many country meetings it can organize. After their evaluation and comprehensive field work in 2003, for instance, Simon Bagshaw and Diane Paul reported that:

There was some highly creative use of the Principles. In some countries, they were used by agencies and NGOs as the basis for awareness-raising initiatives with displaced communities. In others, country teams were using the Principles in their efforts to strengthen national and local capacity for protection through training of civilian and military authorities and the development of legal and policy frameworks for the displaced.[20]

But not all peoples or their governments have lined up enthusiastically to endorse the Guiding Principles. Our story would be incomplete without indicating ongoing efforts to impede progress as well as measures to counteract this negativism. Egypt, India, Algeria, Sudan, China, and other formidable defenders of nonintervention in the Third World continue to object that the principles have not been drafted by governments or formally approved by them. They complain about "legislating through the back door." India also takes exception to the inclusion of large-scale development projects under the prohibition of arbitrary displacement (Principle 6), arguing that this issue is strictly a matter of state sovereignty and does not belong in the international arena.

At ECOSOC in 2000, Egypt prevented the adoption of any resolution on humanitarian issues, filibustering late into the night, in part because of objections to the Guiding Principles. That same year at the General Assembly, the Egyptian delegate forced a vote on a paragraph mentioning the principles in a resolution reaffirming support for UNHCR on its 50th anniversary. The paragraph won over 100 votes in approval, but the Egyptian maneuver garnered 31 abstentions—a clear warning that a substantial number of governments continued to harbor reservations about the Guiding Principles and international efforts on behalf of IDPs. Egypt and India also tried but failed to block a paragraph encouraging use of the Guiding Principles from the plan of action adopted by the World Conference Against Racism at Durban, South Africa, in September 2001.

In the General Assembly's Third Committee debate in 2001, Algeria pursued a subtler approach when asking whether broad application of the Guiding Principles might be enhanced through their being discussed in an intergovernmental forum. Deng parried the Algerian maneuver with the answer that "considering that the Guiding Principles had been developed in response to successive requests from the Commission on Human Rights and the General Assembly and the wide support they have received it would not be strictly correct to assume that they have not been discussed in pertinent inter-governmental bodies."[21]

The failure of these initiatives notwithstanding, Deng and Cohen were worried that Egypt, Algeria, and others might seek to win the Group of 77 and the Non-Aligned Movement, the two prominent clubs of Third World countries, over to more active opposition to the principles.[22] The precise reasons for Egypt's opposition were never clear, for it had no internally displaced persons and, unlike Algeria and India, did not have a history of public opposition to international human rights and humanitarian covenants. Deng recalled ambassadors from both countries, as well as China, telling him that their governments were not really against the Guiding Principles because there was no question of outside intervention against them, but they wanted "to protect smaller and less powerful developing countries from Western intervention."[23]

The stances by major Third World powers coincided with similar negative reactions to the debates about humanitarian intervention and the ICISS's responsibility-to-protect framework. Deng met with the Egyptian and Algerian ambassadors in New York. Jeno Staehlin, the permanent representative of Switzerland, organized luncheon meetings for him with representatives of other key Third World and Western governments; and as an expert on the Guiding Principles and compatriot, Walter Kälin was enlisted to help. OCHA's under-secretary-general Kenzo Oshima organized another session with several developing countries in 2003. The sessions targeted both those developing countries that continued to oppose or harbor serious reservations toward the Guiding Principles as well as those that supported them.

Objections by nay-sayers began to fade as they realized that the principles enjoyed substantial backing among many developing countries; and even India and Egypt retreated from their earlier obstinacy. Their ranks were further thinned in 2000 when Mexico's first free elections in many decades brought Vicente Fox to the presidency with an accompanying shift away from reservations toward the Guiding Principles. Deng and Cohen were gratified, and also somewhat amused, to see the same Mexican official who in Geneva had attacked the principles earlier suddenly become a warm supporter. Elections and a move toward more democratic government in Turkey in 2002—and the continued prospects for EU membership—also brought a more welcoming official attitude in Ankara toward the Guiding Principles and Deng's mandate, together with an end to the earlier policy of denying the existence of IDPs in Turkey.

In recognition of their changed attitudes, both Mexico and Turkey extended invitations to Deng in 2002, the 10th anniversary of his mandate. And perhaps most surprisingly of all, during Deng's mission to Russia in 2003, the government acknowledged the Guiding Principles as applicable to the displaced in Chechnya.

The missions to Turkey and Russia, in particular, can be considered achievements after years of patience in pressing for invitations to meet with the governments. Cohen reinforced these breakthroughs as a public member of the U.S. delegation to the OSCE Human Dimension Implementation Meeting in October 2003, at which time she pressed Turkey and Russia on the Guiding Principles—"right on the mark" according to U.S. ambassador Pamela Hyde Smith.[24] In response to RSG and PID initiatives, along with U.S. and EU backing, the OSCE's Maastricht Declaration of December 2003 referred to the principles "as a useful framework for the work of the OSCE and the endeavors of participating states in dealing with internal displacement."[25] Given the OSCE's consensus decision-making, this decision further reflected Turkey's and Russia's acknowledgment of the principles. Backsliding is always a possibility, but the Guiding Principles are now a firmly established point of reference for international actions to assist and protect IDPs, as was further evidenced by the heads of state and government meeting at the 2005 World Summit who "recognize[d] the Guiding Principles on Internal Displacement as an important international framework for the protection of internally displaced persons."[26]

As Kälin reminds us, their power comes from "their usefulness in the field and not their strictly legal character."[27] Put another way, "they are helpful to aid workers to know what rights IDPs theoretically have," said Dennis McNamara who heads the IDD. At the same time, as his division now concentrates on the eight worst crises, "the Guiding Principles . . . have little value in dealing with lawless governments."[28] When asked about such a judgment in his work in Nepal for OHCHR, Ian Martin drew upon his long experience in protection, including as the secretary-general of Amnesty International, and remarked "that is what critics would say about any international agreement."[29]

Institutional foundations

As we saw in Chapter 5, the institutional foundations to guarantee adequate assistance and protection for IDPs are shaky. This one of Deng's pillars is the weakest because only makeshift arrangements exist, which leave much to be desired. While the RSG and the PID have over the years successfully gotten international organizations and NGOs to concentrate on this category of war victim and make specific provisions for IDPs, the feebleness of central coordination remains an enormous shortcoming in mounting international responses to internal displacement. The period from 1999 to 2005 witnessed numerous developments resulting in what is now called the "collaborative approach" under OCHA's auspices. Whether humanitarian action to help IDPs is noticeably better remains an open question.

The "absence of a focal point within the United Nations system" to ensure that IDPs were assisted and protected was pointed out in the CHR's original resolution 1993/95. Providing a more adequate institutional base was also articulated as a priority by the RSG, for which he presented three options: creation of a specialized institution; designation of an existing agency; or enhanced collaboration. As we saw earlier, however, little headway has been made toward effective organizational responses. The third option, which entails the hope of getting more from a better orchestrated but profoundly decentralized international humanitarian system, remains by default, as it requires no real action and relies on the most powerful dynamic within the United Nations—inertia.

It is worth recapitulating what we noted at the outset. Journalists and the proverbial woman in the street tend to think of "refugees" as all forced migrants whether or not they have actually left their home country. There is little recognition, outside of specialist circles, that a person merits the label only if he or she has crossed internationally recognized borders to escape a well-founded fear of persecution,[30] the classic convention definition. The distinction matters because those who have crossed an international boundary benefit legally from the 1951 international Convention Relating to the Status of Refugees and 1967 Protocol as well as from the institutional ministrations of the UNHCR, one of the most professional and best financed parts of the UN's machinery.

Those displaced within a country often are at least as vulnerable, and perhaps more so, but they receive less attention and can call upon no special international agency. The lot of refugees is hardly attractive, but they may actually be better off than IDPs whose existence customarily causes the issue of sovereignty to raise its ugly head—that is, traditionally international involvement is precluded. Many regimes actively and blatantly manipulate protection and assistance to the internally displaced as leverage to manipulate political actors and outside humanitarian agencies. Indeed, while Principle 25 of the Guiding Principles points to the "right" of aid agencies to come to the rescue of IDPs, it only meekly counsels states not to view such help as "an unfriendly act."

These institutional lacunae have been, of course, repeatedly lamented by the RSG, but their enumeration in report after report has resulted in far too few meaningful institutional adaptations. While substantive knowledge and norms have improved markedly, predictable turf-consciousness within the UN system and among NGOs, along with donor disarray, has prevented the creation of more viable organizational mechanisms to meet the needs of IDPs. This is the simple and sad reality.

The present cobbled-together arrangements simply do not address operational realities, but it is worth recording recent developments in order to bring the historical record up to date. In April 2002, an MOU was signed by the ERC and the RSG, which made IDP advocacy the latter's business but assigned operational coordination to the Internal Displacement Unit (IDU) within OCHA.[31] The Inter-Agency Standing Committee, which is chaired by the ERC, provides one way to fulfill the coordination role. The ERC was formally mandated to serve as the focal point for IDP activities carried out in the field by the resident/humanitarian coordinators. At headquarters, the IDU was to promote coordination but its institutional wherewithal was feeble. Although specifically charged with the responsibility of addressing humanitarian issues that fall between the cracks of existing mandates, it did not have the necessary authority to effectively coordinate the activities of the larger and financially well-established operational agencies.

Two years after the IDU was set up in January 2002 to help the ERC promote better interagency coordination on the ground, two independent evaluators recalled reactions to that birth: "Some saw the Unit as the best solution the international system would allow at that point in time. Critics saw the decision to create the Unit as a common denominator so low as to be meaningless—in essence, a non-decision."[32] Over the next two years, its professionals were mostly drawn from other UN agencies, complemented by consultants; even so, the full-time staff rarely got into double digits. The IDU's terms of reference spelled out an extremely ambitious set of tasks that included: to promote and support advocacy efforts; to monitor situations of internal displacement; to identify operational gaps in the response; to provide training, guidance, and expertise to resident and humanitarian coordinators, UN country teams, and others involved; to formulate strategies to address the protection, assistance, and development needs of IDPs; to develop linkages between humanitarian response and security, political, and development spheres of activity; to mobilize resources to assist IDPs; and to further develop interagency policies on IDP issues.

In all of these activities, the IDU was supposed to work closely with the RSG. It is obvious to anyone familiar with the UN system that, in order to operate effectively, the unit would have required substantial support from the large operational agencies, which was rarely forthcoming, in addition to strong back-up from the ERC and the UN secretary-general.

The Government of Canada organized a February 2004 session in Geneva to examine a scathing evaluation of the IDU. "Those who argued that the creation of the Unit was an arrangement too flimsy to really address the inadequacy of the UN's response to the problem of the internally displaced, yet one that relieved pressure for real change, made a powerful point, one that comes to resonate," wrote Elizabeth Stites and Victor Tanner. "The Unit's record of the past 22 months has so far failed to prove them wrong." Rarely has an evaluation been so clear about the characterization of an administrative performance. The IDU lacked an "impact on the UN system . . . strategic vision . . . [and] follow-through."[33]

As a result of discussions in Geneva, donors accepted the judgment that the IDU had been "scattered" and should either focus better in the future on advocacy and coordination within the UN system, or it should disappear. As the level of determination by the head of OCHA was viewed as the central indicator of the possibility to save the day and maintain OCHA's role,[34] ERC Jan Egeland made a decision to upgrade the unit to a "division." In July 2004, the Internal Displacement Division (IDD) resulted, a bureaucratic indication of increased importance within the UN hierarchy. Egeland is a forceful personality, and his own passionate interest supposedly augured well for the practical work of this new division. And his nomination of Dennis McNamara, a long-time practitioner with decades of service in UNHCR to direct the initial efforts of the division, also was interpreted positively by many commentators. In 2005, the approved staff consisted of some 15 professionals with six borrowed from UNHCR, WFP, OHCHR, UNDP, Habitat, and Save the Children-U.S.

Judgments differ about how precisely to evaluate initial efforts by the IDD, and perhaps it is too early to tell. The IDD was set up to assist in developing more systematic responses to field operations and has focused on only eight of what it sees as the toughest cases: Sudan, Colombia, Uganda, Somalia, the Congo, Liberia, Nepal, and Burundi. That Chechnya is not a priority country for the IDD seems to be largely an issue of avoiding political sensitivities; and the focus on only some of the countries with large displaced populations leaves open whether anyone is really focusing, and how effectively, on ensuring effective responses to the dozens of other cases of conflict-induced IDP crises.

The IDD has increased its presence by posting field staff to a number of countries. One of the division's main emphases has been to define more clearly who does what. In November 2004, the members of what donors often refer to as the "IDP troika"—OCHA's IDD (McNamara), the RSG (Kälin), and the Norwegian Refugee Council (Rasmusson)—signed a memorandum of understanding. The division of labor builds on the September 2004 report of the Inter-Agency Standing Committee:[35] for the IDD—orchestrating inputs from the UN system and making it accountable for actions along with advocacy with governments; for the RSG—engaging in coordinated advocacy and dialogues with governments along with continued research, training, and consciousness-raising; and for the NRC—monitoring internal displacement worldwide and conducting training. The "package" contains a detailed "road map" for implementing the collaborative approach—including checklists for humanitarian coordinators and country teams and an outline of roles and tasks for both UN and NGO agencies.

However, the discrepancy between the enormous requirements for program support to field operations on behalf of IDPs and the paucity of resources and OCHA's actual institutional authority to pull together the UN system could hardly be more glaring. "What is the value added?" asked ICVA coordinator Ed Schenkenberg.[36] In addition, the overall operational challenge involves not only engaging the major actors in the United Nations drama but also developing working partnerships with regional organizations and key international and indigenous NGOs.

The creation of a "division" to replace a "unit" has not altered the January 2004 evaluation's main argument: "The United Nations continues to fall short in its response to the internally displaced . . . and more pointedly, the UN system is not ready for change."[37] The collaborative approach—which Stites and Tanner argued "by and large does not work," and no other independent evaluation would contradict them[38]—consists of begging UN agencies, based on their mandates and available resources, to assist, protect, and help return IDPs to their homes. None of the main operational players—UNHCR, UNICEF, WFP, and UNDP—is in charge. As Richard Holbrooke sardonically remarked several years ago, "Co-heads are no-heads."[39]

The leadership role is supposed to be played by OCHA, which as each new crisis comes on stream asks each agency what it can do. "[T]en years after Rwanda, the United Nations had still not adopted the protection of civilians and the prevention of displacement as a core part of its mandate," wrote Bagshaw and Paul. "The UN's approach to the protection of internally displaced persons is still largely ad hoc and driven more by the personalities and convictions of individuals on the ground than by an institutional, system-wide agenda."[40] OCHA's creation of the IDD has not changed this fundamental reality.

In what turned out to be his last ECOSOC report in March 2004, Deng addressed once again the question of "promoting effective institutional arrangements," which amounted to his overall grade for the collaborative approach. "Notwithstanding the formation of this formal structure to ensure collaboration, the international community's response to internal displacement remains problematic." Deng's own frustration after 12 years of reciting the same mantra was diplomatically hidden behind citing the results of four separate evaluations of the collaborative approach done in the preceding year, which found it seriously wanting. Perhaps the most ironic citation was the one that led, counter-intuitively, to the decision to transform the IDU into the IDD: "The evaluation concluded that the collaborative approach was not working in the field as hoped and that the Unit was not having the hoped-for effect on the system."[41]

In short, OCHA is an extremely slender reed on which to lean. The exceptional circumstances of the December 2004 tsunami provided an opportunity to pull together the many moving parts of UN machinery, but this was not an exception that disproves the rule because natural disasters, whatever their magnitude, have very different politics from wars. OCHA simply has too little bureaucratic leverage and extremely limited financial resources. And if familiarity with the field is a concern, this part of the UN secretariat was supposed to be stripped of its operational mandate and field-based personnel in the so-called reform of 1997. Nonetheless, since that time OCHA has fielded a multitude of operational missions, and tensions around its operational presence have implications for turf-battles over institutional responsibility for IDPs. Moreover, the new IDD is partially composed of personnel temporarily borrowed from UN agencies whose loyalties are thus divided. Without a career humanitarian track in the international civil service,[42] continued promotion and career development is based on the home agency and not performance in OCHA although the theory is that agencies "buy-in" to the experiment by financing the salaries of personnel.

Given the largely operational challenge of satisfying IDP assistance and protection requirements, the only serious candidate for this assignment remains the UNHCR, as was detailed in our earlier discussion of the rejected 1997 reform package.[43] Yet as one senior OCHA official bluntly puts it, "UNHCR is saddled with an inappropriate mandate."[44] While some valid criticisms were leveled against the advisability of such an approach because it coincided with a wave of efforts to restrict asylum, on balance revising UNHCR's mandate and operational profile was the only logical way to proceed. And had it been implemented, this proposal would have provided a sensible temporary home for specific assistance activities for IDPs pending the creation of a "UN Humanitarian Organization for Casualties of War-Affected Populations."[45] Without such a mandate, however, even UNHCR's response to IDPs—according to a March 2005 internal study—"is uncertain, inconsistent and unpredictable . . . This hampers not only UNHCR but the effectiveness of the collaborative response."[46]

Other proposals are in the air. For example, before his death in the August 2003 bombing of UN headquarters in Baghdad, Arthur Helton put forward his recommendations for an intergovernmental mechanism outside the UN system called Strategic Humanitarian Action and Research.[47] Susan Martin and the Georgetown University's Institute for International Migration have developed a proposal for a "UN High Commissioner for Forced Migrants."[48] The Global Commission on International Migration (GCIM) has suggested a merger of IOM and UNHCR to deal with both voluntary and forced migration.[49]

The advantage of the consolidation and centralization proposals, whatever the nomenclature, is obvious. The mandate and operational work would include individuals internally and externally displaced especially because of repression and war, but also because of natural disasters, environmental degradation, and development. For forced migrants, the work of the new agency would be governed by the 1951 Refugee Convention and the 1998 Guiding Principles.

The real question is whether donors will eventually see the necessity to get more from the UN system and insist upon the type of top-down coordination whose absence they continually lament. Within the humanitarian arena, a fundamental consolidation and centralization should be more feasible than for other kinds of reform because all the main players are *de jure* part of the United Nations proper and not separate specialized agencies. There thus is no need for formal constitutional change. The humanitarian components of UNICEF, WFP, and UNDP could be combined with UNHCR—the only one of the big four that is exclusively devoted to aiding and protecting civilian war victims.

However, this would require consistency and constancy from the Western donors who pay the bills. On the one hand, virtually all donors have committed themselves to improving the system of international responses for IDPs, many have earmarked funds for them, and USAID became the first donor organization to issue an official policy for them.[50] On the other hand, the group would be required to communicate with a single voice instead of speaking out of both sides of their mouths—that they are supposedly interested in better delivery of aid and protection for IDPs and other victims of armed conflict, but simultaneously they also wish to maintain the extant, decentralized system. Perceived political and national interests is one explanation, and differences about maintaining the autonomy of favorite UN organizations and NGOs is another.

In any case, for IDPs the "UN system" remains far more a collection of feudal fiefs than a meaningful collective enterprise. While the heads of state and government agreed at the 2005 World Summit "to take effective measures to increase the protection of internally displaced persons," no institutional alterations were considered. Although the secretary-general cogently argued that "internally displaced persons and their needs often fall into the cracks between different humanitarian bodies," he counter-intuitively recommended strengthening the interagency approach.[51]

Perhaps the most startling indication of this reality comes from the long-standing tensions between the RSG and the OHCHR, which have come to the fore rather than diminished over time. It should be recalled that the original mandate of the RSG came from the Commission on Human Rights, and that a staff member of the Centre for Human Rights in Geneva was assigned during Deng's tenure. In the early years, the relationship worked reasonably well. There was an appreciation for what the mandate was about and flexibility to locate external resources to get the job done. That reality lasted until 1998, the year that the Guiding Principles were accepted as well as when the two Brookings books were published and the NRC database created—and also the year that Georg Mautner-Markoff left the Centre for Human Rights. Thereafter, rather than appreciate the entrepreneurial success and visibility of the RSG with the PID's support, the OHCHR tried to control and restrict the mandate, albeit without success.

The operational home moved to the OHCHR after its establishment following the Vienna World Conference on Human Rights in 1993. The logic was sensible, but the atmosphere was never totally supportive. In addition to treating all rapporteurs badly—that is, providing virtually no staff or resources—in this case institutional rivalry was never far from the surface. While "beggars can't be choosers" is an apt proverb, it is an unsatisfactory explanation for the bureaucratic responses frequently emanating from Geneva. While neither the RSG nor rapporteurs receive adequate back-stopping or funds to do a professional job, Deng was able to raise substantial resources in pursuit of his mandate. Many other rapporteurs also raised resources, but none was as successful and none set up an equivalent PID. As such, he and the Brookings project, rather than the OHCHR, were in control. Resentment resulted from the flexibility and visibility of the RSG. The Geneva bureaucracy viewed the mandate of the RSG as merely one slice of a "big pie"—meaning that each mandate should have an equal amount of attention, or rather inattention. Somehow, the existence of 25 million IDPs in desperate need and the necessity to think about an equivalent of UNHCR for the internally displaced got lost in the bureaucratic insistence on treating all mandates equally. That OHCHR working methods developed for other, types of mandates might not be applicable to IDPs seemed alien. The thought that the mandate of the RSG might be different or might become independent was vigorously resisted.

Perhaps the best illustration results from the fact that part of Deng's mandate referred to humanitarian assistance. The OHCHR never really grasped the interagency dimensions of internal displace-, ment, which required different working methods for the RSG mandate. The OHCHR's important shift in rhetoric toward the "main-streaming of human rights" within the UN system thus was not matched by changes in its operational culture. Deng engaged intensely with the various humanitarian actors of the UN system. For example, he became a regular participant in the Inter-Agency Standing Committee, while OHCHR did not generally participate and preferred to see the RSG as part of the human rights side of the house only. Both narrow vision and fear of losing control resulted in OHCHR's resenting Deng's role in the IASC where he had the same say as the high commissioner for human rights.

The essence of Deng's work for the OHCHR involved country missions and reports. An examination of internal correspondence between the RSG and the PID's staff with various personnel at the OHCHR demonstrates an absence of support by the latter for the RSG's work. In what seemed a never-ending battle of memos, Deng argued continually for modest support and even for office space. He complained that he did not control the personnel who worked for him who were often pulled away from their responsibilities for IDPs and assigned to other UN tasks. Exacerbating the problem was a chronic lack of stability—several former staff pointed to unacceptable three-month contracts that sometimes were not extended until after they had expired. Increasingly, Deng and the PID began to add staff to the office who were paid for by extra-budgetary resources that they raised.

"The preparation of country missions and reports has been the activity most closely associated with the Office of the High Commissioner," began one diplomatic exchange by Deng. "But even here, it is difficult for one person to always handle all the responsibilities involved. Indeed, over the years, quite a number of reports, missions and other important activities have benefited from the supplementary support made available by staff members outside the High Commissioner's office."[52]

In short, the OHCHR was unable to support even the country missions, supposedly the essence of the reporting called for by the mandate from the CHR. The PID in response basically shrugged its institutional shoulders and got on with the job, but success in turn led to additional resentment within the OHCHR, which lost control of the missions and was bitter about the autonomy exercised by the RSG in acting without its supervision. On another occasion, Deng pointed out that "Over the years, although the principal officer has been responsible for the first draft, other colleagues, in particular Roberta Cohen, have been pivotal in raising and maintaining the quality of our reports."[53] In other words, the OHCHR's responsibilities were being done regularly by PID staff. With tongue in cheek, Cohen described the creative gyrations to work around the constraints and ensure that the country missions went smoothly as an "arrangement around the mandate of the Representative [that] is not bureaucratically traditional."[54]

Indeed, OHCHR is absent from most emergencies and envisages its role more as passively monitoring and reporting rather than engaging more actively in actual protection efforts. At the same time, it resented the fact that the RSG and the PID moved forward vigorously into such arenas outside of OHCHR's control. Somehow it was able to overlook the fact that internal displacement affected millions of people, and that other human rights, humanitarian, and development agencies should be coming together to help and protect them.

Even for a seasoned UN observer, it is hard to understand how this theater has lasted so long. In one of his early communications to the first high commissioner for human rights, Deng complained that even the staff assigned to his mandate and paid by the PID were "frequently assigned other responsibilities," but nonetheless he hoped that in the future personnel working on IDPs from what was then the Centre for Human Rights would be "given and firmly integrated into plans for the restructuring."[55]

Part of the uneasiness between the OHCHR, on the one hand, and the efforts by the RSG and the PID, on the other, can be gleaned from

Bagshaw and Paul's comments about the failure of the OHCHR to understand the relationship between humanitarian and human rights issues (or simply to relate to humanitarian emergencies). For example, they noted the OHCHR's inability "to take steps to raise awareness among UN and NGO field staff of the special procedures of the UN Commission on Human Rights, which are a largely unknown and under-utilized channel through which to raise protection concerns with governments." They continue: "Similarly, more effective use should be made of the UN human rights treaty bodies. Here too, it is OHCHR's job to raise awareness of the existence of these bodies among UN country teams and national NGOs and civil society groups."[56] Why these basic steps have been lagging has as much to do with myopia as with a lack of resources.

Deng's mandate was not renewed in July 2004. Gimena Sanchez-Garzoli stated clearly what others had described, namely his "instant credibility in his human rights diplomacy."[57] The reason cited was that the mandates for rapporteurs are now limited to two terms, usually a total of six years, and that Deng had already been in the RSG saddle for twice that long.[58] Many of the traditional supporters among member states (especially Austria and Canada, but also Nigeria and Mexico), together with the humanitarian side of the UN led by the ERC, lobbied the secretary-general. According to one anonymous donor representative, official letters went from chancelleries with a common theme: Deng had unusual credentials and had seemingly done the impossible; the mandate of the RSG had always been considered "unique" and "special" (by governments and the ERC, witnessed most notably by Deng's role in the IASC); the rules that applied to "rapporteurs" did not to a "special representative" of the secretary-general; and the Guiding Principles were "accepted but fragile," requiring Deng's continued attention.[59]

While usually the UN Secretariat tends to listen to member states—indeed, officials normally claim that they are slaves to their views—in this case a CHR resolution adopted by consensus followed by efforts from individual governments were to no avail. OHCHR insisted on holding this mandate to the same requirements as all its other mandates (maintaining the "one pie") and teamed up against the ERC with the legal office so that a purely procedural argument held sway. Moreover, "the Geneva-based NGOs were divided," according to ICVA's Manisha Thomas. The NRC supported Deng's extension, but several outspoken human rights NGOs apparently thought it was time for a change and a more outspoken RSG—including Human Rights Watch, Amnesty International, the Jesuit Refugee Service, and the

Quakers. During nine months of going back and forth in what more than one person described as an "undignified" process, the RSG's effectiveness diminished—for instance, he had to cancel a mission to the DRC. The OHCHR again turned to the Office of Legal Affairs to provide an opinion, apparently with the assent of the UN's front office, which had other preoccupations in fending off the scandals from the oil-for-food program and sexual abuse by peacekeepers. Asking the New York legal bureaucracy for its views was "the kiss of death" according to ICVA's coordinator Ed Schenkenberg. The ruling from UN lawyers was predictably to uphold term limits for Deng.[60]

A "new" mandate was approved for two years in July 2004 by the Commission on Human Rights. Walter Kälin had a few words added to his title—the representative of the secretary-general on *the human rights of* internally displaced persons—which sought to underscore his connection to the human rights agenda of the United Nations. However, it was clear that the new RSG was called upon because of his long association with the ongoing work of Deng and the Project on Internal Displacement. And his job description did not change.

The new representative underscored continuity in his mandate and made clear that he would assume his responsibilities only if the Brookings project continued to support his mandate. The OHCHR continued to house the RSG in its offices but in characteristic OHCHR style then removed the staff member assigned to the mandate and sent him to the field just when the RSG needed him. This was followed by a decision, made on obscure bureaucratic grounds, to cease assigning a specific PID staff member within the OHCHR to back-stop the new RSG but instead to make ad hoc arrangements depending on the overall work load of professional staff. Appointed in September 2004, Kälin was unable to obtain a personal meeting with High Commissioner Louise Arbour until April 2005. Shortly thereafter, UNHCR agreed to provide office space for a PID staff member; future arrangements at OHCHR, however, remain unclear as of this writing. The so-called collaborative approach appears the only likely institutional arrangement for the foreseeable future.[61] This means that data will continue to be gathered by the Norwegian Refugee Council, which will also do training, and that most of the research, seminars, and advocacy will be the continued responsibility of the Project on Internal Displacement (still based at Brookings but now also including as a partner the University of Bern, where Kälin teaches). The UN "home" for the current RSG in the OHCHR will remain awkward. In spite of the mandate emanating from the Commission on Human Rights, there are numerous expected activities that the OHCHR has not and cannot regularly fund—including even such basic assignments as attending IASC meetings, undertaking country missions beyond a limited few, and participating in international seminars. If the 2005 World Summit recommendation is implemented to double the allocation to OHCHR from the UN's regular budget over the next five years, perhaps the independent experts will receive more adequate back-stopping and funding.

But more importantly still, under the collaborative approach adopted by the UN, the operational requirements for emergency help and protection for IDPs will continue to reflect largely ad hoc arrangements. While the RSG and the PID have over the years successfully gotten international organizations and NGOs to concentrate specifically on this category of war victim, it simply is impossible to compensate for the absence of a centralized UN presence. When UN mechanisms work, it is because of good faith and compatible personalities rather than a centralized structure to ensure the actual services from the international humanitarian system.

The comprehensive evaluation of January 2004 damned in no uncertain terms OCHA's lack of strategic vision, but it nonetheless recommended a few years' grace in which to turn performance around: "If, on the other hand, after a period of two to three years there is still no progress in the collaborative approach, the Unit [now Division] should be shut down—at that point it will have become a veil masking inherent failures of the system."[62] The notion that within a few years OCHA will improve the actual assistance and protection of IDPs calls to mind the characterization of second marriages by Oscar Wilde—the triumph of hope over experience.

We have examined in the previous two chapters the last half-decade of Francis Deng's tenure as RSG and the adaptation of the Project on Internal Displacement to new needs and demands. Chapter 6 and the first half of this chapter documented improvements in the knowledge base, advocacy, and awareness about internal displacement; the mainstreaming of sovereignty as responsibility; and the gradual acceptance of the Guiding Principles in a variety of settings. The last half of this chapter illustrated the largely unsuccessful efforts to ameliorate the scattered institutional delivery of assistance and protection to IDPs. Where does that leave the new representative of the secretary-general on the human rights of internally displaced persons? We sketch answers to that question in the concluding chapter.

8 Whither and whether, inside-outsiders or outside-insiders?

The previous chapters have documented the history of conceptualizing internal displacement and the consequences of framing the idea of sovereignty as responsibility, including the international protection of these victims of war and human rights violations. This book concentrates on the intertwined mandate of the representative of the secretary-general and the Project on Internal Displacement's contributions between Francis Deng's first appointment as RSG and his replacement by Walter Kälin in September 2004.

The conceptualization of internal displacement has made a notable contribution to contemporary thinking about international relations, in particular by reframing the central component of theory and practice—state sovereignty. In addition to recapping the argument here, we also look toward the future. In this context, an important variable is that the RSG has always had a foot in two camps—taking advantage of being both within the intergovernmental system of the United Nations and outside it. He has made good use of having both official and private platforms. As someone who has thought about how to get research applied, Richard Haass—now the president of the Council on Foreign Relations but formerly director of policy planning at the State Department and vice-president of Brookings—summed up: "Many of us spend a lot of time figuring out how to get ideas into policy-makers' hands, but Francis had a ready-made solution."[1] The impact of individuals on the development of a previously unacceptable framework, policies, and legal standards is worth pondering.

The mandate and the project are intertwined to such an extent that it is difficult to say definitively whether the RSG and the PID are outside-insiders or inside-outsiders. Indeed, they collectively wear whichever hat is most convenient and effective in advancing a particular issue. In the words of the former deputy high commissioner for human rights, Bertram Ramcharan, the success of this effort represents "the power of the voice of the UN system mixed with independence."[2] In adapting to changed political and institutional landscapes, the role of inside-outsiders and outside-insiders is one that could be emulated by others, perhaps with a comparable impact on research, policy, and norms.

What Walter Kälin aptly labels a "hybrid"[3] position undoubtedly has affected the lives of IDPs. As mentioned at the outset, however, we leave to others the measurement of what real impact these policy efforts have had on operations in the field. Nonetheless, it is at least worth mentioning here that evaluations of UNHCR's work on behalf of the internally displaced in Angola, Sri Lanka, and Colombia from 2000 to 2003 suggest institutional learning. We cite a joint DfID-UNHCR conclusion as an illustration:

> The review team was convinced that UNHCR has enhanced the protection and security of IDPs in Sri Lanka by acting to prevent or limit the scale and severity of the human rights violations taking place and by strengthening and supporting national human rights organizations. In addition, UNHCR has improved the material circumstances of IDPs by providing services and additional resources to the population that the parties to the conflict are unable or unwilling to provide. It has also made substantial steps towards finding solutions for the IDPs through its engagement in and input to the relocation/resettlement process.[4]

But we should go back to the beginning of our story. Without an official and assessed UN budget, Deng and since 1994 his colleague Roberta Cohen have compiled an impressive record of achievement mixed with frustrations. One of the reasons for the discussion of the details of this experiment is to trace the path of how a controversial idea, namely the succor and protection of IDPs that clashed directly with the high politics of state sovereignty, moved quickly in the intergovernmental arena largely as a result of research and pressure from outside of the United Nations. As a small and identifiable entity, the Project on Internal Displacement has supported a voluntary position within an official UN mandate. Thus, we have a window into the world of normative and policy change in the international arena in relationship to the fundamental, underlying concept for international relations and organization.

Perhaps "model" is too grandiose a description, but this history is an attempt to get a better grasp of international normative and institutional change, and the PID provides an unusual case study of people who have made a difference. Of special relevance to the "model" throughout this volume is the financial autonomy to develop a strategy and accompanying tactics to pursue the mandate of the RSG. On the one hand, the central approach to the phenomenon of internal displacement is to get governments to take seriously their responsibilities for human rights; and so Deng's work had to be associated intimately with the United Nations. On the other hand, there is a genuine necessity to defend what he has described as "quasi-independent" status.

The fact that an official UN mandate has only moved ahead because of support from and initiatives by the private Project on Internal Displacement is crucial to our understanding of progress to date. The PID's base at a public policy think-tank working in tandem with universities provides a respectable distance from governments and from predictable multilateral diplomatic pressure, processes, and procedures. Rather than maintaining the status quo, the expectation is that the project's activities extend the outer limits of what passes for conventional wisdom in mainstream diplomatic circles. At the same time, and when useful, the RSG also can make use of the UN's official platform.

Such an approach requires "soft" resources because policy institutes and universities rarely devote "hard" tuition income or endowments to subsidize researchers and non-instructional personnel working on a particular problem. For its very existence, the PID required support from a wide range of private and public donors. Their diversity and generosity over the last decade is encouraging. Financial disbursements and in-kind contributions have been made by 10 governments (Austria, Canada, Denmark, Japan, Luxembourg, the Netherlands, Norway, Sweden, United Kingdom, and United States) and five foundations (Ford, MacArthur, McKnight, Mellon, and Schurgot). Support has also come from several parts of the UN system (Office of the Secretary-General, OHCHR, UNICEF, UNHCR, and OCHA) and partner universities and research institutions (Brookings Institution, Ralph Bunche Institute for International Studies of The CUNY Graduate Center, Georgetown University, SAIS of Johns Hopkins University, and the University of Bern). Japan's contributions are through the United Nations in order to finesse parliamentary regulations. But Tokyo's decision to provide multi-year support followed London's, which first made it possible for the PID to hire staff and consultants to undertake enhanced research agendas and also to support the work of local partners in regions of conflict.

Thus, the 2004 and 2005 budgets for direct costs rose to approximately $2 million, but annual operating budgets typically varied from

$500,000 to $800,000 during the earlier period under discussion. By any standard, these are trivial sums for what the PID accomplished in support of the RSG's mandate. This is not the only topic on the international agenda for which resources do not match the long list of responsibilities in UN resolutions. However, internal displacement lies at the far end of a spectrum: an extremely ambitious mandate virtually without any guaranteed regular funds.

The blend of inside-outsider and outside-insider offers advantages that could be replicated for other controversial issues where independent research is required, institutional barriers are high, normative gaps exist, and political hostility is widespread. For instance, the successful negotiation of the landmine ban contains some of the same elements of independently getting a controversial issue on the agenda and then developing a political constituency around an emerging norm. In a final chapter of his treatment of the issue, "Towards a Model for Humanitarian Advocacy,"[5] Don Hubert specifically compares the Ottawa process leading to the ban of anti-personnel landmines with that leading to the Guiding Principles.

It is worth speculating, for instance, whether the work on child soldiers would have advanced far more quickly if Olara Otunnu, until mid-2005 the UN's special representative for children and armed conflict, had been based at a research institute outside of the UN Secretariat rather than within it. Iain Levine, who worked on these issues at UNICEF before moving to Human Rights Watch, remarked that one would have expected more movement on the child soldiers front than on IDPs rather than the opposite—"What is easier to sell than the prohibition of child soldiers?"

In fact, a possible replication of the PID experience is under way with Juan E. Méndez, the president of the International Center for Transitional Justice but who is also part-time the UN's special adviser on the prevention of genocide. Indeed in the displacement arena, the International Organization for Migration's insistence on maintaining its autonomy by being an intergovernmental institution that is outside of the UN but that participates in many activities—including the IASC and consolidated appeals—may reflect a similar calculation.[6] In short, evaluating the pluses and minuses of inside-outsiders and outside-insiders with support from sympathetic governments and foundations is an important topic for further research. Alternative ways of doing business are essential.

If independent ideas matter, so do people. Current and previous project personnel have a mixture of national backgrounds and expertise.[7] The story in these pages also is encouraging for those of us who believe that the development of the next generation is perhaps our greatest legacy. The work on the mandate by the PID provided the opportunity to create a cadre of young experts well versed about the phenomenon of internal displacement. The most prominent examples include: Maria Stavropoulou (now a protection officer at UNHCR who worked for the project as an OHCHR staff member in the early years); Simon Bagshaw (now an adviser with the IDD who worked with the project in Geneva and did his Ph.D. on IDPs); Gimena Sanchez-Garzoli (now the Colombia Project representative of Peace Brigades International where she continues her field work on the Americas begun with the PID); Sivanka Dhanapala (now a UNHCR officer in Myanmar who worked in the New York liaison office); David Fisher (now at the International Federation of the Red Cross and Red Crescent Societies (IFRC) who has prepared a handbook soon to be published of remedies for IDPs and who helped the PID get the national human rights institutions of South Asia to take the issue seriously); and, Erin Mooney (now a senior UN protection officer for IDPs in Africa and formerly the deputy director who developed benchmarks for national responsibility and criteria for ending displacement, and worked with the RSG and PID for a decade, first as an intern for the RSG, then as a consultant and staffer for OHCHR).

Over the last decade, the PID has also engaged numerous short- and longer-term consultants from most regions of the world to work on research, outreach, and capacity-building. This group should be viewed along with a larger network from research institutions and humanitarian NGOs worldwide who have participated in formal or informal sessions organized over the years under the auspices of the PID. There are very few knowledgeable specialists whose work involves internal displacement, who have not worked with or been consulted by the project staff and who are not part of their global network. Some prominent examples are Paula Banerjee, Michael Cernea, Georgi Chkeidze, Kieren Fitzpatrick, Robert Goldman, Mario Gomez, Khoti Kamanga, Julia Kharashvili, Miloon Kothari, James Kunder, Zachary Lomo, Susan Martin, Manfred Nowak, Bahame Tom Nyanduga, William O'Neill, Diane Paul, Courtland Robinson, Carlos Rojas, Ranabir Samaddar, Jeevan Thiagarajah, and Roger Winter. The new RSG, Walter Kälin, summarized this impact when he wrote to Deng and Cohen after they had won the Grawemeyer Prize: "None of us would have worked on the issue had you not taken up the issue of displacement and pushed us."[8]

Financial support from outside the United Nations has made it possible, indeed obligatory, to act autonomously. This took two somewhat unusual forms. First, "partnerships" of all sorts were formed, not just with other units of the UN system but also with regional organizations as well as with international and indigenous NGOs and associations of IDPs. Second, the RSG and the PID have consistently been more forthright and openly critical than would be the case for "normal" international civil servants. At the same time that this independence is generally accepted and admired at UN head-quarters, it also is at times misunderstood by staff whose more bureaucratic approaches prevent their appreciating the benefits and applying the same logic to their own work. As one former foundation official noted in looking back at the decision to make a grant: "The people were solid. Their research materials were high quality. The PID was really the only game in town."[9] Another echoed, "They were incredibly hard-working and produced high-quality work. The only problem was the lack of visibility because they are so self-effacing."[10]

We have argued that this operating model has made a noticeable difference on three of Francis Deng's four pillars. Chapter 3 and the first part of Chapter 6 documented the visible progress in improving the knowledge base and raising international awareness of the prob-lems and prospects for IDPs, two pillars that have been essential for effective international advocacy with governments, IGOs, and NGOs. In the judgment of a February 2005 multi-volume evaluation of its projects for refugees and IDPs, the UK's Department for International Development says it well: "It is widely recognized that RSG-IDP has done a great deal to raise public and political awareness of the plight of IDPs, and to persuade states and international organizations of the need for more effective action in this area . . . and to increase interna-tional understanding of the legal, human rights and relief issues involved."[11] Starting from a point in the early 1990s when there was a question as to whether IDPs were even a special category, it is no small feat to have brought intergovernmental organizations (both UN and regional) and NGOs to take IDP programming seriously and donors to insist on their doing so.

A down-to-earth advocacy has resulted, an essential contribution to what may be as significant a normative change in the Westphalian system as the two dramatic developments following the Second World War, the Nuremberg trials and the Convention on Genocide. The first report to the CHR already highlighted the normative agenda by confronting the tensions between state sovereignty and human rights that are central to the IDP issue. Deng's earlier work on Sudan and Africa[12] had laid the groundwork for "sovereignty as responsibility."[13] His central premise is squarely bounded by *realpolitik*—states are very much the bedrock of international order for the foreseeable future. Any notion of the "erosion" of state sovereignty thus is carefully finessed. At the same time, movement can nonetheless take place toward overcoming the traditional reluctance to intrude into so-called sovereign prerogatives.

Deng sought pragmatically to reconcile the possibility of vigorous international intervention with the UN Charter regime. And picking up on the passion of Roberta Cohen for international protection of IDPs, the approach expanded: if the abuses of human rights are grave enough, a government could lose its legitimacy and its sovereignty could temporarily wane and the prospects for outside interference, including the deployment of outside military forces, increase. The evolution of the notion of sovereignty has been dramatic and affects the ability of humanitarian organizations to come to the rescue in both international and civil wars. The experience of the last decade and a half underscores higher expectations on sovereign political authorities to respect fundamental human rights. In his classic treatment of the role of power in international affairs in the interwar years, E. H. Carr noted: "Some recognition of an obligation to our fellow-men as such seems implicit in our conception of civilisation; and the idea of certain obligations automatically incumbent on civilised men has given birth to the idea of similar (though not necessarily identical) obligations incumbent on civilised nations."[14]

Beginning in 1992, the approach to the implementation of the RSG mandate has involved the kind of mixture of utopia and power that Carr recommended to ensure that international relations did not stagnate in either wishful thinking or despair. As a result of efforts to hone the idea of sovereignty as responsibility and advocate for its wider acceptance, the usual barriers of domestic jurisdiction have been lowered over the years. There has been a perceptible change in thinking and approach toward helping and protecting persons who are suffering but have not crossed a border. Factors now routinely viewed as legitimate to justify Security Council action, for instance, include a range of humanitarian disasters, especially those involving large exoduses by persons displaced within their countries of origin as well as across borders.

As civil wars became the standard bill-of-fare in the 1990s, the cumulative impact of decisions in which rights trumped government policy means that sovereignty as responsibility has become a far more widespread concept even if not yet accepted as conventional wisdom. Such authors as David Rieff may contest whether the spread of the idea has been productive by questioning "the extent to which faith in the idea of imposing human rights or alleviating humanitarian suffering norms at the point of a gun remained a powerful and compelling idea."[15] Nonetheless, state authorities are increasingly seen as having the responsibility to protect the citizens whose rights are being violated. While sovereignty still is an important protection for small states, it should not, as Kofi Annan asserted at the Millennium Summit in 2000, "be a shield for crimes against humanity."[16]

If a state is unwilling or unable to protect the rights of its own citizens, it temporarily forfeits a moral claim to be treated as legitimate. Its sovereignty, as well as its right to nonintervention, is suspended; and a residual responsibility necessitates vigorous action by outsiders to protect populations at risk. The heads of state and government who attended the High-level Plenary Meeting of the General Assembly in September 2005 were the latest to sign on: "We are prepared to take collective action, in a timely and decisive manner, through the Security Council, in accordance with the UN Charter, including Chapter VII . . . should peaceful means be inadequate and national authorities manifestly failing to protect their populations from genocide, war crimes, ethnic cleansing and crimes against humanity."[17]

This does not mean, however, that nothing remains to be done or that various analyses could not have been done better. In order to reduce the divergence between what states are saying and what they actually are doing, effective advocates should adopt a separate agenda for influencing larger publics about the phenomenon of internal displacement. Making realistic proposals about the media is always challenging—for an amateur or expert. There is debate about what pushes the media to cover an issue and why their gatekeepers allocate resources or jump on a particular bandwagon. This is consequential because more must be done to address the extremely limited public understanding of the issue of internal displacement, including among journalists.

A potentially important precedent was set in October 2002 with the publication by the PID of *The Internally Displaced People of Iraq*.[18] This document took the highly visible issue of Iraq—a possible war to enforce a commitment to disarm—and examined the likely repercussions on IDPs. John Fawcett and Victor Tanner's report garnered more media interest than previously commissioned publications. Its analysis and style were more confrontational and openly critical of a sitting government as well as the United Nations, including the Oil-for-Food Programme, than the standard country reports of the RSG or even previous PID publications.

Similar framings of issues might elicit better coverage for the IDP issue because, traditionally, the plight of IDPs rarely has received specific coverage. Some references to internally displaced persons have begun to appear, but a handicap to further progress is the fact that the wider public, even the most literate and concerned members, have very little appreciation either for the scope of humanitarian and development problems that are peculiar for IDPs, or for the need to adapt and create appropriate institutional mechanisms. The plight of IDPs is palpable, but the framing of issues often still appears esoteric. When asked about what to do next in the United States, Donald Steinberg, a former U.S. ambassador to Angola who is vice-president of the International Crisis Group, notes that "IDPs are not on the political agenda." He argued that media attention and advocacy were necessary so that IDPs "are on the same level as narcotics in Colombia or public relations with Museveni in Uganda."[19] The same type of reframing and visibility are undoubtedly necessary to enhance the political salience of IDPs in virtually all countries.

Part of the agenda should be to think through options to enhance visibility and overcome the lack of international attention normally given to RSG country reports. One possible strategy, which is bound to elicit negative reactions from many host governments, is routinely designating international and local media representatives to be part of the RSG's country missions. Media exposure during and between field visits is decisive for building awareness about the mandate and follow-up. Under the right conditions, and by using various modes of promotion and public exposure, it would be helpful for the RSG to catalyze, from the outset, linkages among countries and organizations concerned with the human rights situation of a target country. Public debate in many Western countries would be better informed if the print and electronic media were able to cover his missions. This might also be the case in some target countries although governments that produce IDPs in the first place are unlikely to tolerate much critical local media coverage. Care would obviously be required not to compromise the confidentiality, safety, and candor of either IDPs or local and national officials whose testimony is essential to maintain the integrity of the RSG's human rights mandate.

The media might also help ensure more systematic follow-up for country missions. There is no established procedure or automatic mechanism within the international humanitarian system to track situations in the countries previously visited by the RSG. In Deng's understated prose, internal displacement "is a global phenomenon warranting a more extensive system of on-site monitoring and follow-up than the present resources of the representative will allow."[20] There is no way to ensure that purported points of agreement are implemented or that points of disagreement are revisited. In his reports to the CHR, Deng repeatedly stressed the need "to sustain the momentum of the visits and to ensure active collaboration between the government and the United Nations agencies on the ground." As with so much of the UN's human rights machinery, there is not only no institutional where-withal to secure compliance, but there also are inadequate resources even systematically to sustain embarrassment.

Perhaps part of a media strategy might involve finding a punchier term, one that rolls off the tongue more easily than "internally displaced persons." After the devastation of Hurricane Katrina in New Orleans in August and September 2005, for instance, "refugees" was bandied about loosely by journalists before being abandoned as indicating the "other" rather than U.S. citizens. The term "displacees" became more commonplace among some covering those evacuated from that city. It is not only shorter and snappier, it also rhymes with "refugees." A case could be made to adopt this term over time with appropriate adjectives: "war displacees," "environmental displacees," or "development displacees."

In any event, the most powerful impact of the RSG and his colleagues at the PID has resulted from the subtle but growing support for recasting sovereignty as responsibility, a concept endorsed by the last two secretaries-general, especially by Kofi Annan. The International Commission on Intervention and State Sovereignty also blessed the concept in the opening sentence of its report. Sovereignty and nonintervention are not timeless principles cast in concrete but rather products of actions and resistance by parliamentarians, aid workers, and intellectuals.

Indeed, with the possible exception of the prevention of genocide after the Second World War, no idea has moved faster in the international normative arena than what is now commonly referred to as the "responsibility to protect," the title of the 2001 ICISS report.[21] In fact, as José Alvarez tells us, "traditional descriptions of the requisites of custom—the need for the passage of a considerable period of time and the accumulation of evidence of the diplomatic practices between sets of states reacting to one another's acts—appear increasingly passé."[22] In essence, occasionally human beings count more than the sacrosanct sovereignty enshrined in UN Charter Article 2(7) with its emphasis on noninterference in domestic affairs. As Kofi Annan graphically told a 1998 audience at Ditchley Park, "state frontiers . . . should no longer be seen as a watertight protection for war criminals or mass murderers."[23] Over time, domestic and international jurisdictions are blurring, which became most evident with the willingness to override sovereignty by using military force for humanitarian purposes in the 1990s.

The momentum began in the early 1990s with Francis Deng's "sovereignty as responsibility," formulated to help internally displaced persons by finessing sovereignty and then expanded to reflect the clear need for international protection.[24] This conceptualization to address the phenomenon of internal displacement gained momentum with Annan's own articulation of "two sovereignties" in the late 1990s and the formulation of the responsibility to protect in 2001. "Abuse it and lose it" is a bumper sticker proposed by Richard Haass, whose own recent writing makes specific use of the idea and credits his former Brookings colleagues with it. He remarked: "The idea has had a big impact, and not just on humanitarians."[25] In short, the conditional or contractual nature of sovereignty is now in the mainstream. The three characteristics of a sovereign—territory, authority, population—spelled out in the 1934 Montevideo Convention on the Rights and Duties of States have been complemented by another, a modicum of respect for human rights.

State sovereignty is considerably less sacrosanct today than in 1945. While some members of the Non-Aligned Movement can continue to reiterate their rejection of the so-called right of humanitarian intervention, the bottom line is clear: when a state is incapable or unwilling to do so and peaceful means fail, the resort to outside military force remains a possibility. The threshold for forceful intervention is high— not merely substantial human rights abuses but genocide or ethnic cleansing—but that it remains a policy option represents significant new middle ground in international relations.

A consensus thus is emerging about a state's responsibilities and accountabilities to both domestic *and* international constituencies. A state is not able to claim the prerogatives of sovereignty unless it meets internationally agreed responsibilities, which include protecting the human rights of, and providing life-sustaining assistance to, all those within its jurisdiction. Failure to meet obligations on behalf of IDPs legitimizes intrusion and outside intervention by the United Nations and the community of responsible states, or a coalition of them, against a member of their club that misbehaves egregiously. The improvements in knowledge, advocacy, and international awareness certainly are direct consequences of the PID team's efforts over the last decade to give concrete meaning to the RSG's mandate.

This pillar's impressive fortification, promulgating international law, was detailed in Chapter 4 and the first section of Chapter 7. The normative framework provided by the Guiding Principles on Internal

Displacement now constitutes the point of departure for virtually all public and private efforts for this category of forced migrant. It is worth citing again the independent February 2005 evaluation for DfID, which has funded the Project on Internal Displacement from 2001. In referring to the Guiding Principles and the accompanying *Manual on Field Practice in Internal Displacement* and the *Handbook for Applying the Guiding Principles on Internal Displacement*, a team from Oxford University's Queen Elizabeth House summarized that they "are increasingly used by governments and international and national humanitarian agencies to raise awareness and to guide policy and practice in countries with IDP populations."[26]

Because of inadequate international legal provisions governing the treatment of IDPs, substantial energies have been devoted to filling this lacuna. This does not mean, of course, that they are uncontested. Practical as well as academic criticisms come from those who see the dangers of diluting UNHCR's mandate, which have been referred to repeatedly, as well as the lack of precision in who qualifies and especially as to when one ceases being an IDP without a cessation clause.[27] The arguments from the "refugee fundamentalists" and "containment conspiracy" theorists against any UNHCR task expansion have faded somewhat over time as the numbers of converts to the IDP cause have grown, but they are still a significant drag on UNHCR's task expansion.

In short, the widespread acceptance of the Guiding Principles since their release in 1998 is a success story. Existing norms applicable to this category of forced migrant—prior to and during displacement, as well as during return, resettlement, and reintegration—are conveniently brought together in a single document that guides political authorities and humanitarians.

The process leading to the adoption of the Guiding Principles was itself a key tactical decision. It took half a decade and involved international lawyers and experts from all over the world, regional organizations, IGOs, the ICRC, and NGOs. Consequently, they became the process and then were ready, for the most part, to promote them or at least not to lobby too aggressively against them.

The evolution from an idea to a set of principles to guide governments, militaries, humanitarian agencies, and nonstate actors was a substantial achievement in half a decade, especially because many Third World countries initially viewed any external scrutiny of domestic human rights as an unacceptable assault on their sovereignty. Countries that have actually applied the Guiding Principles to the development of laws and court decisions include Angola, Colombia, Georgia, Peru, Uganda, and Sudan. "Incorporating the Guiding

Principles into domestic law does not necessarily lead to better government policies or to automatic improvements in the rights of IDPs," wrote three evaluators, "but at least there is legislation in place against which governments can be held to account."[28] And representatives of civil society in places as diverse as Sierra Leone, Sri Lanka, Colombia, India, Russia, Liberia, and the SPLM/A in Sudan have been empowered by the principles to seek better assistance and protection from governments and aid agencies.

The outreach to civil society in recent years could be considered a new pillar, and the long-term impact of involving civil society in the work of the PID should not be underestimated. As Ranabir Samaddar summarizes: "The Calcutta Research Group has gained enormously from their work, writings, unstinted assistance, and guidance. Orientation courses have developed, training programmes have evolved, direct knowledge has increased, and an awareness of the legal principles involved in protection of the IDPs has progressed substantially."[29]

Considerable differences in opinion remain about possible next steps. Partisans of proceeding with negotiations for an international convention for IDPs confront those who see a more likely pay-off from pursuing a less direct path toward the gradual acceptance of the Guiding Principles as customary law instead of an emerging norm. Given the bitterness that characterized intergovernmental debates about that document, a frontal attack on recalcitrant states is highly unlikely to be productive in the immediate future. In fact, the overall approach for the Guiding Principles may actually be preferable to negotiating a new convention. As José Alvarez explains, "soft law is no longer just a precursor to a hard rule (whether established by treaty or custom), it is sometimes regarded as a preferable alternative to law-making by treaty or as its complement."[30]

At the same time, particular regions may provide more propitious targets of opportunity on the legal front, which is one reason why the PID has invested in trying to influence them. For example, the African Union has begun drafting provisions for a legally binding instrument on internal displacement, and Commissioner Bahame Tom Nyanduga has been appointed as special rapporteur on refugees, asylum seekers, and internally displaced persons in Africa. The OAS has long had a special representative for IDPs (until recently Robert Goldman) to monitor respect for the Guiding Principles in Latin America. And the OSCE has a number of countries with IDPs so that an emphasis upon the principles could help especially since Moscow has usually dismissed the IDP issue as an anti-Russian stance vis-à-vis Chechnya. The project has had less success in South Africa and the Middle East owing to strong government opposition.

A more fruitful approach in most regions, however, would be the slower and more evolutionary effort to build up precedents through state usage, the development of national laws, and even writings by legal specialists. For instance, the heads of state and government gathered at the 2005 World Summit recognized "the Guiding Principles on Internal Displacement as an important international framework for the protection of internally displaced persons and resolve to take effective measures to increase the protection of internally displaced persons."[31] While they backed away from the earlier text that had called for a more specific term, "standard," nonetheless this acknowledgment was significant.

Moreover, it is striking in this context to note how little creative thinking was done by the High-level Panel and the secretary-general before the summit about possible changes in the UN's humanitarian delivery mechanisms. In comparison with some rather bold new thinking on a Peacebuilding Commission and a more business-like Human Rights Council, the machinery for humanitarian action was basically ignored, resorting to the usual plea for better coordination.[32]

Whatever states decide to do or not to do, the RSG and the PID can contribute directly by helping governments with national laws and policies and by continuing low-key dissemination and raising awareness. New translations are highly desirable, not only of the Guiding Principles themselves but also of the *Handbook* and *Annotations*.[33] In addition, the development of materials suited to the local level—for example, comic strips, PowerPoint presentations, booklets in local languages—could be important. The new RSG is developing a manual for legislators to help with drafting national laws based on the Guiding Principles.

The final pillar, the institutional foundation, remains the one for which progress has been difficult, as both Chapter 5 and the latter section of Chapter 7 demonstrated. The architects have come up with several blueprints and designs, but very little significant new construction has taken place. Indeed, the foundations of the current system—built upon overlapping as well as missing responsibilities and confusing divisions of labor—are unstable and inadequate. While virtually every type of major humanitarian institution—governmental, intergovernmental, nongovernmental—now takes the IDP issue more seriously than a decade ago and has redesigned projects and programs, the dispersal of efforts and wasted energy nonetheless remain critical shortcomings.

Until a centralized structure is available, effective aid and protection for IDPs will remain an aspiration instead of reality. In October 2005 the Global Commission on International Migration was the latest to indicate the reasons for the "lack of inter-agency cooperation," ranging from responsibilities "spread across different institutions" to the involvement by "organizations that were not traditionally involved" to the fact that UN organizations "straddle the somewhat indistinct line between 'migration' and 'humanitarian.'" After pointing out numerous longer-term advantages of merging IOM and UNHCR—efficiency, policy consistency, and pooling of expertise— the members of the GCIM were divided. And so, they backed away from a logical conclusion and proposed instead "better cooperation and coordination" and the creation of yet another layer of bureaucracy, the Inter-agency Global Migration Facility.[34]

"Is it really sensible," asked UK secretary of state for international development Hilary Benn, "that we have different systems for dealing with people fleeing their homes dependent on whether they happen to have crossed an international border?"[35] This most fundamental institutional question—establishing a centralized mechanism to guarantee the best possible assistance and protection to IDPs—remains a distant dream. The failed efforts in the 1997 UN reform have given way to today's so-called collaborative approach under OCHA's umbrella. The 2005 World Summit was unable to address the question posed by Minister Benn. The presidents, prime ministers, and monarchs gathered in New York were not even agreeable to approving the meek language that had appeared in the penultimate draft "to strengthen inter-agency and country-level responses to the needs of internally displaced persons."[36]

This is a poor disguise for the fact that UN institutions and many NGOs value institutional autonomy and market share more than the quality of assistance and protection for IDPs. Consolidation and centralization are in order rather than ad hoc and makeshift responses. As one group of analysts unkindly noted with specific reference to the lack of a dedicated mechanism for IDPs: "When everyone is responsible for a particular population or set of activities, no one can be held accountable for failures."[37] There is little need to reiterate the details of this sad tale here, but we simply repeat Elizabeth Stites and Victor Tanner's bottom line: "No one can ensure the effectiveness of the collaborative approach, and indeed by and large it does not work."[38] Restructuring the extremely decentralized UN system to aid and protect IDPs may be an intractable problem—the more colloquial term UN "family" may be more apt because in other contexts the description is preceded by "dysfunctional."

There is hope among a few insiders that the UN family's previous pathologies and inconsistencies may change modestly as a result of an IASC decision on 12 September 2005, "to designate a lead for each of the clusters . . . accountable for ensuring preparedness and response that is both adequate and predictable."³⁹ The system is supposed to be tested in 2006 for the first emergency with over 500,000 victims; and IDPs are to be included along with all affected populations. This is the latest attempt to ensure for IDPs a response from the UN system that Jan Egeland would like to make "predictably effective."⁴⁰

Without acknowledging the fact openly, it may be that Deng and Cohen's preferred outcome may be realized, namely permitting UNHCR to get on with the job and letting the results speak for themselves. UNHCR could become a *de facto* lead agency for assisting and protecting IDPs in the eye of the storm as it has become the cluster leader for camp coordination and management, emergency shelter, and protection. The decision to assign these responsibilities by sector in advance—essentially the main assistance and protection challenges to IDPs—and to have individual agencies report through UNHCR on them is an attempt to break new operational ground. As a part of the agreement, UNHCR insisted that the assignments be based on "clusters" and not "sectors" (although the actual tasks are by sector) because "protection" cuts across sectors. This battle of words, however, hardly bodes well; and considerable initial energy was spent identifying agencies to take the lead for eight "sub-clusters."

Moreover, if UNHCR is supposed to be the first port of call for IDPs, this arrangement is certain to reignite earlier objections that assuming responsibility for persons in their countries of origin could undermine UNHCR's capacity to achieve its primary mission to protect and aid refugees.⁴¹ The possibility of diminishing the agency's traditional role and diluting its protection mandate would seem to be a modest risk that could be countered by vigilance and a commitment to protecting the rights of all forced migrants. The desire by potential asylum countries to keep large numbers of potential refugees away should not be minimized, but neither should the need to protect and assist IDPs as well as UNHCR's comparative advantage in mounting a unified approach.

Optimists are betting against high odds that this decision may be more promising than those of the past, mainly because UN high commissioner for refugees Antonio Guterres appears keenly interested. "UNHCR is a different place now," summarized Roger Winter. "What's more, their past reluctance is being overridden by a business decision. They are looking, for example, to open twenty-six offices for IDPs in Sudan."⁴² Walter Kälin and others agreed, noting that "UNHCR is running out of refugees."⁴³ Following the IASC decision, for instance, Guterres told Reuters that the UN's inability to protect and aid IDPs "is undoubtedly the international community's biggest failure in terms of humanitarian action." He continued: "You cannot refuse to act just because they have not crossed a frontier."[44]

The day following the IASC decision, Roberta Cohen in addressing UNHCR staff in Geneva at one of their periodic "food for thought" seminars laid out the case for the refugee agency's assuming the mantle for IDPs.[45] In early October during the UNHCR's annual Executive Committee meeting, Guterres and Egeland presented a united front during a panel to delegates from the 68-country body. The latter went so far as to refer to the IASC's "barrier-breaking proposal" that would result in a "more effective, cost-efficient and predictable response using a strengthened collaborative approach."[46] Secretary-General Annan followed suit and called it a "landmark" because "the internally displaced must not be seen as an optional extra."[47] As the emergency relief coordinator, Egeland also now reports bi-annually to the Security Council on the protection of civilians, which in principle provides him with the opportunity to increase accountability and at least expose agencies, including UNHCR, if they do not perform.

The PID has been pushing such a solution for more than a decade. Perhaps the threat of a separate entity may actually be useful in this battle—Susan Martin joked that her proposal for a new agency provides such a "stalking horse."[48] What are the chances that it will work? Ken Bacon argues that there is a greater chance in the future than there was in 1997 because "there is a greater recognition of the problem . . . and a more critical mass behind the change."[49] And Dennis McNamara adds, "I am cynical after all of these years in the business, but in organizational terms the proposed changes amount to revolutionary change." He went so far as to argue that the division that he heads in OCHA could disappear and be merged in the near future if the sectoral approach worked.[50]

Before heaving any sigh of relief, we should recall the terms of reference for a March 2005 study: "Critics, both within and outside UNHCR, have described the UNHCR approach to IDP situations as unilateral, unpredictable, not clearly articulated and not sufficiently linked to existing criteria."[51] Bill Frelick, who attended the October UNHCR Executive Committee as Human Rights Watch refugee policy director, agrees that the cluster approach is "inching toward Richard Holbrooke's lead-agency solution." At the same time, he comments that Guterres and Egeland are likely "to hit a brick wall, three inches from their noses." The reinforced layers of this brick wall consist of "the need for UNHCR not to dilute its refugee mandate; the overlapping mandates of UN agencies and the perennial turf problems of coordination; and the lack of any centralized funds for such a task expansion."[52]

The International Council of Voluntary Agencies—a non-UN member of the IASC along with ICRC, InterAction, and IOM— issued a provocative newsletter following the consultation. "Will all the cluster talk actually lead to more effective humanitarian response in crises or will it just result in the creation of additional layers of coordination and bureaucracy?" The newsletter pointed out several obvious shortcomings from the lack of involvement of NGOs and of centralized funding to the perennial lack of accountability of the UN system, asking "if the cluster approach is not simply putting a band-aid on the symptom." Perhaps their most scathing criticism resulted from the condition that UNHCR could take the lead as long as it did not call into question the protection mandate for refugees. In noting that the agency can opt out when the right to asylum might be undermined, the ICVA document comments:

> [W]hat is probably needed is a crystal ball that the High Commissioner can look into to see if the organisation's involvement with IDPs, could at some point, undermine the right to seek asylum. However, given the dearth of reliable crystal balls, UNHCR will have to develop further its criteria of when not to get involved so that mere mortals can determine the impact on the right to seek asylum.[53]

In the end, as is the case in so many UN matters, success will depend on personalities and on the skills of the humanitarian coordinator. Hoping for the right personal chemistry of top officials is hardly the best way to design international responses—ones that in this case Hugo Slim noted "can't accommodate real life."[54]

Without a centralized power of the purse and firm direction from donors, this new twist to the so-called collaborative approach has very little chance of improving substantially the actual protection of IDP rights and the delivery of life-saving succor to them. As Jeff Crisp— who commissioned the March 2005 UNHCR study and who chaired the IDD retreat in September 2005 while director of policy and research for the Global Commission on International Migration— summarized: "The new division of labour for IDPs all looks good on paper, but does not necessarily address the operational realities: funding, access, security, host government consent and inter-agency competition. In addition, the division of labour agreed to by the agencies has not yet been discussed with donors and has not gone through governing boards such as UNHCR's ExCom." When asked whether the decision seemed like a familiar tune, he added: "The same old waltz sums it up nicely; and those of us who have been on the dance floor since the early 1980s are getting either bored, dizzy, or both."[55]

The oft-heard criticism is of sclerosis of the UN system, but the evolution of the system is actually never ending. In February 2006, the secretary-general set up a 15-member High-level Panel on UN system-wide coherence in the areas of development, humanitarian aid, and the environment. Whether this effort—co-chaired by the prime ministers of Mozambique, Norway, and Pakistan—will result in tinkering of the 1997 variety or actually lead to a centralization of emergency assistance and international protection remains to be seen.

In summary, we can state unequivocally that certain major goals set out at the beginning of the RSG's mandate in 1992 have been achieved—international discourse is different, a clear normative framework is in place, guiding principles are circulating with new coalitions behind them, and individual institutions emphasize to varying degrees the particular problems of IDPs within their programs and projects. The four ways spelled out in the introduction that ideas matter have been illustrated by the pursuit of the RSG's mandate with the assistance of the Project on Internal Displacement.

However, a voluntary position with paltry and impermanent human and financial resources does not provide the capacity to undertake systematic monitoring of situations, or to follow up previous visits to those countries that continue to pose thorny problems of internal displacement or flaunt international norms. Further in-depth research and analyses are prerequisites for ongoing policy and advocacy efforts, to be sure, but the most glaring gaps are practical rather than conceptual. In what qualifies as one of the understatements of the decade, a report in the mid-1990s noted "a considerable gap between the aspirations of the mandate of the representative and his capacity to pursue them."[56]

In order to narrow this gap, four institutional options have been on the international agenda since the outset,[57] but they assume that the RSG mandate become permanent and the RSG serve full-time and with an assured funding base. As attractive as it sounds, the solution could well diminish rather than enhance the effectiveness of the RSG and the PID, for the only practical way of establishing a long-term assured funding base would be to bring both inside the UN system. We have earlier pointed out the benefits, both to the RSG's mandate and to the UN's human rights and humanitarian effort as a whole, of the independence derived from having one foot inside the UN system and one outside. The system needs someone with insider-outsider status to prod it and help correct course.

The innovations under Francis Deng's stewardship need to be carried forward and consolidated. Walter Kälin, the new RSG, is ideally positioned to undertake this task with the back-up of the Brookings-Bern Project on Internal Displacement. Although his position, like that of his predecessor, is voluntary, he has infused his mandate with a renewed energy that promises new achievements. To do so he will need the same level of independence that his predecessor enjoyed. Freedom has its price. A volunteer supported by a PID living from one grant to the next may at this point be, to paraphrase Winston Churchill's remark about democracy, the worst solution except for all the others.

A final word of caution should be introduced when considering the impact of the RSG and the PID. At the end of this volume, one might ask, "Is learning possible within the international humanitarian system?" Any military historian anxious to avoid fighting the last war knows that lessons are difficult enough to identify in the first place, let alone apply afterwards. Political, temporal, military, strategic, and geographic translations from one situation to another are methodologically arduous and operationally problematic. Public policy analysts often overlook the three stages of learning: identification, when problems are observed and data collected; diagnosis, when information is analyzed and underlying beliefs questioned; and implementation, when revised policies and procedures are actually institutionalized and public and bureaucratic support is mobilized on behalf of changes.

Scholars and practitioners who are members of the international conference circuit frequently employ the conventional vocabulary of "lessons learned," but decision-makers and bureaucrats too infrequently implement corrective measures. Lessons are usually identified by people who are not responsible for changing the rules. And decision-makers rarely understand the details and policy implications of major studies. Analysts and administrators are good at taking the first two learning steps. However, what is commonplace and essential in the business literature—the third step, specific changes in policy and behavior—often is missing within the international humanitarian enterprise.

Why is there a gap between lessons compiled and actually learned, between "rhetoric" and "reality"? Cynics would point to hypocrisy and leave it at that. Sometimes they are right, but often there are more complex reasons. Governments and agencies are not monoliths, but this reality is often overlooked when examining applied research.

Those who conduct evaluations, draft resolutions, and make statements usually have not secured political backing from important actors. Competing interests dominate bureaucratic decision-making. And even when policy changes formulated to reflect lessons appear to have been agreed in headquarters, they can prove extremely difficult to translate into practice on the ground.

To the extent that lessons remain relegated to file-drawers, coffee tables, and book jackets, the concept of learning is perverted. In spite of the proliferation of "lessons-learned units," it would be more accurate to speak of "lessons spurned." Scholars and policy analysts should be humble about how little the system of assistance delivery and protection for IDPs has changed over the 1990s.[58]

In closing, it would be appropriate to give the final word to the two persons who have appeared throughout these pages. In a hand-written note after the end of his mandate, Francis Deng wrote to Roberta Cohen: "I honestly believe that you have been the real champion of this accomplishment. Yes, I probably have been the software, but you have been the hardware. And that is probably not even a fair apportionment. In any case, together, we have been an effective couple."[59] This judgment explains why Richard Holbrooke introduced the pair at a conference as "Mr. and Mrs. IDP."[60]

"Although Francis Deng's and my contributions to this progress have been gratifying," wrote Roberta Cohen, "they constitute small steps toward dealing with a monumental global crisis."[61] In thinking about his own experience over 12 years, Francis Deng thoughtfully added: "The UN is ineffective in dealing with the symptoms of displacement, but we should be dealing with the deeper problems of state collapse."[62]

In short, we have a long way to go. There are clear limits to analysis and advocacy without the political will by major donors to act on lessons. How else could one explain the collective yawn beginning in early 2003 at the United Nations in the face of a slow-motion genocide in Darfur in the country with a quarter of the world's total of IDPs?[63] As Roger Winter, now the State Department's special representative on Sudan, notes: "The emperor has no clothes."[64]

Our hope is that we are better placed—we are certainly not worse—to make a difference in the future. People and ideas matter.

Appendix 1
Key UN publications concerning IDPs, 1992–2005

Commission on Human Rights, *Analytical Report of the Secretary-General on Internally Displaced Persons*, UN document E/CN.4/1992/23.

Commission on Human Rights, *Comprehensive Study by the Representative of the Secretary-General on the Human Rights Issues relating to Internally Displaced Persons*, UN document E/CN.4/1993/35.

General Assembly, *Report Prepared by the Representative of the Secretary-General on Internally Displaced Persons*, 1993, UN document A/48/579.

Commission on Human Rights, *Report of the Representative of the Secretary-General on Internally Displaced Persons*, UN document E/CN.4/1994/44.

Commission on Human Rights, *Profiles in Displacement: Sri Lanka*, UN document E/CN.4/1994/44/Add.1.

General Assembly, *Report Prepared by the Representative of the Secretary-General on Internally Displaced Persons*, 1994, UN document A/49/538.

Commission on Human Rights, *Report of the Representative of the Secretary-General on Internally Displaced Persons*, UN document E/CN.4/1995/50.

Commission on Human Rights, *Profiles in Displacement: Colombia*, UN document E/CN.4/1995/50/Add.1.

Commission on Human Rights, *Profiles in Displacement: Burundi*, UN document E/CN.4/1995/50/Add.2.

Commission on Human Rights, *Compilation of Legal Norms*, UN document E/CN.4/1995/50/Add.3.

Commission on Human Rights, *Profiles in Displacement: Rwanda*, UN document E/CN.4/1995/50/Add.4.

General Assembly, *Report Prepared by the Representative of the Secretary-General on Internally Displaced Persons*, 1995, UN document A/50/558.

Commission on Human Rights, *Report of the Representative of the Secretary-General on Internally Displaced Persons*, UN document E/CN.4/1996/52.

Commission on Human Rights, *Profiles in Displacement: Peru*, UN document E/CN.4/1996/52/Add.1.

Commission on Human Rights, *Compilation and Analysis of Legal Norms*, UN document E/CN.4/1996/52/Add.2.

General Assembly, *Report Prepared by the Representative of the Secretary-General on Internally Displaced Persons*, 1996, UN document A/51/483.

General Assembly, *Profiles in Displacement: Tajikistan*, 1996, UN document A/51/483/Add1.

Commission on Human Rights, *Report of the Representative of the Secretary-General on Internally Displaced Persons*, UN document E/CN.4/1997/43.

Commission on Human Rights, *Profiles in Displacement: Mozambique*, UN document E/CN.4/1997/43/Add.1.

General Assembly, *Report Prepared by the Representative of the Secretary-General on Internally Displaced Persons*, 1997, UN document A/52/506.

Commission on Human Rights, *Report of the Representative of the Secretary-General on Internally Displaced Persons*, UN document E/CN.4/1998/53.

Commission on Human Rights, *Compilation and Analysis of Legal Norms, Part II*, UN document E/CN.4/1998/53/Add.1.

Commission on Human Rights, *Guiding Principles on Internal Displacement*, UN document E/CN.4/1998/53/Add.2.

Guiding Principles on Internal Displacement, New York: Office for the Coordination of Humanitarian Affairs, 1998 (in booklet form). Translated from English into Abkhaz, Albanian, Arabic, Armenian, Assamese, Azeri, Bahasa Indonesia, Bengali, Burmese, Cebuano, Chin, Dari, Dinka, French, Georgian, Hausa, Kirundi, Kurdish, Luo, Macedonian, Maguindanaon, Mandarin, Nepali, Nuer, Pashtu, Portuguese, Russian, Rutoro, Serbo-Croatian, Serbo-Croatian Cyrillic, Sgaw Karen, Sinhala, Somali, Spanish, Swahili, DRC Swahili, Tagalog, Tamil, Tetum, Thai, Turkish, Urdu, Yoruba.

Commission on Human Rights, *Report of the Representative of the Secretary-General on Internally Displaced Persons*, UN document E/CN.4/1999/79.

Commission on Human Rights, *Profiles in Displacement: Azerbaijan*, UN document E/CN.4/1999/79/Add.1.

150   *Appendix 1*

Commission on Human Rights, *Report of the Workshop on Internal Displacement in Africa*, UN document E/CN.4/1999/79/Add.2.

General Assembly, *Report Prepared by the Representative of the Secretary-General on Internally Displaced Persons*, 1999, UN document A/54/409.

Commission on Human Rights, *Report of the Representative of the Secretary-General on Internally Displaced Persons*, UN document E/CN.4/2000/83.

Commission on Human Rights, *Profiles in Displacement: Follow-up Mission to Colombia*, UN document E/CN.4/2000/83/Add.1.

Commission on Human Rights, *Summary Report of Workshop on Implementing the Guiding Principles on Internal Displacement (Colombia)*, UN document E/CN.4/2000/83/Add.2.

Commission on Human Rights, *Profiles in Displacement: East Timor*, UN document E/CN.4/2000/83/Add.3.

General Assembly, *Report Prepared by the Representative of the Secretary-General on Internally Displaced Persons*, 2001, UN document A/56/168.

Commission on Human Rights, *Report of the Representative of the Secretary-General on Internally Displaced Persons*, UN document E/CN.4/2001/5.

Commission on Human Rights, *Profiles in Displacement: Forced Relocation in Burundi*, UN document E/CN.4/2001/5/Add.1.

Commission on Human Rights, *Summary Report of the Regional Workshop on Internal Displacement in the South Caucasus*, UN document E/CN.4/2001/5/Add.2.

Commission on Human Rights, *Profiles in Displacement: Armenia*, UN document E/CN.4/2001/5/Add.3.

Commission on Human Rights, *Profiles in Displacement: Georgia*, UN document E/CN.4/2001/5/Add.4.

Commission on Human Rights, *Profiles in Displacement: Angola*, UN document E/CN.4/2001/5/Add.5.

Commission on Human Rights, *Report of the Representative of the Secretary-General on Internally Displaced Persons*, UN document E/CN.4/2002/95.

Commission on Human Rights, *Report of the Mission to the Sudan*, UN document E/CN.4/2002/95/Add.1.

Commission on Human Rights, *Profiles in Displacement: Indonesia*, UN document E/CN.4/2002/95/Add.2.

Commission on Human Rights, *Report of the Seminar on Internal Displacement in Indonesia*, UN document E/CN.4/2002/95/Add.3.

General Assembly, *Report Prepared by the Representative of the Secretary-General on Internally Displaced Persons*, 2003, UN document A/58/393.

Commission on Human Rights, *Report of the Representative of the United Nations Secretary-General on Internally Displaced Persons*, UN document E/CN.4/2003/86.

Commission on Human Rights, *Profiles in Displacement: Follow-up Mission to Sudan*, UN document E/CN.4/2003/86/Add.1.

Commission on Human Rights, *Profiles in Displacement: Turkey*, UN document E/CN.4/2003/86/Add.2.

Commission on Human Rights, *Profiles in Displacement: Mexico*, UN document E/CN.4/2003/86/Add.3.

Commission on Human Rights, *Profiles in Displacement: Philippines*, UN document E/CN.4/2003/86/Add.4.

Commission on Human Rights, *Report on the International Conference on Internal Displacement in the Russian Federation*, UN document E/CN.4/2003/86/Add.5.

Commission on Human Rights, *Report on the International Conference on Internal Displacement in Southern Sudan*, UN document E/CN.4/2003/86/Add.6.

Commission on Human Rights, *Report of the Representative of the United Nations Secretary-General on Internally Displaced Persons*, UN document E/CN.4/2004/77/Add.4.

Commission on Human Rights, *Report of the Representative of the United Nations Secretary-General on Internally Displaced Persons: Mission to the Russian Federation*, UN document E/CN.4/2004/77/Add.2.

Commission on Human Rights, *Report of the Representative of the United Nations Secretary-General on Internally Displaced Persons: Mission to Uganda*, UN document E/CN.4/2004/77/Add.1.

Commission on Human Rights, *Report on the Conference on Internal Displacement in the IGAD Sub-Region, Experts Meeting (30 August–1 September 2003)*, UN document E/CN.4/2004/77.

Commission on Human Rights, *Report of the Representative of the United Nations Secretary-General on Internally Displaced Persons*, UN document E/CN.4/2004/77.

Commission on Human Rights, *Report of the Representative of the United Nations Secretary-General on Internally Displaced Persons: Mission to the Sudan-Darfur Crisis*, UN document E/CN.4/2005/8.

Commission on Human Rights, *Report of the Former Representative of the Secretary-General on Internally Displaced Persons, Francis M.*

Deng, on the Regional Seminar on Internal Displacement in the Americas, UN document E/CN.4/2005/124.

Commission on Human Rights, *Report of Walter Kälin, Representative of the Secretary-General on the Human Rights of Internally Displaced Persons*, UN document E/CN.4/2005/84.

General Assembly, *Report of Walter Kälin, Representative of the Secretary-General on the Human Rights of Internally Displaced Persons*, 2005, UN document A/60/150.

Appendix 2
Principal UN decisions concerning IDPs, 1992–2005

Commission on Human Rights resolution 1992/73, "Internally Displaced Persons" (requested secretary-general to appoint a representative to undertake a comprehensive study on the issue of internally displaced persons).

Commission on Human Rights resolution 1993/95, "Internally Displaced Persons" (extended the mandate by two years).

General Assembly resolution A/RES/48/135, 1993, "Internally Displaced Persons."

Commission on Human Rights resolution 1994/68, "Internally Displaced Persons."

Commission on Human Rights resolution 1995/57, "Internally Displaced Persons" (extended mandate for further three years).

General Assembly resolution A/RES/50/195, 1995, "Protection of and Assistance to Internally Displaced Persons."

Commission on Human Rights resolution 1996/52, "Internally Displaced Persons."

Commission on Human Rights resolution 1997/39, "Internally Displaced Persons."

General Assembly resolution A/RES/52/130, 1997, "Protection of and Assistance to Internally Displaced Persons."

Commission on Human Rights resolution 1998/50, "Internally Displaced Persons" (extended mandate for further three years).

Economic and Social Council resolution 1998/1; 1998/2, "Agreed Conclusions."

Commission on Human Rights resolution 1999/47, "Internally Displaced Persons."

General Assembly resolution, A/RES/54/167, 1999, "Protection of and Assistance to Internally Displaced Persons."

Commission on Human Rights resolution 2000/53, "Internally Displaced Persons."

Security Council, *Presidential Statement on Promoting Peace and Security: Humanitarian Assistance to Refugees in Africa*, 13 January 2000, UN document S/PRST/2000/1.

Commission on Human Rights resolution 2001/54, "Internally Displaced Persons" (extended mandate a further three years).

General Assembly resolution A/RES/56/164, 2001, "Protection of and Assistance to Internally Displaced Persons."

Commission on Human Rights resolution 2002/56, "Internally Displaced Persons."

Economic and Social Council, resolution E/2002/L.34, "Strengthening of the Coordination of Emergency Humanitarian Assistance of the United Nations."

Commission on Human Rights resolution 2003/51, "Internally Displaced Persons."

General Assembly resolution A/RES/58/177, 2004, "Protection of and Assistance to Internally Displaced Persons."

Commission on Human Rights resolution 2004/55, "Internally Displaced Persons."

Commission on Human Rights resolution 2005/46, "Internally Displaced Persons."

In addition to the resolutions specific to the mandate of the representative, a number of thematic or country-specific resolutions of the Commission on Human Rights, the Economic and Social Council, the General Assembly, and the Security Council refer to the issue of internal displacement. For example: General Assembly resolutions on Assistance to Refugees, Returnees and Displaced Persons in Africa; on the United Nations High Commissioner for Refugees; on Sudan; and a Security Council president's statement and resolution on Burundi. There are also references to internal displacement in the final documents of UN meetings, for example the *Plan of Action of the World Conference Against Racism*, the *Madrid International Plan of Action on Ageing*, and the *World Summit Outcome Document*.

Appendix 3

Selected publications by staff and consultants of the Project on Internal Displacement, 1993– 2005

Books

Protecting the Dispossessed: A Challenge for the International Community, by Francis M. Deng (Brookings Institution, 1993).

Masses in Flight: The Global Crisis of Internal Displacement, by Roberta Cohen and Francis M. Deng (Brookings Institution, 1998).

The Forsaken People: Case Studies of the Internally Displaced, co-edited by Roberta Cohen and Francis M. Deng (Brookings Institution, 1998).

Exodus Within Borders: An Introduction to the Crisis of Internal Displacement, by David A. Korn (Brookings Institution, 1999).

The Handbook for Applying the Guiding Principles on Internal Displacement, by Susan Martin, jointly published with the OCHA, 1999 (translated from English into Albanian, Arabic, Bahasa Indonesia, French, Macedonian, Portuguese, Russian, Spanish, and Thai).

Guiding Principles on Internal Displacement: Annotations, by Walter Kälin, jointly published with ASIL, June 2000.

Guiding Principles on Internal Displacement and the Law of the South Caucasus, Georgia, Armenia and Azerbaijan, edited by Roberta Cohen, Walter Kälin, and Erin Mooney, jointly published with ASIL, the OSCE, and the Georgian Young Lawyers Association, June 2003.

Forced Migration in the South Asian Region: Displacement, Human Rights and Conflict Resolution, edited by Omprakash Mishra, Centre for Refugee Studies, Jadavpur University (Calcutta), published in collaboration with the Brookings-SAIS Project on Internal Displacement by Manak (New Delhi), Spring 2004.

Protect or Neglect: Toward a More Effective United Nations Approach to the Protection of Internally Displaced Persons, by Simon Bagshaw and Diane Paul, jointly published with the Internal Displacement Division of the OCHA, 2004.

Internal Displacement in South Asia: The Relevance of the UN's Guiding Principles, edited by Paula Banerjee, Sabyasachi Basu Ray Chaudhury and Samir Kumar Das, published in collaboration with the Brookings-Bern Project on Internal Displacement by Sage (New Delhi), 2005.

A Guide to International Human Rights Mechanisms for Internally Displaced Persons and Their Advocates, by David Fisher, Brookings-Bern Project on Internal Displacement (forthcoming).

Papers

"Improving Institutional Arrangements for the Internally Displaced," by Roberta Cohen and Jacques Cuénod, jointly published with the RPG, 1995.
"Refugee and Internally Displaced Women: A Development Perspective," by Roberta Cohen, jointly published with the RPG, 1995.
"Rethinking 'Relief' and 'Development' in Transitions from Conflict," by Steven Holtzman, January 1999.
"The U.S. Government and Internally Displaced Persons: Present, But Not Accounted For," by James Kunder, jointly published with the USCR, November 1999.
"The Consolidated Appeals and IDPs: The Degree to Which UN Consolidated Inter-Agency Appeals for the Year 2000 Support Internally Displaced Populations," by James Kunder, jointly published with UNICEF, August 2000.
"Internally Displaced Persons and Political Participation: The OSCE Region," by Simon Bagshaw, September 2000.
"Internal Displacement in the Americas: Some Distinctive Features," by Roberta Cohen and Gimena Sanchez-Garzoli, May 2001. This is the English version of an article published in Spanish by the Inter-American Institute for Human Rights and UNHCR in *Derechos Humanos y Refugiados en las Américas: Lecturas Seleccionadas*, Costa Rica, 2001.
"Selected Bibliography on the Global Crisis of Internal Displacement," by Gimena Sanchez-Garzoli, December 2001.
"The Need for a More Focused Response: European Donor Policies Toward Internally Displaced Persons," by Phillip Rudge, jointly published with the NRC and the USCR, January 2002.
"Recent Commentaries about the Nature and Application of the Guiding Principles on Internal Displacement," by Walter Kälin, Francis Deng, and Roberta Cohen, April 2002.
"National Human Rights Commissions and Internally Displaced Persons, Illustrated by the Sri Lankan Experience," by Mario Gomez, July 2002.
"The Internally Displaced People of Iraq," by John Fawcett and Victor Tanner, October 2002.
"Risks and Rights: The Causes, Consequences and Challenges of Development-Induced Displacement," by W. Courtland Robinson, May 2003.
"Practitioner's Kit for Return, Resettlement, Rehabilitation and Development: An Agenda for a Call to Action," by Consortium of Humanitarian Agencies (Sri Lanka), published in collaboration with the Brookings Institution-SAIS Project, March 2004.
"A New Challenge for Peacekeepers: The Internally Displaced," by William G. O'Neill, April 2004.

"The Voting Rights of Internally Displaced Persons: The OSCE Region," by Erin Mooney and Balkees Jarrah, October 2004.

"Protection of Internally Displaced Persons in Situations of Natural Disaster: A Working Visit to Asia," by Walter Kälin, 27 February–5 March 2005.

"Addressing Internal Displacement: A Framework for National Responsibility," by Erin Mooney, April 2005.

"Protecting Two Million Internally Displaced: The Successes and Shortcomings of the African Union in Darfur," by William G. O'Neill and Violette Cassis, November 2005.

Seminar reports

Report of a Workshop on Internal Displacement in Africa, jointly published with UNHCR and the OAU, October 1998.

Summary Report of Internal Displacement in Colombia: Workshop on the Dissemination and Implementation of the Guiding Principles on Internal Displacement, jointly published with the USCR and GAD, May 1999.

Summary Report of the Regional Meeting on Internal Displacement in the South Caucasus, jointly published with the Office for Democratic Institutions and Human Rights of the OSCE and the NRC, May 2000.

Report of the Vienna Colloquy on the Guiding Principles on Internal Displacement, Brookings Institution Project on Internal Displacement, Representative of the UN Secretary-General on Internally Displaced Persons. Hosted by the Government of Austria, Vienna, Austria, September 2000.

Report of the Seminar on Internal Displacement in Indonesia: Toward an Integrated Approach, Brookings Institution-CUNY Project on Internal Displacement, Center for Research on Inter-Group Relations and Conflict Resolution (University of Indonesia), National Commission on Human Rights, OCHA, UNDP, UNHCR, June 2001.

Report of the Brainstorming Session on When Displacement Ends, jointly published with Georgetown University Institute of International Migration, Washington, D.C., April 2002.

Report of the International Conference on Internal Displacement in the Russian Federation, jointly published with the Institute of State and Law of the Russian Academy of Sciences and Partnership on Migration, Moscow, April 2002.

Report of the Seminar on Internal Displacement in Southern Sudan, Brookings Institution-SAIS Project on Internal Displacement, the Representative of the UN Secretary-General on Internally Displaced Persons, UNICEF, November 2002.

Report on the International Symposium on the Mandate of the Representative of the UN Secretary-General on Internally Displaced Persons: Taking Stock and Charting the Future, Brookings Institution-SAIS Project on Internal Displacement. Hosted by the Governments of Austria and Norway, Vienna, December 2002.

Conference on Internal Displacement in the IGAD Sub-Region, Report of the Experts Meeting, Brookings Institution-SAIS Project on Internal Displacement, the Representative of the UN Secretary-General on Internally Displaced Persons, OCHA. Hosted by the Government of the Republic of Sudan, Khartoum, 30 August–2 September 2003.

Report of the Regional Seminar on Internal Displacement in the Americas, Brookings Institution-SAIS Project on Internal Displacement, the Representative of the UN Secretary-General on Internally Displaced Persons. Hosted by the Government of Mexico, Mexico City, February 2004.

Report of the Seminar on Internal Displacement in the SADC Region, Brookings-Bern Project on Internal Displacement, the Representative of the UN Secretary-General on the Human Rights of Internally Displaced Persons, UNHCR. Hosted by the Government of Botswana, Gaborone, August 2005.

Articles

Project staff have published numerous articles on the subject of internal displacement in journals such as *Bulletin of the Atomic Scientists, Ethnopolitics, Forced Migration Review, Foreign Affairs, Georgetown Journal of International Affairs, International Journal of Refugee Law, Global Future, Global Governance, Harvard International Review, International Studies Perspective, International Migration, Journal of Refugee Studies, Refugee Survey Quarterly, United Nations Chronicle*; chapters in various books on the subject of displacement; and op-eds in a variety of newspapers including the *Baltimore Sun, Christian Science Monitor, International Herald Tribune, Miami Herald, New York Times, Newsday, Philadelphia Inquirer*, and the *Washington Post*.

Websites

For a complete listing of all the reports, articles, and other activities of the Brookings-Bern Project on Internal Displacement, see www.brookings.edu/idp.

For a 2001 bibliography on internal displacement by Gimena Sachez-Garzoli, see www.brookings.edu/fp/projects/idp/resources/bibliography.htm.

See also *Collection of Global Course Syllabi Relating to Internally Displaced Persons*, by Gimena Sanchez-Garzoli, 2004, at www.brookings.edu/fp/projects/idp/resources/syllabi.htm.

Notes

Prelims

1   The Institute for Intercultural Studies, which was founded by Margaret Mead in 1944, has been unable to locate when and where this admonition was first cited, but it has become a motto for many organizations and movements. However, it was firmly rooted in her professional work and reflected a conviction that she expressed often, in different contexts and phrasings. Mead's fullest exploration of cultural transmission and of the place of small groups in cultural change and innovation was in *Continuities in Cultural Evolution*, first published in 1964.

Introduction

1   See David A. Korn, *Exodus within Borders* (Washington, D.C.: Brookings Institution, 1999).

2   Norwegian Refugee Council, *Internal Displacement: Global Overview of Trends and Developments in 2004* (Geneva: Global IDP Project, 2005), 9–10. See also USCR, *World Refugee Survey 2005* (Washington, D.C.: USCR, 2005), 11. This is not to say that existing statistics are uncontested because of disputes as to who counts. These statistics reflect the usual practice of referring only to persons uprooted by conflict, but some observers press for much broader notions to encompass millions more uprooted by natural disasters and development. Moreover, there is also no consensus about when displacement ends, thereby inflating figures in some cases. For a discussion, see Erin D. Mooney, "The Concept of Internal Displacement and the Case for IDPs as a Category of Concern," *Refugee Survey Quarterly* 24, no. 3 (2005): 9–26. This entire issue is devoted to "Internally Displaced Persons: The Challenges of International Protection."

3   Roberta Cohen and Francis M. Deng, *Masses in Flight: The Global Crisis of Internal Displacement* (Washington, D.C.: Brookings Institution, 1998), 3. See also Roberta Cohen and Francis M. Deng, eds., *The Forsaken People: Case Studies of the Internally Displaced* (Washington, D.C.: Brookings Institution, 1998); Francis M. Deng, *Protecting the Dispossessed: A Challenge for the International Community* (Washington, D.C.: Brookings Institution, 1993); and Francis M. Deng, "Dealing with

the Displaced: A Challenge to the International Community," *Global Governance* 1, no. 1 (1995): 45–57.
4 Donald Steinberg, *Orphans of Conflict: Caring for the Internally Displaced* (Washington, D.C.: U.S. Institute of Peace, 2005), Special Report #148.
5 Centers for Disease Control, "Famine-Affected, Refugee, and Displaced Populations: Recommendations for Public Health Issues," *Morbidity and Mortality Weekly Report* 41, RR-13 (1992). More recent estimates are essentially unchanged. See Peter Salama, Paul Spiegel, and Richard Brennan, "Refugees—No Less Vulnerable: The Internally Displaced in Humanitarian Emergencies," *The Lancet* 357, no. 9266 (2001): 1430–1431.
6 For ease of reference, this and other key UN publications are found in Appendix 1.
7 This and other UN decisions regarding IDPs are listed in Appendix 2.
8 See, for example, Francis M. Deng, Sadikiel Kimaro, Terrence Lyons, Donald Rothchild, and I. William Zartman, *Sovereignty as Responsibility: Conflict Management in Africa* (Washington, D.C.: Brookings Institution, 1996); and Francis M. Deng, "Frontiers of Sovereignty," *Leiden Journal of International Law* 8, no. 2 (1995): 249–286.
9 Louis Emmerij, Richard Jolly, and Thomas G. Weiss, *Ahead of the Curve? UN Ideas and Global Challenges* (Bloomington: Indiana University Press, 2001), 214.
10 These are found in Boxes 3.1 and 6.1.
11 These are found in Box 6.2.
12 Key publications are listed in Appendix 3.
13 See Hedley Bull, *The Anarchical Society: A Study of Order in World Politics* (New York: Columbia University Press, 1977) and the more recent Robert H. Jackson, *The Global Covenant: Human Conduct in a World of States* (Oxford: Oxford University Press, 2000).
14 See, for example, Ramesh Thakur and Thomas G. Weiss, *The UN and Global Governance: An Idea and Its Prospects* (Bloomington: Indiana University Press, forthcoming).
15 Stephen Krasner, *Sovereignty: Organized Hypocrisy* (Princeton, N.J.: Princeton University Press, 1999).
16 See, for example, David Held and Anthony McGrew, David Goldblatt and Jonathan Perraton, *Global Transformations: Politics, Economics and Culture* (Stanford, Calif.: Stanford University Press, 1999); and David Held and Anthony McGrew, *The Global Transformations Reader: An Introduction to the Globalization Debate* (Cambridge: Polity Press, 2000).
17 Thomas S. Kuhn, *The Structure of Scientific Revolutions* (Chicago: University of Chicago Press, 1962), 53.
18 See, for example, Karl Popper, *The Logic of Scientific Discovery* (New York: Harper & Row, 1968).
19 This is the working assumption behind a major research undertaking for which one of the authors has been a co-director, the United Nations Intellectual History Project. See www.unhistory.org. The discussion of ideas is based on Thomas G. Weiss, Tatiana Carayannis, Louis Emmerij, and Richard Jolly, *UN Voices: The Struggle for Development and Social Justice* (Bloomington: Indiana University Press, 2005), 1–11.
20 For a discussion, see Morten Bøås and Desmond McNeill, *Global Institutions and Development: Framing the World?* (London: Routledge, 2004).

21 Judith Goldstein and Robert O. Keohane, eds., *Ideas and Foreign Policy* (Ithaca, N.Y.: Cornell University Press, 1993).

22 Kathryn Sikkink, *Ideas and Institutions: Developmentalism in Argentina and Brazil* (Ithaca, N.Y.: Cornell University Press, 1991).

23 Peter M. Haas, "Introduction: Epistemic Communities and International Policy Coordination," *International Organization* 46, no. 1 (1992): 1–36; and Peter M. Haas, Robert O. Keohane, and Marc A. Levy, eds., *Institutions for the Earth: Sources of Effective International Environmental Protection* (Cambridge, Mass.: MIT Press, 1992).

24 Peter A. Hall, ed., *The Political Power of Economic Ideas: Keynesianism Across Nations* (Princeton, N.J.: Princeton University Press, 1989).

25 Ernst B. Haas, *When Knowledge is Power: Three Models of Change in International Organizations* (Los Angeles: University of California Press, 1994); and Peter M. Haas and Ernst B. Haas, "Learning to Learn: Improving International Governance," *Global Governance* 1, no. 3 (1995): 255–284.

26 Kathryn Sikkink, *Activists Beyond Borders: Advocacy Networks in International Politics* (Ithaca, N.Y.: Cornell University Press, 1998).

27 See Anne-Marie Slaughter, *A New World Order* (Princeton, N.J.: Princeton University Press, 2004).

28 Alexander Wendt, *Social Theory of International Politics* (Cambridge: Cambridge University Press, 1999).

29 John G. Ruggie, *Constructing the World Polity* (New York: Routledge, 1998).

30 See, for example, Robert W. Cox, ed., *The New Realism: Perspectives on Multilateralism and World Order* (New York: St. Martin's, 1997); Robert W. Cox with Timothy J. Sinclair, *Approaches to World Order* (Cambridge: Cambridge University Press, 1996); Quintin Hoare and Geoffrey N. Smith, eds. and trans., *Selections From the Prison Notebooks of Antonio Gramsci* (London: Lawrence & Wishart, 1971).

31 *The Economist*, 17 January 2004, 80.

32 See Catherine Phuong, *The International Protection of Internally Displaced Persons* (Cambridge: Cambridge University Press, 2004).

33 Office for the Coordination of Humanitarian Affairs, *Guiding Principles on Internal Displacement* (New York: OCHA, 1998).

Chapter 1

1 Commission on Human Rights, *Analytical Report of the Secretary-General on Internally Displaced Persons*, UN document E/CN.4/1992/23.

2 Andrew Mack, ed., *Human Security Report 2005* (Vancouver: Human Security Centre, 2005), 104. See especially pages 103–107, "The Plight of the Displaced."

3 Will H. Moore and Stephen M. Shellman, "Refugee or Internally Displaced Person? To Where Should One Flee?", *Comparative Political Studies* 39 (2006), forthcoming.

4 "Statement by Ambassador Richard C. Holbrooke, United States Permanent Representative to the United Nations, on Promoting Peace and Security: Humanitarian Assistance to Refugees in Africa," in the Security Council, 13 January 2000.

5 "Africa in Statistics," *National Geographic*, September 2005, no page.
6 United States Committee for Refugees, *World Refugee Survey 1982* (Washington, D.C.: USCR, 1982), 4–5 and 41.
7 See the Independent Commission on International Humanitarian Issues, *Winning the Human Race* (London: Zed Books, 1987), 97–120.
8 *Report on Refugees, Displaced Persons and Returnees, Prepared by Mr. Jacques Cuénod, Consultant*, UN document E/109/Add.1, 27 June 1991, para. 118 (hereafter "Cuénod report"). This is an excellent source for the early history and activities.
9 *Ibid.*, para. 30.
10 *Ibid.*, para. 118.
11 *Ibid.*
12 *Ibid.*, para. 122.
13 Jarat Chopra and Thomas G. Weiss, "Sovereignty Is No Longer Sacrosanct: Codifying Humanitarian Intervention," *Ethics & International Affairs* 6 (1992): 95–117.
14 See Larry Minear in collaboration with Tabyiegen A. Aboum, Eshetu Chole, Koste Manibe, Abdul Mohammed, Jennefer Sebstad, and Thomas G. Weiss, *Humanitarianism Under Siege: A Critical Review of Operation Lifeline Sudan* (Trenton, N.J.: Red Sea Press, 1991).
15 Thomas G. Weiss and Leon Gordenker, eds., *NGOs, the UN, and Global Governance* (Boulder, Colo.: Lynne Rienner, 1996).
16 Cuénod report, para. 109.
17 Lance Clark, "Internal Refugees—The Hidden Half," in *World Refugee Survey 1988* (Washington, D.C.: USCR, 1989), 18–24.
18 Interview, 11 October 2005.
19 Roberta Cohen, *Introducing Refugee Issues into the United Nations Human Rights Agenda* (Washington, D.C.: RPG, 1990), 34–35.
20 Letter from Elizabeth Ferris to Dennis Gallagher, 11 January 1990.
21 Letter covering a draft memorandum, the World Council of Churches, Programme Unit on Justice and Service, Commission on Inter-Church Aid, Refugee and World Service, 23 November 1989.
22 Roberta Cohen, "U.N. Human Rights Bodies Should Deal with the Internally Displaced," presented at meeting organized for delegates to the UN Commission on Human Rights by the Quaker United Nations Office and the World Council of Churches, Geneva, 7 February 1990.
23 Letter from Martin Macpherson to Roberta Cohen, 16 March 1990.
24 Circulated as E/CN.4/1991/NGO/1.
25 Interview, 27 October 2003.
26 Interview, 4 November 2003.
27 See David P. Forsythe, *The Humanitarians: The International Committee of the Red Cross* (Cambridge: Cambridge University Press, 2005), 33–50; and Mary B. Anderson, "You Save My Life Today, But for What Tomorrow? Some Moral Dilemmas of Humanitarian Aid," in *Hard Choices: Moral Dilemmas in Humanitarian Intervention*, ed. Jonathan Moore (Lanham, Md.: Rowman & Littlefield, 1998), 137–156.
28 Quoted by Elizabeth Becker, "Red Cross Man in Guantanamo. A 'Busybody,' but Not Unwelcome," *New York Times*, 20 February 2002.
29 Roberta Cohen, "The Displaced Fall Through the World's Safety Net," *Christian Science Monitor*, 6 February 1997; Roberta Cohen and Francis M. Deng, *Masses in Flight: The Global Crisis of Internal Displacement*

(Washington, D.C.: Brookings Institution, 1998), 10; and "Exodus within Borders," *Foreign Affairs* 77, no. 4 (1998): 15. Their thoughts about the necessity for protection are found in *Masses in Flight*, 162–166, 176–181, and 254–284.

30 Roberta Cohen, *Human Rights Protection for Internally Displaced Persons* (Washington, D.C.: RPG, 1991), Refugee Policy Group Paper.

31 *Ibid.*, 14.

32 See, for example, Francis M. Deng and I. William Zartman, eds., *Conflict Resolution in Africa* (Washington, D.C.: Brookings Institution, 1991); Francis M. Deng and Terrence Lyons, eds., *African Reckoning: A Quest for Good Governance*, (Washington, D.C.: Brookings Institution, 1998); and Francis M. Deng, "Reconciling Sovereignty with Responsibility: A Basis for International Humanitarian Action," in *Africa in World Politics: Post-Cold War Challenges*, ed. John W. Harbeson and Donald Rothschild (Boulder, Colo.: Westview, 1995): 295–310.

33 Interview, 11 October 2005.

34 It is rarely fruitful to attempt to identify exactly when an idea is born. For some lawyers, for instance, the notion of sovereignty as responsibility began to evolve with the arbitration decision by Judge Max Huber on 4 April 1928, over "The Island of Palmas (or Miangas)" for the International Bureau of the Permanent Court of Arbitration at The Hague. In judging against the United States and in favor of the Netherlands, Huber wrote that the formal U.S. sovereignty over the island that "has not yet received any concrete form of development" was less important than the effective Dutch exercise of responsibility "which involves the maintenance of the state of things." In short, "The Netherlands title of sovereignty, [was] acquired by continuous and peaceful display of State Authority." See *American Journal of International Law* 22, no. 4 (1928): 867–912, quote at 910–911. We are grateful to Walter Kälin for drawing this case to our attention.

35 Interview, 11 October 2005.

36 Jarat Chopra and Thomas G. Weiss, "Sovereignty Is No Longer Sacrosanct: Codifying Humanitarian Intervention," *Ethics & International Affairs* 6 (1992): 95–117.

37 Cohen, *Human Rights Protection*, 17.

38 Interview, 18 June 2005.

39 Letter from Elizabeth G. Ferris to Dennis Gallagher, 1 November 1990.

40 Roberta Cohen, "Proposed Lobbying Effort to Achieve Action on Internally Displaced Persons by UN Commission on Human Rights at its 1992 Session," dated 1991.

41 See Mario Bettati, *Le Droit d'ingérence: mutation de l'ordre international* (Paris: Odile Jacob, 1996).

42 See Peter J. Hoffman and Thomas G. Weiss, *Sword & Salve: Confronting New Wars and Humanitarian Crises* (Lanham, Md.: Rowman & Littlefield, 2006).

43 All of the quotes in this paragraph are in a fax from Jacques Cuénod to Dennis Gallagher, 7 February 1992.

44 Fax from Jacques Cuénod to Dennis Gallagher and Roberta Cohen, 12 February 1992.

45 Memo from Roberta Cohen to Dennis Gallagher, 24 February 1992.

46 Interview, 27 October 2003.

164   *Notes*

Chapter 2

1 Interview, 19 October 2003.
2 Interview, 11 October 2005.
3 Interview, 31 October 2003.
4 *Ibid.*
5 Interview, 12 November 2003.
6 *Comprehensive Study Prepared by Mr. Francis M. Deng*, UN document E/ CN.4/1993/35, 21 January 1993, para. 12.
7 Memorandum for the record prepared by Roberta Cohen, 9 October 1992.
8 Interview, 8 November 2005.
9 Quotes in this paragraph are from Francis Deng, *Protecting the Dispossessed* (Washington, D.C.: Brookings Institution, 1993), 46, 48, and 61.
10 See Francis M. Deng and Larry Minear, *The Challenges of Famine Relief: Emergency Operations in Sudan* (Washington, D.C.: Brookings Institution, 1992).
11 Deng, *Protecting the Dispossessed*, 74–75.
12 *Ibid.*, 88 and 91.
13 Roberta Cohen, memorandum for the record, luncheon meeting with Francis Deng, 26 October 1992.
14 Note from Roberta Cohen to Francis Deng, 26 November 1992.
15 Diplomatic note from the Permanent Mission of Pakistan, Geneva, 13 November 1992.
16 Diplomatic note from the Permanent Mission of the People's Republic of China, Geneva, 12 October 1992.
17 Letter from Ambassador Morris Abrams to Francis M. Deng, 17 November 1992.
18 Diplomatic note from the Ministry of Foreign Affairs of the Republic of Estonia, 29 September 1992.
19 Diplomatic note from the Norwegian government, 10 May 1992.
20 See Catherine Phuong, *The International Protection of Internally Displaced Persons* (Cambridge: Cambridge University Press, 2004).
21 Quotes in this paragraph are from Commission on Human Rights, *Comprehensive Study by the Representative of the Secretary-General on the Human Rights Issues relating to Internally Displaced Persons*, UN document E/CN.4/1993/35, 21 January 1993, paras. 129 and 127.
22 Interview, 12 October 2005.

Chapter 3

1 Commission on Human Rights, *Comprehensive Study by the Representative of the Secretary-General on the Human Rights Issues relating to Internally Displaced Persons*, UN document E/CN.4/1993/35, 21 January 1993, para. 294.
2 Stephen Castles and Nicholas Van Hear with Jo Boyden, Jason Hart, Christian Wolff, and Paul Ryder, *Developing DfID's Policy Approach to Refugees and Internally Displaced Persons*, vol. 1 (Oxford: Queen Elizabeth House, University of Oxford, February 2005), 77.
3 "In Bosnia's Fog," *The Economist*, 23 April 1994, 16.

4 See Michael Barnett and Martha Finnemore, "The Politics, Power and Pathologies of International Organizations," *International Organization* 53, no. 4 (1999): 699–732; and *Rules for the World: International Organizations in Global Politics* (Ithaca, N.Y.: Cornell University Press, 2004).

5 Interview, 23 July 2005.

6 "Displacement Studies and the Role of Universities," lecture by Francis Deng to a Conference of the German Academic Exchange Service, University of Kassel, Germany, June 2002.

7 Francis M. Deng, *Protecting the Dispossessed* (Washington, D.C.: Brookings Institution, 1993), 77.

8 This lengthy quote and the next two come from "Displacement Studies and the Role of Universities."

9 Interview, 26 September 2005.

10 Interview with Francis Deng, 11 October 2005. Ironically, Boutros-Ghali was not re-elected in 1997, and so Kofi Annan wrote the foreword for what became *Masses in Flight*.

11 Interview, 8 November 2005.

12 One is reminded of the ICRC's early years and an unlikely combination of the careful and lawyerly Gustave Moynier along with the passionate and eccentric Henri Dunant. See Caroline Moorehead, *Dunant Dream War, Switzerland and the History of the Red Cross* (New York: HarperCollins, 1998).

13 Speaking notes dated February 1996 for a session at the Brookings Institution.

14 Interview, 11 October 2005.

15 Interview, 11 October 2005.

16 Interview, 12 October 2005. For a discussion, see Cecilia M. Bailliet, *Between Conflict & Consensus: Conciliating Land Disputes in Guatemala* (Oslo: NRC, 2002), 75–77.

17 Letter from Francis Deng to Kofi Annan, 10 November 2004.

18 Interview, 12 October 2005.

19 *Internally Displaced Persons, An Interim Report to the United Nations Secretary General on Protection and Assistance, by Francis M. Deng, Representative of the Secretary General on Internally Displaced Persons,* December 1994, 7.

20 Interview, 12 October 2005.

21 See Julie Mertus, *The United Nations and Human Rights: A Guide for a New Era* (London: Routledge, 2005).

22 Interview, 12 October 2005.

23 Interview, 12 October 2005.

24 For example, see the discussion of refugee data problems in "Technical Notes on Statistical Information," in UNHCR, *The State of the World's Refugees: Fifty Years of Humanitarian Action* (Oxford: Oxford University Press, 2000), 301; and Jeff Crisp, *Who Has Counted the Refugees? UNHCR and the Politics of Numbers* (Geneva: UNHCR, 1999), New Issues in Refugee Research no. 12. For a discussion of IDPs specifically, see Erin Mooney, "The Concept of Internal Displacement and the Case for Internally Displaced Persons as a Category of Concern," *Refugee Survey Quarterly* 24, no. 3 (2005): 9–26.

25 Janie Hampton, ed., *Internally Displaced People: A Global Survey* (London: Earthscan, 1998).

26 A selection of key publications is found in Appendix 3.
27 Published as *Guiding Principles on Internal Displacement*, UN document E/CN.4/1998/53/Add.2, 11 February 1998. They were subsequently reprinted in booklet form as *Guiding Principles on Internal Displacement* (New York: Office for the Coordination of Humanitarian Affairs, 1998).

Chapter 4

1 Commission on Human Rights, *Analytical Report of the Secretary-General on Internally Displaced Persons*, UN document E/CN.4/1992/23, quotes are from paras. 103, 104, and 95.
2 International Committee of the Red Cross, "Internally Displaced Persons, Compilation and Analysis of Legal Norms, Report of the Representative of the Secretary-General on Internally Displaced Persons Mr. Francis Deng, Comments by the International Committee of the Red Cross," Geneva, 10 April 1996, para. 77.
3 "IOM's Internally Displaced Persons (IDP) Programmes," no date.
4 Commission on Human Rights, *Comprehensive Study by the Representative of the Secretary-General on the Human Rights Issues relating to Internally Displaced Persons*, UN document E/CN.4/1993/35, 21 January 1993, para. 87.
5 Otto Linher, ed., *A Compilation of International Legal Norms Applicable to Internally Displaced Persons* (Vienna: Ludwig Boltzman Institute of Human Rights, no date), 6.
6 Roberta Cohen, "The Guiding Principles on Internal Displacement: An Innovation in International Standard Setting," *Global Governance* 10, no. 4 (2004): 465.
7 Janelle Diller, confidential memorandum, copied to Roberta Cohen, 10 February 1995; Robert Goldman, Janelle Diller, and Cecile Meijer, *Internally Displaced Persons and International Law, A Legal Analysis Based on the Needs of Internally Displaced Persons* (Washington, D.C.: International Human Rights Law Group, October 1995).
8 Interview, 28 October 2005.
9 Simon Bagshaw, "Developing the Guiding Principles on Internal Displacement, The Role of a Global Public Policy Network," undated paper.
10 Walter Kälin, remarks to a roundtable on internally displaced persons, 10 April 1996.
11 Roberta Cohen, confidential memorandum to Francis Deng, Robert Goldman, Daniel Helle, Walter Kälin, Manfred Nowak, and Maria Stavropoulou, 20 June 1996.
12 "Statement by Dr. Francis Deng, Representative of the Secretary General for Internally Displaced Persons to the 52nd Session of the United Nations Commission on Human Rights," Geneva, 9 April 1996.
13 The 1993 Vienna Summit on Human Rights had been considered a "success" because there had been no backsliding from the 1948 Universal Declaration of Human Rights.
14 For the full text, see *American Journal of International Law* 89, no. 1 (1995): 215–223.
15 UN document E/CN.4/1992/23, 14 February 1992, para. 17.

16 *Guiding Principles on Internal Displacement*, UN document E/CN.4/1998/53/Add.2, 11 February 1998, para. 2.
17 Erin Mooney, "The Concept of Internal Displacement and the Case for Internally Displaced Persons as a Category of Concern," *Refugee Survey Quarterly* 24, no. 3 (2005): 11.
18 Bagshaw, "Developing the Guiding Principles," para. 4.1.
19 Federal Ministry for Foreign Affairs, Vienna, undated.
20 Interview, 7 November 2005.
21 Interview, 19 October 2005.
22 Bagshaw, "Developing the Guiding Principles," para. 4.2.
23 Fax to Francis Deng from the Austrian Permanent Mission to the United Nations in Geneva, 12 April 1998.
24 The commission had 53 members, but its rules allowed non-member states to co-sponsor resolutions.
25 Roberta Cohen, "Developing an International System for Internally Displaced Persons," *International Studies Perspectives*, forthcoming.
26 Interview, 11 October 2005.
27 Interview, 12 October 2005.
28 Walter Kälin, *Guiding Principles on Internal Displacement: Annotations* (Washington, D.C.: American Society of International Law, 2000), Studies in Transnational Legal Policy No. 32.
29 When Deng assumed positions at The Graduate Center of The City University of New York and then at Johns Hopkins, the project was affiliated with those institutions as well, but the core remained at Brookings.

Chapter 5

1 See Kofi A. Annan, *The Question of Intervention: Statements by the Secretary-General* (New York: UN, 1999); United Nations, Report of the High-level Panel on Threats, Challenges and Change, *A More Secure World: Our Shared Responsibility* (New York: UN, 2004); and International Commission on Intervention and State Sovereignty, *The Responsibility to Protect* (Ottawa: ICISS, 2001), xiii.
2 Kofi Annan, *In Larger Freedom: Towards Development, Security and Human Rights for All*, UN document A/59/2005, 21 March 2005, para. 135; and *Draft Outcome Document of the High-level Plenary Meeting of the General Assembly of September 2005 Submitted by the President of the General Assembly*, UN document A/59/L.70, 13 September 2005, para. 138.
3 Kathleen Newland with Erin Patrick and Monette Zard, *No Refuge: The Challenge of Internal Displacement* (New York and Geneva: OCHA, 2003), 36.
4 Mohammed Ayoob, "Humanitarian Intervention and International Society," *International Journal of Human Rights* 6, no. 1 (2002): 84.
5 See Richard Jolly, Louis Emmerij, and Thomas G. Weiss, *The Power of UN Ideas: Lessons from the First 60 Years* (New York: United Nations Intellectual History Project, 2005); and Thomas G. Weiss, Tatiana Carayannis, Louis Emmerij, and Richard Jolly, *UN Voices: The Struggle for Development and Social Justice* (Bloomington: Indiana University Press, 2005).

168   *Notes*

6 For an earlier treatment of this theme, see Thomas G. Weiss, "International Efforts for IDPs after a Decade: What Next?", in *Taking Stock and Charting the Future*, ed. Brookings Institution-SAIS Project on Internal Displacement (Washington, D.C.: Brookings, 2003), 43–88.

7 Andrew Cooley and James Ron, "The NGO Scramble: Organizational Insecurity and the Political Economy of Transnational Action," *International Security* 27, no. 1 (2002): 5–39.

8 See also Ian Smillie and Larry Minear, *The Charity of Nations: Humanitarian Action in a Calculating World* (West Hartford, Conn.: Kumarian Press, 2004).

9 Francis M. Deng, Sadikiel Kimaro, Terrence Lyons, Donald Rothchild, and I. William Zartman, *Sovereignty as Responsibility: Conflict Management in Africa* (Washington, D.C.: Brookings Institution, 1996), xi.

10 Benchmarks for national responsibility for IDPs were developed by Erin Mooney, *Addressing Internal Displacement: A Framework for National Responsibility* (Washington, D.C.: Brookings-University of Bern Project, 2005).

11 Francis M. Deng, "Frontiers of Sovereignty," *Leiden Journal of International Law* 8, no. 2 (1995): 260–261 and 270.

12 See Thomas G. Weiss, David P. Forsythe, and Roger A. Coate, *The United Nations and Changing World Politics*, 4th edn. (Boulder, Colo.: Westview, 2004), chapters 5–7.

13 Kofi Annan, "Preface," *Masses in Flight: The Global Crisis of Internal Displacement*, ed. Roberta Cohen and Francis M. Deng (Washington, D.C.: Brookings Institution, 1998), xix.

14 Mario Bettati and Bernard Kouchner, eds., *Le Devoir d'ingérence: peut-on les laisser mourir?* (Paris: Denoël, 1987); and Mario Bettati, *Le Droit d'ingérence: mutation de l'ordre international* (Paris: Odile Jacob, 1987).

15 See, for example, Cecilia M. Bailliet, *Between Conflict & Consensus: Conciliating Land Disputes in Guatemala* (Oslo: NRC, 2002), 75–77.

16 Interview, 11 October 2005.

17 Complete listings of missions are found in Boxes 3.1 and 6.1. For a discussion of the reluctance of Turkey (overcome in 2002), Burma, and Algeria, see Roberta Cohen, "Hard Cases: Internal Displacement in Turkey, Burma and Algeria," *Forced Migration Review* 6 (December 1999): 25–28.

18 General Assembly, *Report Prepared by the Representative of the Secretary-General on Internally Displaced Persons*, UN document A/52/5062, November 1997.

19 Cohen and Deng, *Masses in Flight*, 128–129.

20 See Cécile Dubernet, *The International Containment of Displaced Persons: Humanitarian Spaces without Exit* (Aldershot, UK: Ashgate, 2001). For a rebuttal, see Erin D. Mooney, "In-country Protection: Out of Bounds for UNHCR?", in *Refugee Rights and Realities: Evolving International Concepts and Regimes*, ed. Frances Nicholson and Patrick Twomey (Cambridge: Cambridge University Press, 1999), 200–219. For a balanced treatment of the agency, see Gil Loescher, *The UNHCR and World Politics: A Perilous Path* (Oxford: Oxford University Press, 2001).

21 Bill Frelick, "Aliens in Their Own Land: Protection and Durable Solutions for Internally Displaced Persons," in *World Refugee Survey 1998* (Washington, D.C.: USCR, 1998), 30–39; and "Assistance Without

Protection," in *World Refugee Survey 1997* (Washington, D.C.: USCR, 1997), 4–33.

22 Interview, 12 October 2005.

23 Interview, 8 November 2005.

24 For her own discussion, see Sadako Ogata, *The Turbulent Decade: Confronting the Refugee Crises of the 1990s* (New York: Norton, 2005), especially 29–49.

25 Interviews, 11 October 2005.

26 International Organization on Migration, *Internally Displaced Persons: IOM Policy and Activities* (Geneva: IOM, 2002), IOM document MC/INF/258, 3.

27 See Thomas G. Weiss, "UN Responses in the Former Yugoslavia: Moral and Operational Choices," *Ethics & International Affairs* 8 (1994): 1–10; and Thomas G. Weiss and Amir Pasic, "Reinventing UNHCR: Enterprising Humanitarians in the Former Yugoslavia, 1991–1995," *Global Governance* 3, no. 1 (1997): 41–57.

28 InterAction's 2005 position is totally different: "UNHCR should be vested with the authority and resources to be able to coordinate response for internally displaced persons." See "Statement by Dr. Mohammad N. Akhter, President & CEO, InterAction," 16 September 2005.

29 Kofi Annan, *Renewing the United Nations: A Programme for Reform* (New York: UN, 1997). For the details of this story, see Thomas G. Weiss, "Humanitarian Shell Games: Whither UN Reform?", *Security Dialogue* 29, no. 1 (1998): 9–23.

30 See, for example, Antonio Donini, *The Policies of Mercy: UN Coordination in Afghanistan, Mozambique, and Rwanda* (Providence, R.I.: Watson Institute, 1996), occasional paper #22.

31 Interview, 11 October 2005.

32 See Catherine Phuong, *The International Protection of Internally Displaced Persons* (Cambridge: Cambridge University Press, 2004).

33 Interview, 11 October 2005.

34 "Statement by Ambassador Richard C. Holbrooke to the Security Council," 13 January 2000, USUN Press Release #6(00).

35 "Ambassador Richard C. Holbrooke, Statement at Benjamin N. Cardozo School of Law," 28 March 2000, USUN Press Release #44(00).

36 See Thomas G. Weiss and Amir Pasic, "Dealing with Displacement and Suffering from Yugoslavia's Wars: Conceptual and Operational Issues," in *The Forsaken People: Case Studies of the Internally Displaced*, ed. Roberta Cohen and Francis M. Deng (Washington, D.C.: Brookings Institution, 1998), 175–231. A more recent study of the institution calls some of this thinking into doubt. See Barb Wigley, *The State of UNHCR's Organization Culture* (Geneva: UNHCR Policy and Evaluation Unit, 2005), document EPAU/2005/08.

37 Refugee Policy Group, *Human Rights and Humanitarian Emergencies: New Roles for U.N. Human Rights Bodies* (Washington, D.C.: RPG, September 1992), 5–6.

38 Roberta Cohen and Jacques Cuénod, *Improving Institutional Arrangements for the Internally Displaced* (Washington, D.C.: Brookings Institution and RPG, 1995), 54.

39 Roberta Cohen, "Protecting the Internally Displaced," in USCR, *World Refugee Survey 1996* (Washington, D.C.: USCR, 1996), 26.

40 Inter-Agency Standing Committee, *Protection of Internally Displaced Persons: United Nations Inter-Agency Standing Committee Policy Paper* (New York: UN, 2000): 2, 9, and 5.
41 Interview, 11 October 2005.
42 Annan, *Renewing the United Nations*, paras. 78–79 and 194–206.
43 Interview, 11 October 2005.
44 Cohen and Deng, *Masses in Flight*, 127.

Chapter 6

1 Appendix 3 contains a list of key publications.
2 See Simon Bagshaw, *Internally Displaced Persons and Political Participation: The OSCE Region* (Washington, D.C.: Brookings Institution, September 2000); Erin Mooney and Balkees Jarrah, *The Voting Rights of Internally Displaced Persons: The OSCE Region* (Washington, D.C.: Brookings Institution, November 2004); and Erin Mooney and Balkees Jarrah, "Displaced and Disenfranchised: Internally Displaced Persons and Elections in the OSCE Region," *Ethnopolitics* 4, no. 1 (2005): 29–48. See also a summary in Erin Mooney and Balkees Jarrah, "Safeguarding IDP Voting Rights," *Forced Migration Review*, issue 23 (2005): 55.
3 William G. O'Neill, *A New Challenge for Peacekeepers: The Internally Displaced* (Washington, D.C.: Brookings-SAIS Project on Internal Displacement, 2004).
4 William G. O'Neill and Violette Cassis, *Protecting Two Million Internally Displaced: The Successes and Shortcomings of the African Union in Darfur* (Washington, D.C.: Brookings Institution-University of Bern PID, 2005).
5 John Borton, Margie Buchanan-Smith, and Ralf Otto, *Support to Internally Displaced Persons: Learning from Evaluations* (Stockholm: Swedish International Development Agency, 2005), 12.
6 Email, 11 October 2005.
7 Walter Kälin, *Protection of Internally Displaced Persons in Situations of Natural Disasters* (Geneva: OHCHR, 2005), a report of a post-tsunami mission from 27 February–5 March 2005. See also "Tsunami: Learning from the Humanitarian Response," Special Issue of *Forced Migration Review*, July 2005.
8 Interview, 28 October 2005.
9 Interview, 7 November 2005.
10 Interview, 11 October 2005.
11 Interview, 12 October 2005.
12 For a first examination by the PID, see W. Courtland Robinson, *Risks and Rights: The Causes, Consequences, and Challenges of Development-Induced Displacement* (Washington, D.C.: Brookings Institution-SAIS Project on Internal Displacement, 2003). For more general treatments of the issue, see also Richard Black, *Refugees, Environment and Development* (London: Longman, 1998); Christopher McDowell, ed., *Understanding Impoverishment: The Consequences of Development-Induced Displacement* (Providence, R.I.: Berghahn, 1996); and Susan F. Martin, "Development and Politically Generated Migration," in *Determinants of Emigration from*

Mexico, Central America, and the Caribbean, ed. Sergio Diaz-Briquets and Sidney Weintraub (Boulder, Colo.: Westview, 1991), 215–239.

13 Brookings Project on Internal Displacement, *Summary Report of the Conference on Development Induced Displacement, 5 December 2002* (Washington, D.C.: Brookings Institution, 2002): 2.

14 James Kunder, *The U.S. Government and Internally Displaced Persons: Present, But Not Accounted For* (Washington, D.C.: Brookings Institution and USCR, 1999).

15 Interview, 12 October 2005.

16 Mario Gomez, *National Human Rights Commissions and Internally Displaced Persons: Illustrated by the Sri Lankan Experience* (Washington, D.C.: Brookings Institution, 2002).

17 John Fawcett and Victor Tanner, *The Internally Displaced People of Iraq* (Washington, D.C.: Brookings Institution, 2002).

18 James Kunder, *The Consolidated Appeals and IDPs: The Degree to Which UN Consolidated Inter-Agency Appeals for the Year 2000 Support Internally Displaced Populations* (Washington, D.C.: Brookings Institution and UNICEF, 2000).

19 Simon Bagshaw and Diane Paul, *Protect or Neglect? Toward a More Effective United Nations Approach to the Protection of Internally Displaced Persons* (Washington, D.C.: Brookings Institution and OCHA, 2004).

20 Email, 11 October 2005.

21 Omprakash Mishra, ed., *Forced Migration in the South Asia Region: Displacement, Human Rights & Conflict Resolution* (Delhi: Manak Publications, 2004); and Paula Banerjee, Sabyasachi Basu Ray Chaudhury, and Samir Das, eds., *Internal Displacement in South Asia* (New Delhi: Sage, 2005).

22 David A. Korn, *Exodus Within Borders* (Washington, D.C.: Brookings Institution, 1999).

23 Roberta Cohen and Francis M. Deng, *Masses in Flight: The Global Crisis of Internal Displacement* (Washington, D.C.: Brookings Institution, 1998); and Roberta Cohen and Francis M. Deng, eds., *The Forsaken People: Case Studies of the Internally Displaced* (Washington, D.C.: Brookings Institution, 1998).

24 Center for Refugees and Forced Migration Studies, *Exodus Within Borders: The Global Crisis of Internal Displacement* (Skopje, Macedonia: Center for Refugees and Forced Migration Studies, 2001).

25 Gimena Sanchez-Garzoli, ed., *Selected Bibliography on the Global Crisis of Internal Displacement* (Washington, D.C.: Brookings Institution, 2001). A current consolidated bibliography would be more impressive and also more useful were it key-worded and on the internet.

26 Janie Hampton, ed., *Internally Displaced People: A Global Survey* (London: Earthscan, 1998). A shorter version is published annually. The most recent is Global IDP Project, *Internal Displacement: Global Overview of Trends and Developments in 2005* (Geneva: Norwegian Refugee Council, 2006).

27 Interview, 8 November 2005.

28 Interview with Erin Mooney, 23 September 2005.

29 Bagshaw and Paul, *Protect or Neglect?*, 49–50. This is published annually in March.

30 International Commission on Intervention and State Sovereignty, *The Responsibility to Protect* (Ottawa: ICISS, 2001), xi.
31 For further details, see Thomas G. Weiss, *Military-Civilian Interactions: Humanitarian Crises and the Responsibility to Protect*, 2nd ed. (Lanham, Md.: Rowman & Littlefield, 2004), 191–214.
32 Kofi A. Annan, *The Question of Intervention – Statements by the Secretary-General* (New York: UN, 1999); and *"We the Peoples": The United Nations in the 21st Century* (New York: UN, 2000). For a discussion of the controversy surrounding the speech in September 1999, see Thomas G. Weiss, "The Politics of Humanitarian Ideas," *Security Dialogue* 31, no. 1 (2000): 11–23.
33 For an overview, see Mohammed Ayoob, "Humanitarian Intervention and International Society," *Global Governance* 7, no. 3 (2001): 225–230; and Robert Jackson, *The Global Covenant: Human Conduct in a World of States* (Oxford: Oxford University Press, 2000).
34 Commission on Global Governance, *Our Global Neighborhood* (Oxford: Oxford University Press, 1995), 90.
35 Greenberg Research, *The People on War Report* (Geneva: ICRC, 1999), xvi.
36 Antonio Donini, Larry Minear, Ian Smillie, Ted van Baarda, and Anthony C. Welch, *Mapping the Security Environment: Understanding the Perceptions of Local Communities, Peace Support Operations, and Assistance Agencies* (Medford, Mass.: Feinstein International Famine Center, June 2005), 53.
37 World Commission on Environment and Development (the Brundtland Commission), *Our Common Future* (Oxford: Oxford University Press, 1987).
38 Lloyd Axworthy, *Navigating a New World: Canada's Global Future* (Toronto: Alfred A. Knopf Canada, 2003), 414.
39 General Assembly, *Report of the Secretary-General on the Work of the Organisation*, UN document A/54/1 (1999), 48.
40 In addition to Evans, the Northern side included Lee Hamilton, Michael Ignatieff, Klaus Naumann, Cornelio Somaruga, and Gisèle Côté-Harper. In addition to Sahnoun, the South's representatives included Ramesh Thakur, Cyril Ramaphonsa, Fidel Ramos, and Eduardo Stein. Russia's Vladimir Lukin completed the group.
41 Commission on Human Security, *Human Security Now* (New York: Commission on Human Security, 2003).
42 See Thomas G. Weiss and Don Hubert, *The Responsibility to Protect: Research, Bibliography, and Background* (Ottawa: ICISS, 2001), part III.
43 United Nations, Report of the High-level Panel on Threats, Challenges and Change, *A More Secure World: Our Shared Responsibility* (New York: UN, 2004), paras. 199–203; and Kofi Annan, *In Larger Freedom: Towards Development, Security and Human Rights for All*, UN document A/59/2005, 21 March 2005, para. 135.
44 General Assembly, *2005 World Summit Outcome*, UN document A/60/L.1, 15 September 2005, para. 139.
45 U.S. Committee for Refugees, *World Refugee Survey 2005* (Washington, D.C.: USCR, 2005), 11.
46 Ayoob, "Humanitarian Intervention and International Society," 226.

47 David Rieff, *A Bed for the Night: Humanitarianism in Crisis* (New York: Simon & Schuster, 2002), 15.
48 Alex J. Bellamy, "Responsibility to Protect or Trojan Horse? The Crisis in Darfur and Humanitarian Intervention after Iraq," *Ethics & International Affairs* 19, no. 2 (2005): 53.
49 Email, 11 October 2005.
50 Thomas G. Weiss, "The Sunset of Humanitarian Intervention? The Responsibility to Protect in a Unipolar World," *Security Dialogue* 35, no. 2 (2004): 135–153.
51 Interview, 30 November 2005.
52 Email, 29 September 2005.
53 Anthony Lewis, "The Challenge of Global Justice Now," *Dædalus* 132, no. 1 (2003): 8.
54 Letter from Francis Deng to Kofi Annan, 10 November 2004.

Chapter 7

1 Erin D. Mooney, "Towards a Protection Regime for Internally Displaced Persons," in *Refugees and Forced Displacement: International Security, Human Vulnerability and the State*, ed. Edward Newman and Joanne van Selm (Tokyo: UN University Press, 2003), 161.
2 Susan Martin, *The Handbook for Applying the Guiding Principles on Internal Displacement* (New York: OCHA, 1999); and Inter-Agency Standing Committee Working Group, *Manual on Field Practice in Internal Displacement* (Geneva: OCHA, 1999).
3 Martha Finnemore and Kathryn Sikkink, "International Norm Dynamics and Political Change," *International Organization* 52, no. 4 (1998): 887–917.
4 Abkhaz, Albanian, Armenian, Assamese, Azeri, Bahasa Indonesia, Bengali, Burmese, Cebuano, Chin, Dari, Dinka, Georgian, Hausa, Kirundi, Kurdish, Luo, Macedonian, Maguindanaon, Nepali, Never, Pashtu, Portuguese, Rutoro, Serbo-Croat, Serbo-Croat Cyrillic, Sgaw Karen, Sinhala, Somali, Swahili, DRC Swahili, Tagalog, Tamil, Thai, Turkish, Urdu, and Yoruba.
5 General Assembly, *Strengthening of the Coordination of Emergency Humanitarian Assistance of the United Nations, Report of the Secretary-General*, A/53/139-E/1998/67, 12 June 1998, para. 10.
6 General Assembly, *Report Prepared by the Representative of the Secretary-General on Internally Displaced Persons*, 1999, UN document A/54/409, 29 September 1999, para. 6.
7 *Ibid.*, para. 28.
8 For example, see Roberta Cohen, "The Guiding Principles on Internal Displacement: An Innovation in International Standard Setting," *Global Governance* 10, no. 4 (2004): 459–480; "Nowhere to Run, No Place to Hide," *Bulletin of the Atomic Scientists* 58, no. 6 (2002): 37–45; "A New Tool to Protect Internally Displaced Persons: 'The Guiding Principles on Internal Displacement,'" *Human Rights Tribune* 6, no. 1 (1999): 16–23; and "A New Tool for NGOs," *The Mustard Seed*, no. 49 (Fall 1998): 9–11.
9 Interview, 11 October 2005.

10 Susan F. Martin, Patricia Weiss Fagen, Kari M. Jorgensen, Andrew Schoenholtz, and Lydia Mann-Bondat, *The Uprooted: Improving Humanitarian Responses to Forced Migration* (Lanham, Md.: Lexington Books, 2005), 64–66. Endnotes contain comprehensive references to legislative texts.
11 Interview with Roberta Cohen, 9 June 2005.
12 Martin *et al.*, *The Uprooted*, 68–69.
13 Correspondence from Roberta Cohen, 26 September 2005.
14 Interview, 28 October 2005.
15 Quoted by Christian Bourge, "New Internal Refugee Project Launched," *United Press International*, 10 September 2002.
16 Martin, *The Handbook for Applying the Guiding Principles*; and Walter Kälin, *Guiding Principles on Internal Displacement: Annotations* (Washington, D.C.: American Society of International Law, 2000), Studies in Transnational Legal Policy no. 32.
17 The Russian translation was done by a civil society organization called Memorial with the support of the PID, which suggests the importance of such capacity-building and outreach.
18 Interview, 25 August 2005.
19 Parveen A. Gaffar, "Responsibility towards the Displaced," *IDP Newsletter—A Collaborative Effort by CHA, CPA and HRC NPDS for IDPs Project*, issue 1 (July 2005): 7.
20 Simon Bagshaw and Diane Paul, *Protect or Neglect? Toward a More Effective United Nations Approach to the Protection of Internally Displaced Persons* (Washington, D.C.: Brookings Institution and OCHA, 2004), 38.
21 United Nations Commission on Human Rights, *Report of the Representative of the Secretary-General on Internally Displaced Persons, Francis M. Deng*, UN document E/CN.4/2002/95, 16 January 2002, para. 15.
22 The Group of 77 is composed of 132 members. See www.g77.org. The NAM officially lists 115 members, but Yugoslavia is "suspended," making the active membership at 114 states. See www.nam.gov.za.
23 Interview, 11 October 2005.
24 Letter from Pamela Hyde Smith to Roberta Cohen, 30 October 2003.
25 Organization for Security and Co-operation in Europe, Ministerial Council, Decision No. 4/03 "Tolerance and Non-Discrimination," adopted at Maastricht, OSCE document MC.DEC/4/03, 2 December 2003, para. 13.
26 General Assembly, *2005 World Summit Outcome*, UN document A/60/L.1, 15 September 2005, para. 132.
27 Interview, 28 October 2005.
28 Interview, 7 November 2005.
29 Interview, 7 November 2005.
30 For a discussion, see Guy Goodwin-Gill, *The Refugee in International Law*, 2nd edn. (Oxford: Clarendon Press, 1996); and Gil Loescher, *The UNHCR and World Politics: A Perilous Path* (Oxford: Oxford University Press, 2001).
31 United Nations, *Memorandum of Understanding Seals Agreement to Improve UN Assistance to Internally Displaced*, UN document HR/4584, REF/1172, 18 April 2002.

32 Elizabeth Stites and Victor Tanner, *External Evaluation of OCHA's Internal Displacement Unit: Final Report* (New York: OCHA, January 2004), 9.

33 *Ibid.*, 29 and 5–6.

34 Permanent Mission of Canada, "Report of the Workshop on the Future International Response to Internal Displacement," Geneva, 4 February 2004, internal memorandum.

35 See "Memorandum of Understanding," dated 24 November 2004; and Inter-Agency Standing Committee, *Implementing the Collaborative Response to Situations of Internal Displacement: Guidance for United Nations Humanitarian and/or Resident Coordinators and Country Teams* (Geneva: UN, 2004).

36 Interview, 9 November 2005.

37 Stites and Tanner, *External Evaluation*, 12.

38 United Nations Commission on Human Rights, *Report of the Representative of the Secretary-General on Internally Displaced Persons, Francis M. Deng*, UN document E/CN.4/2004/77, 4 March 2004, paras. 24–33 summarizes the results of four such evaluations.

39 Richard C. Holbrooke, "A Borderline Difference," *Washington Post*, 8 May 2000.

40 Bagshaw and Paul, *Protect or Neglect?*, 3.

41 Economic and Social Council, *Specific Groups and Individuals, Mass Exoduses and Displaced Persons, Report of the Representative of the Secretary-General on Internally Displaced Persons, Francis M. Deng*, UN document E/CN.4/2004/77, 4 March 2004, paras. 24 and 29.

42 For a discussion, see Thomas G. Weiss, Peter Hoffman, and David Shorr, *The UN on the Ground* (Muscatine, Ia.: Stanley Foundation, 2003).

43 A recent independent evaluation of the institution's approach to problem-solving suggests that UNHCR may no longer be, at least in the opinion of many staff and some donors, as much ahead of other UN agencies as in the past. See Barb Wigley, *The State of UNHCR's Organization Culture* (Geneva: UNHCR Policy and Evaluation Unit, 2005), document EPAU/2005/08.

44 Interview with Mark Bowden, 19 October 2005.

45 Thomas G. Weiss, "Humanitarian Shell Games: Whither UN Reform?", *Security Dialogue* 29, no. 1 (1998): 9–23.

46 Vanessa Mattar and Paul White, *Consistent and Predictable Responses to IDPs: A Review of UNHCR's Decision-making Processes*, UNHCR Evaluation and Policy Unit, document EPAU/2005/2, March 2005, 1.

47 Arthur Helton, *The Price of Indifference: Refugees and Humanitarian Action in the New Century* (Oxford: Oxford University Press, 2002), 286–293.

48 See Martin *et al.*, *The Uprooted*, and also an accompanying volume of case studies by Nicholas Van Hear and Christopher McDowell, eds., *Catching Fire: Containing Complex Displacement in a Volatile World* (Lanham, Md.: Lexington Books, 2006).

49 Global Commission on International Migration, *Migration in an Interconnected World: New Directions for Action* (Geneva: GCIM, 2005), 75.

50 U.S. Agency for International Development, "USAID Assistance to Internally Displaced Persons Policy," document PD—ACA-558, October 2004, available at www.usaid.gov/policy/ads/200/200mbd.pdf.

51   Kofi A. Annan, *In Larger Freedom: Towards Development, Security and Human Rights for All* (New York: UN, 2005), para. 210.
52   Letter from Francis M. Deng to Jan Cedergren, 4 October 2001.
53   Email from Francis M. Deng to Marlene Alejos, 6 December 2001.
54   Email from Roberta Cohen to multiple OHCHR staff, 18 September 2001.
55   Letter from Francis M. Deng to José Ayala-Lasso, 3 January 1997.
56   Bagshaw and Paul, *Protect or Neglect?*, 6.
57   Interview, 11 October 2005.
58   A new ruling along these lines was made for the first time in 1999—that is, several years after Deng's first appointment.
59   Interview, 16 June 2005.
60   Interview, 9 November 2005.
61   There are a few analysts who see its performance in a better light. See, for example, Catherine Phuong, *The International Protection of Internally Displaced Persons* (Cambridge: Cambridge University Press, 2004); and Monette Zard, "A Comprehensive Approach to Refugee Protection and the Protection of the Internally Displaced: Challenges and Opportunities," in *Towards a Comprehensive Regime for Refugees and Internally Displaced Persons*, ed. Brookings-SAIS Project on Internal Displacement and Migration Policy Institute (Washington, D.C.: MPI/ Brookings Institution, 2005), 26–85.
62   Stites and Tanner, *External Evaluation*, 12.

Chapter 8

1   Interview, 30 November 2005.
2   Interview, 18 June 2005.
3   Interview, 28 October 2005.
4   Nicola Jens, Rachel Lavy, Anthea Mulaka, and Jeff Crisp, *UNHCR's Programme for Internally Displaced Persons in Sri Lanka: Report of Joint Appraisal Mission by the UK Department for International Development and UNHCR* (Geneva: UNHCR, 2002), v–vi. See also reports on Angola (November 2000, May 2001, and May 2002) and Colombia (May 2003) as well as an overview by UNHCR's Evaluation and Policy Analysis Unit (EPAU), *Protection and Solutions in Situations of Internal Displacement: Learning from UNHCR's Operational Experience* (Geneva: UNHCR, 2002). EPAU's predecessor was the Central Evaluation Unit.
5   See Don Hubert, *The Landmine Ban: A Case Study in Humanitarian Advocacy* (Providence, R.I.: Watson Institute, 2000), Occasional Paper # 42, 57–71.
6   IOM's increasing practical involvement in assistance to IDPs led to a series of ad hoc policy papers that was finally formalized in November 2002 in *Internally Displaced Persons: IOM Policy and Activities* (Geneva: IOM, 2002), IOM document MC/INF/258, 2.
7   After the end of Francis M. Deng's mandate, the PID professional staff based at Brookings consisted of: Walter Kälin (University of Bern) and Roberta Cohen, co-directors; Erin Mooney, David Fisher (based at OHCHR, Geneva), Steven Most, Joy Miller, Jessica Wyndham, Molly Browning, and Erin Williams. In addition, assisting the RSG in New York was Claudine Haenni Dale (OCHA). Former PID staff at Brookings

included: Gimena Sanchez-Garzoli, Marianne Makar, Jennifer Marsh, Christen Sewell, Balkees Jarrah, Charles Driest, and Galit Wolfenson; former personnel in New York included Sivanka Dhanapala and Cecilia Piazza; and former staff assisting the RSG in Geneva included Simon Bagshaw, Matthias Behnke, Pablo Espiniella, Marlene Alejos, Juan-Pablo Ordonez, Erin Mooney, Daniel Helle, Bat-Erdene Ayuush, Maria Stavropoulou, and Peter Neussl. Other former staff included Kristin Janson and Kate Brantingham (SAIS, Johns Hopkins); and Phil Orchard and Effie Maclachlan (The CUNY Graduate Center).

8   Letter from Walter Kälin to Roberta Cohen, 2 December 2004.

9   Interview, 18 August 2005.

10 Interview, 25 August 2005.

11 Stephen Castles and Nicholas Van Hear with Jo Boyden, Jason Hart, Christian Wolff, and Paul Ryder, *Developing DfID's Policy Approach to Refugees and Internally Displaced Persons*, vol. 1 (Oxford: Queen Elizabeth House, University of Oxford, February 2005), 77.

12 Francis M. Deng and Larry Minear, *The Challenges of Famine Relief: Emergency Operations in the Sudan* (Washington, D.C.: Brookings Institution, 1992); and Francis M. Deng and I. William Zartman, eds., *Conflict Resolution in Africa* (Washington, D.C.: Brookings Institution, 1991).

13 Francis M. Deng, "Frontiers of Sovereignty: A Framework of Protection, Assistance, and Development for the Internally Displaced," *Leiden Journal of International Law* 8, no. 2 (1995): 249–286; and Francis M. Deng, Sadikiel Kimaro, Terrence Lyons, Donald Rothchild, and I. William Zartman, *Sovereignty as Responsibility* (Washington, D.C.: Brookings Institution, 1996).

14 Edward Hallett Carr, *The Twenty Years' Crisis, 1919–1939* (New York: Harper Torchbooks, 1964), 154.

15 David Rieff, *At the Point of a Gun: Democratic Dreams and Armed Intervention* (New York: Simon & Schuster, 2005), 3. See also *A Bed for the Night: Humanitarianism in Crisis* (New York: Simon & Schuster, 2002).

16 "Statement of United Nations Secretary-General Kofi Annan to the General Assembly on Presenting his Millennium Report," 3 April 2000.

17 United Nations, *2005 World Summit Outcome*, UN document A/60/L.1, 15 September 2005, para. 139.

18 John Fawcett and Victor Tanner, *The Internally Displaced People of Iraq* (Washington, D.C.: Brookings Institution-SAIS Project on Internal Displacement, 2002).

19 Interview 23 September 2005.

20 General Assembly, *Report Prepared by the Representative of the Secretary-General on Internally Displaced Persons*, 1995, UN document A/50/558, 11.

21 International Commission on Intervention and State Sovereignty, *The Responsibility to Protect* (Ottawa: ICISS, 2001).

22 José E. Alvarez, *International Organizations as Law-makers* (Oxford: Oxford University Press, 2005), 591.

23 Kofi A. Annan, *The Question of Intervention: Statements by the Secretary-General* (New York: UN, 1999), 7.

24 The operational meanings of "protection" are an ongoing debate. See, for example, Hugo Slim and Andrew Bonwick, *Protection: An ALNAP Guide*

178   *Notes*

   for Humanitarian Agencies (London: Overseas Development Institute, 2005).
25 Interview, 30 November 2005. See Richard N. Haass, *The Opportunity: America's Moment to Alter History's Course* (New York: Public Affairs, 2005), 41. The endnote (p. 223) reads: "I am indebted to both Francis Deng and Roberta Cohen, who through their work on internally displaced persons first introduced me to the seminal idea of 'sovereignty as responsibility'."
26 Castles and Van Hear with Boyden, Hart, Wolff, and Ryder, *Developing DfID's Policy Approach*, 77.
27 See, for example, Cécile Dubernet, *The International Containment of Displaced Persons: Humanitarian Spaces without Exit* (Aldershot, UK: Ashgate, 2001); and Cecilia Baillet, *Between Conflict & Consensus: Conciliating Land Disputes in Guatemala* (Oslo: NRC, November 2002).
28 John Borton, Margie Buchanan-Smith, and Ralf Otto, *Support to Internally Displaced Persons: Learning from Evaluations* (Stockholm: Swedish International Development Agency, 2005), 12.
29 Email, 29 September 2005.
30 José E. Alvarez, *International Organizations as Law-makers* (Oxford: Oxford University Press, 2005), 599.
31 *2005 World Summit Outcome*, para. 132.
32 See Thomas G. Weiss and Barbara Crossette, "The United Nations, post-Kofi Annan," in *Great Decisions 2006* (New York: Foreign Policy Association, 2006), 9–19.
33 *Manual on Field Practice in Internal Displacement* (New York: OCHA, 1999) is a useful compendium of best practices that complements the *Handbook* and *Annotations* and should also be translated.
34 Global Commission on International Migration, *Migration in an Interconnected World: New Directions for Action* (Geneva: GCIM, 2005), 74–76.
35 Hilary Benn, "Statement before the Overseas Development Institute," London, 15 December 2004.
36 *Draft Outcome Document of the High-level Plenary Meeting of the General Assembly of September 2005 Submitted by the President of the General Assembly*, 5 August 2005, para. 151.
37 Susan F. Martin, Patricia Weiss Fagen, Kari M. Jorgensen, Andrew Schoenholtz, and Lydia Mann-Bondat, *The Uprooted: Improving Humanitarian Responses to Forced Migration* (Lanham, Md.: Lexington Books, 2005), 120.
38 Elizabeth Stites and Victor Tanner, *External Evaluation of OCHA's Internal Displacement Unit: Final Report* (New York: OCHA, January 2004), 29.
39 Inter-Agency Standing Committee, "Draft Statement by IASC Principals," for the Ad Hoc Principals Meeting, "Strengthening Humanitarian Response," 12 September 2005, 2.
40 Interview, 26 September 2006. For a set of short essays with a variety of views as to the effectiveness of the collaborative approach and its future prospects, see "Protecting and Assisting the Internally Displaced: The Way Ahead," Supplement to *Forced Migration Review*, October 2005.
41 For an argument about why to keep UNHCR focused on refugees, see Dubernet, *The International Containment of Displaced Persons*. Catherine

Phuong emphasizes the utility of the current collaborative approach and the need for OHCHR to focus on IDPs rather than the UNHCR in her *The International Protection of Internally Displaced Persons* (Cambridge: Cambridge University Press, 2004). The case for UNHCR's expansion has been made in a number of places, including: Roberta Cohen, "Protecting the Internally Displaced," in USCR, *World Refugee Survey 1996* (Washington, D.C.: USCR, 1996), 20–27; and Erin D. Mooney, "In-country Protection: Out of Bounds for UNHCR?", in *Refugee Rights and Realities: Evolving International Concepts and Regimes*, ed. Frances Nicholson and Patrick Twomey (Cambridge: Cambridge University Press, 1999), 200–219. For a recent report on this controversy, see Project on Internal Displacement and Migration Policy Institute, *Towards a Comprehensive Regime for Refugees and Internally Displaced Persons* (Washington, D.C.: Brookings, 2005); the contrasting views in the two background papers are illustrative of the concerns about diluting UNHCR's mandate. Monette Zard is more reticent in "A Comprehensive Approach to Refugee Protection and the Protection of the Internally Displaced: Challenges and Opportunities," 26–85, while Susan Martin is more bullish in "Protecting Refugees and Internally Displaced Persons: The Need for Comprehensive Reform," 86–141. For a discussion of the economics of the recipients, see Karen Jacobsen, *The Economic Life of Refugees* (West Hartford, Conn.: Kumarian Press, 2005).
42 Interview, 12 October 2005.
43 Interview, 28 October 2005.
44 Quoted by Richard Waddington, "UN Refugee Boss Says World Tackling Past Failures," *New Brisbane News*, 27 September 2005, available at www.leadingthecharge.com/stories/news-0078154.html.
45 A special issue of the UNHCR journal, *Refugee Survey Quarterly* 24, no. 3 (2005), is devoted to "Internally Displaced Persons: The Challenges of International Protection—Articles, Documents, Literature Survey."
46 UNHCR, "UN Agency Chiefs Outline New Approach to Provide Better Care for Internally Displaced People," 4 October 2005.
47 UNHCR, "Secretary-General Applauds UNHCR's Commitment to the Internally Displaced," 6 October 2005.
48 Interview, 11 October 2005.
49 Interview, 12 October 2005.
50 Interview, 7 November 2005.
51 Vanessa Mattar and Paul White, *Consistent and Predictable Responses to IDPs: A Review of UNHCR's Decision-making Processes*, UNHCR Evaluation and Policy Unit, document EPAU/2005/2, March 2005, 53.
52 Interview, 12 October 2005.
53 International Council of Voluntary Agencies, *Talk Back* 7, no. 3 (3 October 2005), Special Issue on "Humanitarian Reforms," available at www.icva.ch/cgi-bin/browse.pl?doc = doc00001467.
54 Interview, 8 November 2005.
55 Email, 21 September 2005.
56 *Secretary-General's Representative Report on Displaced Persons*, UN document A/50/558, 25.
57 These options were spelled out by Roberta Cohen and Jacques Cuénod, *Improving Institutional Arrangements for the Internally Displaced* (Washington, D.C.: Refugee Policy Group, October 1995), 81–86. They

were debated by a group of experts on 30 September 1998, at the Brookings Institution. See "Roundtable Report on New Directions for the Mandate of the Representative of the Secretary-General on Internally Displaced Persons," unpublished document. For additional analysis, see Thomas G. Weiss, "Whither International Efforts for Internally Displaced Persons?", *Journal of Peace Research* 36, no. 3 (1999): 363–373.

58 For a discussion of the failures to change as a result of analyses, see Nicola Reindorp and Peter Wiles, *Humanitarian Coordination: Lessons from Recent Experience* (London: Overseas Development Institute, 2001); A. Wood, R. Apthorpe, and J. Borton, eds., *Evaluating International Humanitarian Action: Reflections from Practitioners* (London: Zed Books, 2001); and Ian Smillie and Larry Minear, *The Charity of Nations: Humanitarian Action in a Calculating World* (West Hartford, Conn.: Kumarian Press, 2004).

59 Letter from Francis Deng to Roberta Cohen, 3 December 2004.

60 Interview with Francis Deng, 11 October 2005.

61 Roberta Cohen, "Developing an International System for Internally Displaced Persons," *International Studies Perspectives*, forthcoming.

62 Interview, 23 July 2005.

63 The number is between 5.3 and 6.7 million according to the U.S. Committee for Refugees, *World Refugee Survey 2005* (Washington, D.C.: USCR, 2005), 11. See also Gérard Prunier, *Darfur: The Ambiguous Genocide* (Ithaca, N.Y.: Cornell University Press, 2005).

64 Interview, 12 October 2005.

Index

184   *Index*

120–1, 125–6; restrictions on 41–2; summary 129–30

Gallagher, Dennis 18, 24, 25, 26, 48–9
Geneva Conventions 56; *see also* Additional Protocols
Geneva legal meeting 1995 59
Georgia 93
Global Commission on International Migration (GCIM) 120, 140–1
Global Ecumenical Network 110
global governance 98
Global IDP Project 53
Goldman, Robert: expertise 57, 58, 59, 131; guiding principles 62, 66, 68; Washington Conference (1991) 25
Goldstein, Judith 7
Gomez, Mario 93, 131
Grant, James P. 25
grants 42–3
Grawemeyer Award 5
Guiding Principles on Internal Displacement 55–70; acceptance of 7; development of 9; dissemination of 103–14; elections 90; first draft 62–5; General Assembly presentation 54; national legislation 109–10; natural disasters 91; opposition to 55–6, 67, 112–13; overview 137–40; in publications 110; resolution 1998 67–8; support for 55; translations 104–5, 110; "unfriendly acts" 115; workshops and seminars 105–8, 109; worldwide discussions 94
Guterres, Antonio 142–3

Haas, Ernst B. 8
Haas, Peter 8
Haass, Richard 101, 127, 137
Habitat 117
Hall, Peter 8
Hall, Tony 25
Handbook for Applying the Guiding Principles (Martin) 104, 111, 138
Hargrove, Lawrence 57
Harvard Law School 42
Helle, Daniel 43

Helton, Arthur 111, 120
Henkin, Alice 18
High Commissioner for Refugees: *see* UNHCR (UN High Commissioner for Refugees)
High-level Panel on Threats, Challenges and Change 71, 99, 140
HIV/AIDS 8
Holbrooke, Richard 14, 82, 118, 147
Hubert, Don 130
human rights: Centre for Human Rights 62, 69; humanitarian issues 17, 23, 71–2, 124; IDPs 23; Inter-American Commission on Human Rights 108; Inter-American Institute of Human Rights 60, 63, 66, 110; International Human Rights Law Group 57, 58; Lawyers Committee for Human Rights 39; monitors 83; refugees 19; research 26; Universal Declaration of Human Rights 77; *see also* Commission on Human Rights (CHR)
Human Rights and Humanitarian Emergencies (Cohen) 84
Human Rights Council 140
Human Rights Internet 94, 110
Human Rights Protection (Cohen) 84
Human Rights Tribune 110
Human Rights Watch 76–7, 110, 124
humanitarian intervention, right of 17, 73–4, 97; *see also* International Commission on Intervention and State Sovereignty (ICISS) and responsibility to protect
Hurricane Katrina 15, 91, 136
Hyde Smith, Pamela 114

ICJ Review 110
ideas, role of 7–10
identity crises 46
Improving Institutional Arrangements (Cohen and Cuénod) 84
Independent Commission on International Humanitarian Issues 15
India 28, 67, 100, 112
influence on public policy 92–3